WORDS AS SWORDS:
VERBAL VIOLENCE AS A CONSTRUCTION OF AUTHORITY IN RENAISSANCE AND CONTEMPORARY ENGLISH DRAMA

SILA SENLEN

Sıla Şenlen

WORDS AS SWORDS:

VERBAL VIOLENCE AS A CONSTRUCTION OF AUTHORITY IN RENAISSANCE AND CONTEMPORARY ENGLISH DRAMA

ibidem-Verlag
Stuttgart

Bibliografische Information der Deutschen Nationalbibliothek
Die Deutsche Nationalbibliothek verzeichnet diese Publikation in der Deutschen Nationalbibliografie; detaillierte bibliografische Daten sind im Internet über http://dnb.d-nb.de abrufbar.

Bibliographic information published by the Deutsche Nationalbibliothek
Die Deutsche Nationalbibliothek lists this publication in the Deutsche Nationalbibliografie; detailed bibliographic data are available in the Internet at http://dnb.d-nb.de.

Cover photo: © Burak Güvenç

∞

Gedruckt auf alterungsbeständigem, säurefreien Papier
Printed on acid-free paper

ISBN-10: 3-89821-982-8

ISBN-13: 978-3-89821-982-2

Printed in Germany

For Prof. Dr. Ayşegül Yüksel

ACKNOWLEDGEMENTS

My deepest gratitude goes to my mentor Prof. Dr. Ayşegül Yüksel, one of the greatest rhetoricians I have had the pleasure of meeting in my life, for sparing a great deal of time and thought in order to help me actualize the I wished to produce.

I would also like to extend my sincere appreciation to Prof. Dr. Belgin Elbir, Assoc. Prof. Dr. N. Selda Öndül, Dr. Hasan İnal, Assist. Prof. Dr. Nazan Tutaş, Prof. Dr. Yusuf Eradam, Assist. Prof. Dr. Evrim Doğan, Prof. Dr. Serap Alsancak, Dr. Hatice Oruç, Zeynep Gültekin, Kağan Çöğender and Kaya Sezer for their invaluable suggestions, and my family Ali Tuncay and Elmas Şenlen, Erol and Hatice Güvenç, Ali and Perihan Göktekin, Turgay and İnci Kayaoğlu Kubilay Şenlen, Aziz Şenlen, Evrim and Ebru Şenlen, Bahadır Güvenç, Leyla and Sılay Kandemir, Bilgin and Ahu Ersözlü, Gamze Aksoy, Sibel Kaya, and my deceased grandfather Kandemir Yılmaz Kandemir, for their endless support.

And last but not least, I wish to thank Burak Güvenç, a Shakespearean 'villain' with the soul of Prometheus, for the help and inspiration he extended.

CONTENTS

INTRODUCTION

A lot has been written on the connection between 'power' and 'violence', but their relationship with 'language' and to what extent language contributes to the infliction of violence in drama, however, has not yet been clearly set. The main focus of this book will be the contribution of language to the violence created on the stage, its relationship with power, and its function in the creation of a discourse of authority. To this end, this study proposes to dwell on dramatic works from distinct periods in the history of English drama, namely, two tragedies in verse from the English Renaissance, Christopher Marlowe's *Tamburlaine, Part I* (1587) and William Shakespeare's *King Richard III* (1593), and three works in prose portraying three different phases of contemporary English drama; Bernard Shaw's *Pygmalion* (1914) produced in the realistic vein at the beginning of the 20th century, Harold Pinter's *The Birthday Party* (1957) representing absurdism in drama in the mid-20th century and Anthony Neilson's *The Censor* (1997), an example of in-yer-face theatre written at the threshold of the 20th century.

First, it would be best to define the terms 'violence' and 'power', and to set their connection with 'language' within the framework of this study. 'Violence' comes from the Latin word 'violentia' deriving from 'vis' symbolizing power, violence and physical strength (Unsal, 1996: 30). Although 'violence' is generally defined as the exercise of physical force in order to cause bodily harm, J. Salmi points out that "any act that threatens a person's physical or psychological integrity is a form of violence" (1993: 16). Since violence offers a foundation for the construction of power, it is certainly a "latent ingredient" in the forming of social relationships (Aijmer, 2000: 1).

In comparison to violence, 'power' is a more abstract and ambiguous term. 'Power' is regarded as the ability of a manipulator (person, group, organization or nation) to get others to act in the desired fashion (Macmillan, 1986: 14). In *An Anatomy of Power,* John Kenneth Galbraith summarises the types of power as being 'condign' (submission based on infliction or threat of physical punishment), 'compensatory' (submission by the offer of reward such as payment or a share of products etc.) or 'conditioned' (submission as a result of persuasion, education, or social commitment to what seems natural or proper) (1985: 4-6). In both 'condign' and 'compensatory' power, the individual being persuaded is aware of his/her submission. 'Conditioned' power, in contrast to the other two, causes an individual to submit to the will of another/others without being aware of it (Galbraith, 1985: 6). In this respect, 'conditioned' power is particularly important for this study because it involves non-physical actions such as persuasion, influence and manipulation.

Galbraith points out to different kinds of power as religious power, political power, economic power, corporate power and military power (1985: 7-8). Power may be held through 'delegated authority', 'social class', 'gender', 'race', 'persuasion' (direct, indirect, or subliminal), 'knowledge', 'money', 'force', 'tradition', and manifests itself as 'authority', 'pressure', 'influence on opinion' and 'domination'. The sources of power, however, are not fixed and can change according to the period and form of government in question. For example, countries/empires in the Renaissance Europe were ruled by kings. The theory of 'Rights of Kings' argued that certain kings ruled because they were chosen by God and therefore were accountable to no person except God[1]. The authority and ultimate power held by such monarchs are reflected clearly by rulers in *Tamburlaine, Part I* and *Richard III.* In these two Renaissance tragedies, power is defined as skill in oration. In the contemporary period, however, power is held by the 'state' instead of rulers and exercised through its social institutions and dominant social class. Thus, in plays such as *Pygmalion*, *The Birthday Party* and *The Censor*, power is exerted through language and discourse standardized by means of education, dominant social classes, censorship etc.

There is a close relationship between 'power', 'violence' and 'language' because these terms exist in correlation with each other. Power can be established by the use of violence, as Machiavelli puts forth in *The Prince*[2], or it might manifest itself as the right to inflict violence on others. In the latter case, violence can both exist in a physical form or in a more hidden fashion through language. Since language is used to force one's own views or inflict one's power upon others without resorting to physical force, it is evidently the most implicitly effective instrument of power.

Language functions as one of the ways individuals or groups are manipulated or persuaded by arguments addressed to the reason, without resorting to physical

---

[1] In terms of the hierarchical order, the "Great Chain of Being" popular in the seventeenth and eighteenth centuries organized the creatures of nature in a hierarchy from innate objects at the bottom, proceeding to 'plants', 'fish', 'birds', 'mammals', 'humans', 'angels' and 'God' at the very top. The category of 'humans' was further divided into the 'King' at the top, followed by 'aristocratic' lords and 'peasants' situated below them.

[2] In Chapter VIII entitled "Those who come to power by crime", Machiavelli expresses his views on the proper use of cruelty (1995: 26-30).

force. As J. A. C. Brown states, "attempts to change the opinions of others" started with the development of "speech":

> [...] through speech comes the power to manipulate or persuade without necessarily resorting to physical force, [...]. Unlike direct violence, thoughts are created and modified primarily by the spoken or written word and are essential weapons aimed at psychological. (1963: 9)

Similar to Brown's opinion of language as a weapon aimed at the psychological, the German philosopher Martin Heidegger argued that language was potentially very dangerous because a silent world is simply what it is, whereas a world experienced through, or represented by, language is radically unstable and open to multiple and conflicting interpretations. Since man exists in language, he creates this danger and brings the destruction it threatens (Heidegger, 1971: 50-53). Furthermore, language resembles a live being that changes and adjusts, and everything that is abstract or concrete is defined and categorized through the medium of language. In this respect, Heidegger points out that it is language which speaks, not man, and thus human beings speak to the extent that they skilfully conform to language (1971: 51-55). Language becomes especially dangerous when the person on the receiving end is not aware of the system, patterns of discourse, and its persuasive tactics. Similar to this view, Hanke defines the relationship between language and man as one of torture, pain, and coercion (in Malkin, 1992: 10)

There is a famous children's rhyme in which language is compared to weapons: "Sticks and bones can break my bones, but words will never hurt me", which implies that physical pain cannot be compared to verbal abuse. Contrary to this popular rhyme, however, language has the potential to be as violent as, and even more damaging than physical force exerted by people upon others. The reason why language is not immediately connected to violence is because it is generally considered a vehicle for communication, used daily to express feelings and thoughts. For this reason, Pierre Bourdieu suggests that language is misrecognized "due to its very familiarity which renders it invisible" (in Hughes, 1999: 30). As Ludwig Wittgenstein observed, the things that are hardest to perceive are those that are right before our eyes and therefore taken for granted (1999: 47-50) [3].

[3] As Andersen points out, language is not immediately recognized as an instrument of power and violence because it "reflects, creates and distorts our experience and our knowledge." (1988: 25)

The language people are born into is an already existing and constructed system created by authority transferred to them to be learned and consumed. It embodies all the cultural codes of a group of people, country, nation which are passed on to others through discourse. This aspect of the system of language is implied in Samuel Beckett's novel *The Unnamable* when the narrator says "I have to speak, whatever that means. Having nothing to say, no words but the words of others, I have to speak" (1965: 314).

In *The Power and The Word,* Roger Andersen states that although power has been examined by specialists in philosophy, politics and sociology, and language in linguistics, psychology and philosophy, power and language have seldom been examined together (1988: 17). Since language reflects and creates social power, it provides a good starting point for the analysis of that power (Andersen, 1988: 15).

Through examples from English drama, namely two plays from the Renaissance and three plays from the contemporary times, this study aims to demonstrate the point that language (whether in the form of rhetoric which "enslaves everything in voluntary, unconstrained submission to itself:" [Plato, 1982: 133] or in the form of daily language), in representing the process of power struggle on the stage, can serve as powerful a weapon as that produced by physical force. For this reason, language in both Renaissance and contemporary drama, when employed by the masters of the art, functions to trick, to persuade, to manipulate and to establish authority and dominance.

Rhetoric is closely associated with constructing authority over a person or group of people, through persuasion. Consideration of the rhetorical approach to language represents a problem, since the term 'rhetoric' has acquired many shades of meaning and is used with both complimentary and pejorative force (Prior, 1964: 8-9). To secure as a background for the rhetorical analysis of plays, Part I, Chapter 1 will be devoted to a historical survey of rhetoric, with special reference to Classical texts on rhetoric. Part I, Chapter 2 will concentrate on the use of verbal violence in the form of rhetoric in Christopher Marlowe's blank-verse play *Tamburlaine, Part I (1587)* and Chapter 3 will be devoted to another play in blank verse, William Shakespeare's *Richard III (1593).* The focus will be on the employment of rhetoric by characters in order to attain power and to torture, trick, abuse, or manipulate others.

Part II will study verbal violence in contemporary English plays written in prose. Part II, Chapter 1, will be dealing with contemporary discussions concerning 'power', including those by Michel Foucault, one of the most important philosophers in this area. The same chapter will also include an introduction to English plays in which the use of contemporary colloquial English will be studied in connection to social class and identity, and how it serves to create verbal violence. Chapter 2 will focus on Bernard Shaw's *Pygmalion* (1914), Chapter 3 will examine Harold Pinter's *The Birthday Party (*1957), and the last chapter will deal with Anthony Neilson's *The Censor* (1997).

PART I:
VERBAL VIOLENCE AS A MEANS OF CONSTRUCTING AUTHORITY THROUGH THE USE OF RHETORIC IN RENAISSANCE DRAMATIC DIALOGUE

CHAPTER 1
POWER AND THE WORD: RHETORIC

The term 'rhetoric'[4] comes from the Greek word 'rhetör', meaning "speaker in the assembly", and is defined as the art of using language for persuasion, in speaking or writing, and especially in oratory (Cuddon, 1998: 747).

In mid-fifth century B.C., Athens was governed by democracy. Thus, the ability of orators to move the crowds in the assemblies through rhetoric was closely associated with the concept of power. It was the sophists[5] who appreciated the art of rhetoric and understood the importance of being able to transform effective reasoning into persuasive public speech. Sophists, thus, laid the groundwork for the next generation of thinkers including Plato and Aristotle (Dillon and Gergel, 2003: ix). Some of the major Classical works on rhetoric include Aristotle's *Treatise on Rhetoric*, Marcus Tullius Cicero's *De Inventione* and *De Oratore,* and Marcus Fabius Quintilian's *Istitutio Oratoria* (Cuddon, 1998: 748).

Aristotle's *Treatise on Rhetoric* has been one of the most influential works on rhetoric and oratory. In *Treatise on Rhetoric*, Aristotle defines rhetorical discourse as a faculty of considering all the possible means and devices of persuasion used by an orator in order to make an intellectual and emotional impact on an audience so as to persuade them to accede to the orator's point of view (1995: 11) Rhetoric, like logic, is present in all sciences, but is not a distinct science itself. It is instead an art (Aristotle, 1995: 1). As Socrates also points out in *Phaedrus,* it is a "universal art of enchanting the mind by arguments" (Plato, 1993: 74). Aristotle states that each art is suitable to inform or persuade respecting its own subject[6], but persuasion itself is the business of no art except rhetoric[7] (Aristotle, 1995: 11).

---

[4] According to Abrams, rhetoric, in the broad sense, is the study of language in its practical uses, focusing on the persuasive and other effects of language, and on the means by which one can achieve those effects on auditors or readers (1999: 268-269).

[5] A sophist is an 'expert' or 'pundit', one who is skilled or 'wise' (sophos) such as Protagoras, Gorgias, Prodicus, Hippias, Antiphon, Thrasymachus, Critias, Euthydemus, Dionysodorus, Alcidamas, and the anonymus Iamblici (Dillon and Gergel, 2003: "Introduction", x). Other definitions of a 'sophist' are a rhetorician who has no concern for 'truth', or one who teaches rhetoric to students lacking 'truth' in exchange for money.

[6] A good example can be found in Plato's *Gorgias*. When Socrates asks Gorgias what kind of power rhetoric has, Gorgias compares an orator with a doctor:

Aristotle argues that there are three kinds of rhetoric, 'deliberative', 'judicial', and 'demonstrative' (or 'epideictic'). The business of 'deliberative' rhetoric is partly exhortation to persuade and partly dissuasion on what is either expedient or inexpedient[8], and adopts the future tense because it is directed towards things to come, such as finance, war and peace, safeguard of the territory, imports and exports and legislature. 'Judicial'[9] rhetoric concerns itself with accusation and defence. Its object is justice and injustice and it employs the past tense, for it is on the subject of actions already done. The third kind of rhetoric, which is 'demonstrative'[10] is about

---

> You might well be amazed, Socrates, if you knew the whole truth and realized that oratory embraces and controls almost all other spheres of human activity. I can give you a striking illustration of this. It has often happened I have gone with my brother and other doctors to some sick person who refused to drink his medicine or to submit to surgery or cautery, and when the doctors could not persuade him I have succeeded, simply by the use of the art of oratory. I tell you that, if any city that you like to name, an orator and a doctor had to compete before the Assembly or any other body for the appointment of medical officer, the man who could speak would be appointed by an overwhelming vote if he wanted the post, and the doctor would be nowhere. (1960: 34)

[7] In Plato's *Phaedrus*, Socrates compares rhetoric to medicine:

Socrates:	Rhetoric is like medicine
Phaedrus:	How is that?
Socrates:	Why, because medicine has to define the nature of the body and rhetoric of the soul-if you would proceed, not empirically but scientifically, in the one case to impact health and strength by giving medicine and food, in the other to implant the conviction which you require by the right use of words and principles (1993: 83).

[8] What is advisable or not advisable.

[9] In judicial oratory, the narrator must clearly narrate the subject by avoiding long and rapid narration, and bias the audience in favour of the orator. Proof in judicial should be demonstrative and should rely on facts, emphasize the point that there was no harm, in the degree of the importance supposed, and stress the moral action of the action (Aristotle, 1995: 262).

[10] In Act III, scene ii, of Shakespeare's *Julius Caesar,* Brutus addresses the crowd (after the death of Caesar) stating his reasons for joining the conspiracy. He builds his case on the concept of 'honor' and the benefit of Rome. Then Brutus makes a fatal mistake by leaving the stage to Antony, who captures the attention of the audience by coming to stage with the corpse of Caesar:

> Friends, Romans, countrymen, lend me your ears;
> I come to bury Caesar, not to praise him.
> The evil that men do lives after them,
> The good is oft interred with their bones;
> So let it be with Caesar was ambitious.
> If it were so, it was a grievous fault,
> And grievously hath Caesar answered it.
> Here, under leave of Brutus and the rest-
> For Brutus is an honourable man;

praise and blame with the goal of honouring or disgracing and uses the present tense as it refers to the qualities generally accepted as either praiseworthy or despicable (Aristotle, 1995: 24-29). Of the three kinds of rhetoric defined by Aristotle "judicial" rhetoric seems to be the most commonly employed.

Aristotle goes on to explain the three points that should be considered in the process of 'producing a speech'; Leaving a good 'impression on the audience', 'style', and 'arrangement of parts'.

The first of these points is concerned with the ways that an orator can affect the listeners. This can be done by impressing them "in a certain way", by presenting oneself as a man of character, or by using proven facts in one's arguments (1995: 203).

The second is the subject of style. Aristotle expands on the idea of style by referring to "excellence of style", "purity of style" and "elevation of style". "Excellence" can be achieved through a clear style, which may be possible by

---

So are they all, all honourable men-
Come I to speak in Caesar's funeral.
He was my friend, faithful and just to me;
But Brutus says he was ambitious,
And Brutus is an honourable man.
He hath brought many captives home to Rome,
Whose ransoms did the general coffers fill:
Did this in Caesar seem ambitious?
When that the poor have cried, Caesar hath wept;
Ambition should be made of sterner stuff:
Yet Brutus says he was ambitious,
And Brutus is an honourable man.
You all did see that on the Lupercal
I thrice presented him a kingly crown,
Which he did thrice refuse. Was this ambition?
Yet Brutus says he was ambitious,
And sure he is an honourable man.
I speak not to disprove what Brutus spoke,
But here I am to speak what I do know.
You all did love him once, not without cause,
What cause withholds you then to mourn foe him?
O judgement! Thou art fled to brutish beasts,
And men have lost their reason. Bear with me;
My heart is in the coffin there with Caesar,
And I must pause till it come back to me. (III. ii, 75-108)

By the time Antony has finished, the meaning of the word 'honor' emphasized by Brutus has been weakened.

employing nouns, verbs and metaphors[11] in their general use. For example, Aristotle states that metaphors should be used as an analogy and that one should use positive metaphors to embellish his subject, while using negative metaphors if one wishes to "cry it [the subject] down" (1995: 210-211). Also, in order to create a natural language, one must employ 'high' or 'low' language (1995: 208) appropriate for the subject, and avoid using foreign words, compound words and newly coined words that the audience might not be familiar with.

The "purity of style" depends on assigning the correct connective particles (as 'thus', 'although' etc.) that the sentence requires (Aristotle, 1995: 220), expressing ideas using definite words rather than generals[12], avoiding the use of vague terms, using words in their proper gender (feminine, masculine or neuter) and correctly quoting the plural, dual, and singular numbers (Aristotle, 1995: 221). In short, for "excellence", the style must be natural and easy to understand.

Aristotle puts forth that "elevation of style" is produced by seven expedients. The first two expedients concern the use of the noun or only its definition if it is more to taste[13] (1995: 222). The third is illustration by the use of metaphors (including proverbs and hyperboles) and epithets. The fourth is using the plural for the singular such as the employment of 'Grecian Heavens' instead of 'heaven' (Aristotle, 1995: 222). The fifth is the assignment of each word with its own particle instead of using a common one for all as in: "[t]his woman, this my wife" (Aristotle, 1995: 223). The sixth is the proper use of connectives, such as the case in "Having departed and having spoken to him" or, "having departed, I spoke to him" (Aristotle, 1995: 223). The last expedient is about the depiction of expressions from absent qualities[14] as in saying that "a trumpet" is a "lyreless harmony" (Aristotle, 1995: 223).

Aristotle indicates that there are two kinds of style; "continuous" and "reflex". By "continuous", he refers to a style which does not divide itself into parts and is composed of one whole flow[15]. Aristotle calls it "continuous" because it does not

---

[11] Aristotle indicates that he should use a positive metaphor if one wishes to embellish his subject and employ a negative one if he wishes to "cry it down" (1995: 211)

[12] Aristotle does not expand or provide examples of this aspect.

[13] Aristotle's defines the circle as "a plane superficies, whose circumference is at all points equidistant from the centre." (Aristotle, 1995: 222).

[14] One of the examples that Aristotle provides is from the work of Antimachus celebrating the hill Teumessus, "There is a certain little hill visited by the winds;" (1995: 223)

[15] This is the old style, employed by historians as in the example "this is the exposition of the historical research of Herodotus, of Thurium" (Aristotle, 1995: 229).

have a "termination" (1995: 230). On the other hand, he defines "reflex"[16] as one consisting of 'periods', each of which has a beginning and an end, and a length easily taken in at a glance (1995: 229-230). This division, enriched with instances of 'antithesis' or 'alliteration' as "In his life you spoke ill of him, and now after his death you write ill" (1995: 234-235) etc., is both pleasing and easier to remember.

Aristotle points out that "elegancies and approved beauties [of style]" are derived from presenting information in such a way that it is received with ease and therefore pleasant (1995: 234). This is best achieved by the use of "metaphor"[17] (and similes), "antithesis"[18], and "personification"[19]. In the case of 'metaphor'[20], Aristotle states that when the poet calls old age "stubble,"[21] he produces in us a knowledge and information by means of a "common genus"; for both are past their prime (1995: 234-5). Similarly, 'similes' produce the same effect, because it is a "metaphor with the difference of the addition [of a particle denoting similitude]" (1995: 235). With reference to 'antithesis', Aristotle indicates that it should be used in the wording of expressions. An example of 'antithesis' is "deeming the common peace of the rest, a very war to their individual interests", in which "war" is used in opposition to "peace" (1995: 235-236). The last point is about "personification", which helps "setting forth to the eyes", as in the following example: "having his prime yet blooming" (1995: 239-240).

The third one of the three points that should be considered in the process of 'producing a speech' is the arrangement of the parts. Exordium is the "commencement of the speech; which in poetry is the prologue, and in the performances on the pipe, the prelude: for these are all commencement, and, as it were, an opening of the way for what to succeed." (Aristotle, 1995: 251)[22]. An

[16]Aristotle defines 'reflex' in terms of resembling "antistrophic odes of the old poets" (Aristotle, 1995: 229-230)

[17] Metaphor: "Changing a word from its literal meaning to one not properly applicable but analogous to it; assertion of identity rather than, as with simile, likeness" (Lanham, 1991: 100).

[18] Antithesis: "Conjoining contrasting ideas" (Lanham, 1991: 16).

[19] Personification: "An animal or an inanimate object is represented as having human attributes and addressed or made to speak as if it were human" (Lanham, 1991: 123).

[20] Aristotle also recognizes proverbs, hyperboles as metaphors (1995: 245).

[21] A stump of reaped corn.

[22] The "exordia" of demonstrative rhetoric arise from praise, blame, exhortation, dissuasion, and appeals to the hearers. It may derive praise, like Gorgias does in the Olympic oration: "Men worthy, O Greeks, of admiration among many;" for he is eulogizing those who instituted the general assemblies, or may include blame such as: "because they distinguish by prizes the excellencies of person, while for those who are wise they propose no reward;" and thirdly, from suggesting advice; for instance, "-because it is fitting to honour the good," (Aristotle, 1995: 251).

“exordium” in judicial speech that is “equivalent to the opening scenes of dramas” should awaken the attention of the hearers and excite them (1995: 252). For example, when one is to introduce oneself in the process of making a defence, he should eliminate any negative impression that the judges might have about him and present himself as a person of character (1995: 253). One of the examples that Aristotle suggests for achieving such an end is as follows: “[l]end me your whole attention, for the question does not affect me any more than yourself;” or “for I will relate to you a thing so strange, so wonderful, as you never yet heard.” (1995: 254)[23].

In Chapter XVI on “Narration” Aristotle comments on judicial oratory. He indicates that in judicial oratory, the narration must make the subject clear, and bias the audience in favour of the orator. The defendant’s narration must be brief and convey an impression of his character, which is possible by manifesting a moral purpose, by narration of the concomitant circumstances and by means of speaking with feeling (1995: 259-260). However, if there should be any narration, it should be in order to awaken the recollection of things that have already happened (1995: 262).

As for “proof”, a good number of approaches are available in Aristotle’s work. For example, in demonstrative (‘epideictic’) oratory the proof is made by amplification, while in ‘deliberative’ the “fallacies of the adversary must be observed” (1995: 269).

As for the last part of a speech which Aristotle defines as “peroration” (conclusion of a speech), it serves to make the final impact on the audience’s feelings and thoughts. “Peroration” consists of four things; “Of getting the hearer favourable to one’s self, and ill-disposed towards the adversary”, “of amplification and extenuation”, “of placing the hearer under the influence of the passions” and “of awakening his [person in the audience] recollection” (Aristotle, 1995: 270).

The first surviving treatise produced on rhetoric after Aristotle’s work *Treatise on Rhetoric* (4th B.C.) and *Rhetorica ad Alexandrum* (4th B.C.) is Marcus Tullius Cicero’s[24] *De Inventione* (91-89 B.C.) (Kennedy, 1972: 111). It shows the changes that took place in the two and a half centuries that followed Aristotle’s work. The

[23]Compared with the demonstrative and judicial oratory, “exordia” is employed less in a deliberative speech because the audience are aware of the subject. Thus, deliberate oratory needs no exordium except about the speaker himself or his opponent, or if the audience conceives the importance of the subject matter, either too serious or too trifling, otherwise than he could wish, thinking it. An example of this is panegyric of Gorgias on the Eleans beginning with the following line “O Elis, city blest by fortune!” (Aristotle: 1995: 255).

[24] Quintilian indicates that “the name of Cicero has come to be regarded not as the name of a man, but as the name of eloquence itself” (1998: 63)

first book of *De Inventione* deals with the four constitutions of speech (question of fact, law, nature of the act, and legal procedure) and the parts of an oration as "Exordium"[25], "Narrative"[26], "Partition"[27], "Confirmation"[28], "Refutation"[29], "Digression"[30] and "Peroration"[31]. Book II takes up the three kinds of oratory: epideictic (demonstrative), deliberative and forensic (judicial). Cicero presents the arguments that are appropriate for each kind of speech.

De Inventione is followed by Cicero's *De Oratore* (55 B.C.). *De Oratore* is composed of three books and sets Cicero's ideal of what the perfect speaker should be. Each of the three books of dialogues takes place at various spots of L. Crassus's estate at Tusculum in September 91 B.C. between orators active in the age of Cicero such as Crassus, Antonius, old Augur Scaevola, Sulpicius, Aurelius Cotta, Lutatius Catulus and Julius Caesar Strabo Vopiscus.

The main points under discussion in *Book I* are general knowledge about oration, and the education of the orator. Crassus states that an orator has the ability to express his ideas better than a specialist because he has a wide general knowledge:

> In fact that favourite assertion of Socrates– that every man was eloquent enough upon a subject that he knew– has in it some plausibility but no

---

[25] The "exordium" is divided into 'introduction' and 'insinuation'. An "introduction is an address which directly and in plain language makes the auditor well-disposed, receptive, and attentive. Insinuation is an address which by dissimulation and indirection unobtrusively steals into mind of the auditor."(Cicero, 1993: 43)

[26] The "narrative" is "an exposition of events that have occured or are supposed to have occured." (Cicero, 1993: 55)

[27] In an argument a "partition" correctly made "renders the whole speech clear and perspicious" (Cicero, 1993: 63). This can be done by presenting the agreed and disputed aspects of the subject, or setting forth the matters to be discussed in a methodical way. (Cicero, 1993: 63)

[28] "Confirmation" or 'proof' is "part of the oration which by marshalling arguments lends credit, authority, and support to our case". (Cicero, 1993: 69)

[29] The "refutation" is "that part of an oration in which arguments are used to impair, disprove, or weaken the confirmation or proof in our opponents' speech." (Cicero, 1993: 123)

[30] Cicero defines "digression" with reference to Hermagoras, although he does not believe that it should be a seperate part:

> In this digression he [Hermagoras] thinks a passage should be introduced unconnected with the case and the actual point to be decided; it might contain praise of oneself or abuse of the opponent, or lead to some other case which may supply confirmation or refutation not by argument but by adding emphasis by means of some amplification. (Cicero, 1993: 147)

[31] The "peroration" is "the end and conclusion of the whole speech; it has three parts, the summing-up, the indignatio or exciting of indignation or ill-will against the opponent, and the conquestio or the arousing of pity and sympathy." (Cicero, 1993: 147)

> truth: it is nearer the truth to say that neither can anyone be eloquent upon a subject that is unknown to him, nor, if he knows it perfectly and yet does not know how to shape and polish his style, can he speak fluently even upon that which he does know.
> Accordingly, should anyone wish to define in a comprehensive manner the complete and special meaning of the word, he will be an orator, in my opinion worthy of so dignified a title, who, whatever the topic that crops up to be unfolded in discourse, will speak thereon with knowledge, method, charm and retentive memory, combining with these qualifications a certain distinction of bearing.(Cicero, 1996: 47)

Although Antonius agrees with Crassus, he states that attaining such a wide general knowledge is impossible:

> I do not picture [the orator] as Crassus did, who I thought included, under the single vocation and title of the orator, omniscience in every topic and every art: in fact I take him to be a man who can use language agreeable to the ear, and arguments suited to convince, in law-court disputes and in debates of public business. (Cicero, 1996: 151)

Next, Crassus discusses the nature and training of the orator, describes various categories of rhetorical theory and outlines rhetorical exercises, and concludes with the necessity of studying history and law. Oration is made up of five divisions: invention, arrangement, style, memory and delivery:

> *Crassus*: And, since all the activity and ability of an orator falls into five divisions, I learned that he must first hit upon what to say; then manage and marshal his discoveries, not merely in orderly fashion, but with a discriminating eye for the exact weight as it were of each argument; next go on to array them in the adornments of style; after that keep them guarded in his memory; and in the end deliver them with effect and charm. (Cicero, 1996: 99)

In *Book II*, Antonius discusses the orator on the basis of his own experience. He states that oratory derives from ability, but owes little to art. For, while art is concerned with the things that are known, the activity of the orator has to do with opinion instead of knowledge (Cicero, 1996: 219). Although he admits that oratory is not the highest form of art, he asserts that clever rules may be laid down for "playing upon men's feelings and making prize of their goodwill". He adds that if anyone is to claim that the knowledge of such devices is an art of real significance, "I am not going to quarrel with him" (Cicero, 1996: 221).

Antonius also discusses three functions of the orator, which is to win over the audience's sympathy, to prove what is true, and to stir their emotions to the desired action that become the central concept of Cicero's rhetorical theory (Kennedy, 1927: 207). Antonius further emphasizes the power of oration:

> It is the part of the orator, when advising on affairs of supreme importance, to unfold his opinion as a man having authority: his duty too it is to arouse a listless notion, and to curb its unbridled impetuosity. By one and the same power of eloquence the deceitful among mankind are brought to destruction, and the righteous to deliverance who more passionately than the orator can encourage to virtuous conduct, or more zealously that he reclaim from vicious courses? Who can more austerely censure the wicked, or more gracefully praise men of worth? Whose invective can more forcibly subdue the power of lawless desire? Whose comfortable words can soothe grief more tenderly? (Cicero, 1996: 223)

In *Book III,* Crassus concerns himself primarily with style and delivery, and touches upon the orator's need for a general education and especially knowledge of philosophy. In this respect, he reviews ancient intellectual history blaming Socrates for separating rhetoric and philosophy. At a different point, he states that the orator must have knowledge in order to amplify, or explain something in greater detail (Kennedy, 1972: 208). *De Oratore* ends with a tribute to Hortensius, the rising young orator, a tribute apparently intended as an imitation of the reference to Isocrates at the end of *Phaedrus* (Plato, 1993)

De Institutione Oratoria, or *On the Education of an Orator* (55 B.C.) by M. Fabius Quintilian shares some common features with *Treatise on Rhetoric*, and *De Oratore*, but instead of composing a rhetorical treatise like Aristotle and Cicero, prefers to produce a study of the whole education of the orator. Quintilian is considered the greatest teacher of rhetoric at Rome. He taught *invention*–discovery of the relevant material, *arrangement*–organization of the material into sound structure form, *style*–consideration of the appropriate manner suitable for the subject matter and occasion such as grand style, middle style, and low style or plain style, *memory*–technique on how to memorize, and *delivery*– techniques on how to actually deliver a speech. He is regarded as a teacher of the curriculum rather than as a reformer. The twelve books of *De Institutione Oratoria* reflect ancient rhetorical theory[32], method of teaching, and suggestions to help students understand the rules of rhetoric, increase their power of speech and nourish their eloquence (Quintilian, 1996: 17). In Book X, to benefit the student of rhetoric, he includes a list of Greek and Roman playwrights, among other writers, who are noteworthy for their rhetorical skill. This part of his argument will be mentioned later on in the discussion of rhetoric.

George Kennedy, who has covered many figures used for rhetorical ends in his book *The Art of Rhetoric in the Roman World* (1972), indicates that rhetoric played an important role in education in the Roman period. Students were taught the use of 'apostrophe'[33], 'alliteration'[34], 'assonance'[35], 'tricolon'[36], 'anaphora'[37], 'asyndeton'[38], 'homoeoteleuton'[39], 'polyptoton'[40], 'figura etymologica', 'commutation', the use of

---

[32] Quintilian outlines the structure of these twelve books in the introduction of *Book I*:

> My first will be concerned with the education preliminary to the duties of the teacher of rhetoric. My second will deal with the rudiments of the schools of rhetoric and with problems connected with the essence of rhetoric itself. The next five will be concerned with Invention, in which I include Arrangement. The four following will be assigned to Eloquence, under which head I include Memory and Delivery. Finally there will be one book in which our complete orator will be delineated; as far as my feeble powers permit, I shall discuss his character, the rules which should guide him in undertaking, studying and pleading cases, the style of his eloquence, the time at which he should cease to plead cases and the studies to which he should devote himself after such cessation. (1996: 15-17)

In the earlier books Quintilian tends to address parents and teachers, in the later books he speaks directly to the would-be orator. The concept of nature is important throughout: Quintilian wants to produce a natural style, he wants a speech to grow naturally and organically, and he wants to bring each speaker to his full natural development (Kennedy, 1972: 499).

[33] Apostrophe: "Breaking off a discourse to address some person or personified thing either present or absent." (Lanham, 1991: 20).

[34] Alliteration: "Recurrence of an initial consonant sound [...]". (Lanham, 1991:6-7).

[35] Assonance: "Identity or similarity in sound between internal vowels in neighboring words." (Lanham, 1991: 24).

[36] Tricolon: "The three-unit pattern common in many prose styles." (Lanham, 1991: 154).

[37] Anaphora: "Repetition of the same word at the beginning of successive clauses or verses". (Lanham, 1991: 11).

[38] Asyndeton: "Omission of conjunctions between words, phrases, or clauses." (Lanham, 1991: 25).

[39] Homoeoteleutor: "In English, the use of similar endings to words, phrases, sentences." (Lanham, 1991: 83)

‘synonyms’, ‘antonyms’, ‘oxymoron’[41], paradox[42], innuendo, epigram, point, and declamatory structure. The result was that the rhetoricians put judicial oratory first in their discussion and developed categories applicable to it (1972: 115).

After the Roman Empire, the study of rhetoric continued to be central to the study of the verbal arts. In the Middle Ages, rhetoric became part of the 'trivium'[43], the lower division of the seven liberal arts (arithmetic, astronomy, geometry, and music, in conjunction with grammar, logic, and rhetoric) comprising grammar, rhetoric, and logic. The rules for oral and written composition were divided into five parts: ‘invention’, ‘arrangement’, ‘style’, ‘memory’ and ‘delivery’ as already discussed by Quintilian in *De Institutione Oratoria* (Cuddon, 1998: 748). However, there was virtually no interest in ancient oratory, even though some of Cicero’s speeches and collections of declamations were still extant. It was Petrarch who reclaimed classical oratory by his discovery of Cicero’s *Pro Archia* in 1333. He was followed by other humanists like Giovanni Bussi, who published the first edition of Cicero’s orations in 1471. However, it took longer for the Greek orators to be rediscovered and translated into Latin (Vickers, 1988: 286). By the sixteenth century, oration had already become a literary genre rather than a means of political persuasion and many of those published were epideictic, intended for the reader instead of the audience’ (Vickers, 1988: 287).

The chief medieval authorities on rhetoric were Martianus Capella (5th Century), author of an encyclopaedia of the seven liberal arts entitled *Satyricon, or De Nuptiss Philologiae et Mercurii et de Septem Artibus liberalibus libri novem*, Flavius Magnus Aurelius Cassiodorus (485-585), known for his *Institutiones Divinarum et Humanarum Lectionum*, and Isidore of Seville (560-636), who compiled an encyclopaedic work setting forth the erudition of the ancient world (Bram, 1989: 252).

Renaissance humanism defined itself as disfavoring medieval scholastic logic and dialectic and favoring the study of classical Latin style and grammar, philology and rhetoric. During the Renaissance, the study of rhetoric was again based on the works of such writers of classical antiquity as Aristotle, Cicero, and Quintilian. A

---

[40] Polyptoton: “Repetition of words from the same root but with different endings.” (Lanham, 1991: 117).

[41] Oxymoron: “A condensed paradox [...]”. (Lanham, 1991: 106).

[42] Paradox: “A seemingly self-contradictory statement, which yet is shown to be (sometimes in a surprising way) true”. (Lanham, 1991: 107).

[43] Theory of education, literally meaning ‘three ways’, or ‘three roads’.

number of contemporary books were produced, among them the *Art or Craft of Rhetoryke* (1530s) by the English schoolmaster Leonard Cox, *Art of Rhetorique* (1553) by the English statesmen and writer Thomas Wilson, and treatises by Pierre de Courcelles and André de Tonquelin also stand out. Rhetoric was a prescribed subject in colleges and universities, public disputations and competitive exercises keeping the practice long alive (Bram, 252: 1986).

Desiderius Erasmus was an influential figure in the rebirth of interest in classical rhetoric. His work, *De Duplici Copia Verborum et Rerum* (1512), was widely published and became one of the basic school texts on the subject. Also, Juan Luis Vives helped shape the study of rhetoric in England. He was appointed in 1523 to the Lectureship of Rhetoric at Oxford, and was entrusted by Henry VIII to be one of the tutors of Mary. His writings on rhetoric included *Rhetoricae, De Ratione Dicendi, Libri Tres* (1533) and *De Consultatione* (1533).

The mid-1500s saw the rise of theories on rhetoric written in English rather than in the Classical languages such as John Milton's *Institutiones Oratoriae* (1544), Thomas Wilson's *The Arte of Rhetorique* (1553), Angel Day's *The English Secretorie* (1586), George Puttenham's *The Arte of English Poesie* (1589), Richard Rainholde's *Foundacion of Rhetorike* (1563) and Francis Bacon's *The Advancement of Learning* (1605). Thomas Hobbes also wrote on rhetoric and promoted a simpler and more natural style that used figures of speech sparingly. In addition, he produced a shortened translation of Aristotle's *Rhetoric*.

As Enright and Chickera point out John Dryden is generally credited in creating a new and modern English style. He indicated that 'style' should be suitable to the person, subject and occasion. Parallel to this view, he advocated the use of English words instead of foreign words if possible and his own work became exemplars of this style (1962: 105-9).

In the early eighteenth century, rhetoric declined in importance more on its theoretical than on its practical style and for the following half-century, the art of rhetoric had increasingly fewer exponents. *Lectures on Rhetoric* (1783) by Hugh Blair achieved considerable popularity in the late eighteenth and nineteenth centuries, as did the *Philosophy of Rhetoric* (1776) by George Campell and the *Elements of Rhetoric* (1828) by Richard Whately (Bram, 1986: 252). In the first half of the twentieth century, a revival of the study of formal rhetoric, encouraged largely by the exponents of semantics, occurred throughout the English-speaking countries of the world (Bram, 1986: 252)

Due to renewed importance of language and persuasion in the twentieth century, the study of rhetoric was revived during the period. The rise of advertising and of mass media such as photography, telegraphy, radio, and film brought rhetoric more prominently into people's lives (Berger, 1997: 14). The rhetorical theory in contemporary times is as much influenced by the research done in behavioral sciences and by theories of literary criticism as by ancient rhetorical theory. Early rhetorical theorists attempted to turn the study of rhetoric into a social science focusing primarily on rhetoric as speech, while contemporary rhetorical theorists are interested in the spoken and written word as well as music, film, performance, radio, television, etc. (Berger, 1997: 14). Some of the notable twentieth century writers working in the field of history and theory of rhetoric include Wayne C. Booth, Cleanth Brooks, I.A. Richards and Richard A. Lanham.

Having presented a general overview of rhetoric, it is necessary to next focus on the power and danger of rhetoric. Victoria Kahn states that the term 'rhetoric' refers to "a repertoire of means of persuasion ranging from the figurative language and formal organization of a text" to the modes of persuasion used by the speaker, "which are available for the service of both good and evil" (1994: 5). As rhetoric has always been associated with the concept of speaking persuasively, its relation to "truth" has also been widely discussed by ancient philosophers. Most classical teachers of rhetoric have commented upon the use of rhetoric to various ends, emphasizing the point that although rhetoric is a powerful instrument, it has no regard for truth. Thus, it should be used with caution, and used for truth.

Socrates who emphasizes the importance of truth in *Phaedrus*[44] (427-347 B.C.), points out that mere truth will not make anyone a better orator:

> Perhaps, however, rhetoric has been getting too roughly handled by us, and she might answer: what amazing nonsense is this! As if I forced any man to learn to speak in ignorance of the truth! Whatever my advice may be worth, I should have told him to arrive at the truth first, and then come to me. At the same time I boldly assert that mere knowledge of the truth will not give you the art of persuasion. (Plato, 1993:74)

[44] *Phaedrus* is a dialogue between Socrates and Phaedrus set under a plane tree by the banks of the Ilissus, in which they discuss love, lovers, and non-lovers [friends]. Additionally, they debate about rhetoric, rhetoricians and dialecticians (Plato, 1993)

Socrates goes further to say that a skilful rhetorician has no need for truth:

> *Socrates:* [...] he who would be a skilful rhetorician has no need of truth–for that in courts of law men literally care nothing about truth, but only about conviction: and this is based on probability, to which he would be a skilful orator should therefore give his whole attention. [...] in speaking the orator should run after probability, and say good-bye to the truth. And the observance of this principle throughout a speech furnishes the whole art.
>
> *Phaedrus*: That is what the professors of rhetoric do actually say. (Plato, 1993:85)

In Plato's *Gorgias*, the other rhetorician Gorgias stresses the point that rhetoric is a powerful art that must be used with caution:

> Such is the nature and power of the art of oratory, Socrates, as there are the use of any other accomplishment. Just because a man has acquired such skill in or in-all wrestling or armed combat that can beat anyone, friend or foe, is no reason why he should employ it against all men indiscriminately and strike and wound and kill his friends. And, on the other hand, if a course of physical training has put a man in good condition and made him a boxer, and he then strikes his father or mother or some relation or friend, that is no reason for detesting and banishing trainers and those who teach the use of weapons. [...] The same argument holds good about oratory. The orator can speak on any subject against any opposition in such a way as to prevail on any topic he chooses, but the fact that he possesses the power to deprive doctors and other professional men of their reputation does not justify him in doing so; he is as much bound to make a proper use of his oratory as the possessor of physical superiority. But if a man who has acquired orational skill uses the power which his rat confers to do wrong, that is no reason to detest and banish his teachers. His instruction was given to be employed for good end, and if the uses it for the opposite it is he, not the man who taught him, who deserves detestation and banishment and death. (1960: 34-35)

Aristotle in turn discusses the knowledge of rhetoric, and the dangers that it has in the hands of those who use it unwisely, or without any regard for truth. Aristotle says that if a person "unfairly availing himself of such powers of speaking, may be, in a very high degree, injurious" (Aristotle, 1995: 9). Aristotle blames sophists for teaching rhetoric to anyone who can afford to pay the fee[45] for the lessons[46]:

> Now as logic and rhetoric are in their own indifferent to truth or falsehood, it must require an act of choice in either case to select the former or the latter [...] But when logic is prostituted to the support of false propositions by the bad principles of its professors, it is branded with the name sophistry, and the persons who so misapply it are called sophists; whereas, in the case of rhetoric, no such distinction in reference to the principle of its professors ever obtained; but the name of orator is enjoyed equally by all who are masters of the art, whether they exercise it fairly or not. (1995: 10)

Rhetoric may be used to persuade, manipulate, or propagate ideas. When rhetoric is used to establish power, it becomes closely related to propaganda[47]. It may be a scheme for propagating a doctrine or practice, or systematic attempt by an interested individual to control the attitudes of groups of individuals through the use of suggestion, and, consequently, to control their actions[48]:

> Techniques of persuasion or propaganda involve arguments addressed to reason, deliberately planned and systematic use of symbols, chiefly

[45] The fees quoted for a full course from Protagoras, or Gorgias is 100 minae (around £100,000 or $160,000 in todeys prices) (Dillon and Gergel, 2003: introduction xii).

[46] It should be noted that in Plato's *Meno,* Socrates defines sophists as those "who profess to be teachers of virtue, and declare themselves available to any Greek who wants to learn, and who also set and change a fee for it (Dillon and Gergel, 2003: 8).

[47] The word 'propaganda' takes its origin for the Latin "propagare" meaning "the gardeners' practice of pinning the fresh shoots of a plant into the earth in order to reproduce new plants which will later take on a life of their own" (Brown, 1963: 10).

[48]There are different ways of propaganda ranging from written texts to speeches, but the most effective means of persuasion and propaganda is personal communication due to several reasons. Firstly, personal contacts are more casual, more difficult to avoid compared to mass communication. Secondly, face-to-face contact permits of greater flexibility in that the content can be varied to suit the resistance of the audience by the communicator modifying his line. Thirdly, the direct personal relationship involved in face-to-face relationship can enhance the rewards for accepting the message and the punishment for not doing so. Fourthly, people are more likely to put their trust in someone they know that in an impersonal mass communication. And lastly, by personal contacts the communicator can often achieve his purpose without actually persuading the audience to accept his point of view (Brown, 1963).

through suggestion and related psychological techniques, with the aim of altering and controlling opinions, ideas, and values, and ultimately of changing overt actions along predetermined lines. Persuasion or propaganda may also include the selective control of information to favour a particular viewpoint, and their intention might either be stated clearly, or concealed (Brown, 1963: 10).

When the question of the abuse of rhetoric arises, the name of Niccolo Machiavelli inevitably comes up. Machiavelli attempted to make rhetoric and prudential deliberation generate a new set of priorities in the domain of politics by saving it from ethical norms. For this reason, some identified Machiavelli with the abuse of rhetoric and condemn his divorce of ethics from politics and his merely instrumental use of the virtues as immoral cunning (Kahn, 1994: 10). For example, Cardinal Pole in his *Apologia ad Caralum Quintum* (1539) tells the readers that Machiavelli's works "stink of the malice of Satan" and that *The Prince* was written "by Satan's hand" (in Kahn, 1994: 87).

This 'dark' aspect of Machiavellian rhetoric, which caused it to be criticized[49] by many, is its ethical indeterminacy, its concern with success and its use for the purpose of force and fraud, violence and misrepresentation. Machiavelli's rhetorical politics stand in opposition to the views held by the ancients, and transforms imitation to misrepresentation, persuasion to coercion, means to ends, intention to effect; demonic flexibility to allegorical stability, and virtue or to success (Kahn, 1994: 9).

'Rhetoric' and to a large extent 'Machiavellian rhetoric' have always had an important function, especially in verse drama. In his rhetorical theory illustrated in *The Arte of Poesie* (1589), George Puttenham states that poets were "from the beginning the best perswaders [persuaders] and their eloquence the first Rethoricke [Rhetoric] of the world." (*Book I*, 1529: 83). In fact, rhetoric has been an important part of drama since the very emergence of the genre itself in ancient Greece, and continued its existence from then on. Quintilian, in *De Inventione*, advises students to read the works of certain playwrights, among other writers such as poets, orators,

[49]In the Renaissance, rhetoric was conceives as an "ethically and ideologically neutral technique of argument on the one hand, and on the other, it was seen as the "embodiment of a faculty of practical reasoning or prudential deliberation that is tied to ethical norms." (Kahn, 1994: 9). The possible abuse of rhetoric was acknowledged but it was also believed that a good orator was of necessity a good man (Kahn, 1994: 9).

historians and philosophical writers, in order to improve their skills in oratory (*Book X-XII*, 1998: 1-75) In 'Book X' of *De Inventione,* Quintilian goes through a survey of both Greek[50] and Roman[51] writers that can serve as models for students of rhetoric.

With respect to ancient Greek drama, Quintilian states that Old Comedy, characterized by eloquence and a special power in the denunciation of vice, is almost the only form of poetry which portrays the grace of Attic diction. Also, its lofty, elegant and graceful style resembles oratory: "I am not sure that there is any style which bears a closer resemblance to oratory or is better adapted for forming the orator." (*Books X-XII*, 1998: 38). Examples of Old Comedy include the works of Aristophanes, Eupolis and Cratinus[52] (*Books X-XII*, 1998: 39).

With respect to 'New Comedy' Quintilian praises Menander's (342-291 B.C.) characterization. Quintilian indicates that he is "perfect" in his representation of actual life, rich in his power of invention and has a gift of style, and is able to adapt himself "perfectly" to every kind of circumstance, character and emotion (*Books X-XII*, 1998: 39). According to him, Menander shows his power by creating a number of characters such as 'soldiers', 'peasants', 'rich men and poor men', 'the angry man' and 'the suppliant', 'the gentle' and 'the harsh', and treating each of them according to "appropriateness" (*Books X-XII*, 1998:41)[53].

---

[50] Quintilian's list of Greek writers, apart from playwrights, are as follows: poets (Homer, Hesiod, appolonius, Aratus, Theocritus.), elegiac poets (Callimachus, Philetas, Archilochus of elegias, lyrical poets (Pindas, Stesichorus, Alcaeus, Simonides), historians (Thucydides, Herodotus, Theopompus, Philistus, Ephorus, Clitarchus, Timagenes and Xenophon), orators (Demosthenes, Aeschines, Hyperides, Isocrates, Demetrius of Phalerum) and writers of philosophy (Plato, Xenophon, Aristotle, Theophrastus) [1998: "Introduction"]

[51] With respect to Roman writers, Quintilian also provides a list of poets (Virgil, Macer, Lucretius, Varro of Atax, Ennius, Ovid, Cornelius Severus, Serranus, Valerius Flaccus, Saleius Bassus, Rabirius, Pedo, Lucan, Germanicus Augustus.) and elegiac poets (Tribullus, Propertius, Gallus, Lucilius, Persius, Terentius Varro, Catullus, Bibaculus, Horace, Caesius Bassus.), historians (Sallust, Titus Livius, Servilius, Aufidius Bassus, Cremutius), orators (Cicero, Demosthenes, Asinius Pollio, Messala, Gaius Caesar, Caeliurs, Calvus, Servius Sulpicius, Cassius Severus, Domitius Afer, Julius Africanus, Trachalus, Vibius Crispus, Julius Secundus) and writers of philosophy (Cicero, Brutus, Cornelius Celsus, Plautus, Catius.) [Quintilian, 1998: "Introduction"]

[52] Quintilian points out that even though Aeschylus was first to bring tragedy into prominence, his style is uncouth and inharmonious (1998: 39).

[53] Menander composed a form of light drama based on social activity focusing on the love affairs of the young, the obstacles placed in the way and the means by which such obstacles were overcome. Some of the "characters" mentioned by Quintilian can be seen in *Old Cantankerous.* In this play, Knemon, a bad-tempered man, marries a widow, who had one son from a previous marriage. They have a daughter. Later however, the wife leaves him due to his unpleasant behavior, and he continues to live like a hermit on his farm. Sostratos falls madly in love with the young daughter and comes to ask for her hand in marriage, but he is refused by the cantankerous man. Soon after Knemon falls into a well and is rescued by Sostratos. Finding Knemon quite reformed, his wife

As for Greek tragedy, Quintilian indicates that although both Sophocles and Euripides[54] brought the genre to a far greater perfection, the study of Euripides would have a greater contribution to students who are training themselves in 'judicial oratory' (*Books X-XII*, 1998:39). Comparing the two playwrights, Quintilian stresses the point that:

> Euripides [compared to Sophocles] will be found of far greater service to those who are training themselves for pleading in court. For his language, although actually censured by those who regard the dignity, the stately stride and sonorous of Sophocles as being more sublime, has a closer affinity to that of oratory, while he is full of striking reflections, in which, indeed, in their special sphere, he rivals the philosophers themselves, and for defence and attack may be compared with any orator that has won renown in the courts. Finally, although admirable in every kind of emotional appeal, he is easily supreme in the power to excite pity. (*Books X-XII*, 1998: 39).

Many instances of 'judicial oratory' can be found in Euripides' *Medea,* which illustrates the tragic story of a woman who has been betrayed by her husband. Medea, through her sorcery, helps Jason gain the Golden Fleece and betrays her father and kills her brother in the process. Medea and Jason return to Corinth with their two children and the tragedy begins after Jason decides to marry the daughter of King Creon. Creon, recognizing that Medea and her children will pose a constant threat to his own line of succession, rules that Medea and her children be sent into exile. For

---

comes back to him and he consents to the marriage of the young couple. Then he consents to Sostratos's sister marrying Gordias, his wife's son, and they live happily ever after. The character types that appear in this play are as follows: "Pan, the god of country life", "Sostratos, a young man about town", "Chaireas, his friend", "Pyrrhias, his servant" "Knemon, a cantankerous old farmer", "A Girl, his daughter", "Gorgias, his step-son", "Daos, Gorgias' servant", "Simiche, Kremon's servant", "Kallipides, Sostratos's father", "Getas, his servant", "Sikon, a cook", "Sostratos's Mother "and "Myrrhine, Knemon's estranged wife" also appear (Menander, 1987: 22). Other character types such as "Polemon, a professional soldier", "Glykera, the soldier's mistress" can be found in another play entitled *The Rape of the Lock* (Menander, 1987: 106). These plays were later adapted for the Roman stage by the playwright Plautus and Terence, which is evident by the similarity between Menander's stage types and Plautus's stock characters.

[54] It is said that only eighteen plays out of the ninety plays that Euripides is thought to have composed have survived. These are *Alcestis, Medea, Heracleidae, Hippolytus, Cyclops, Heracles, Iphigeneia in Tauris, Helen, Hecuba, Andromache, The Trojan Women, Ion, The Suppliant Women, Orestes, Electra, The Phoenician Women, Iphigeneia at Aulis, The Bacchae*, and *Alcmaeon at Corinth* (Worthen: 2000:92).

revenge, Medea poisons Jason's new bride and Creon, kills her own sons and flees from Corinth, rising above the scene in a dragon-drawn chariot with the dead bodies of her children.

In *Medea*, Jason is the spokesperson for men while Medea speaks for women, especially those who have been deceived[55]. Jason enters with attendants and begins his speech with an 'exordium'[56] designed to create a negative portrayal of Medea and a positive sketch of himself. He begins by asserting how hopeless it is to deal with "stubborn temper" (435-6) referring to Medea's personality. He insists that he does not mind her telling everyone that he is a "worthless man", but she is being banished for speaking ill of King Creon. After taking pride in his talents as a speaker he says: "As for me, it seems that I be no base speaker." (510) Jason lists his arguments in support of taking a new wife almost as though he were arguing in the courtroom, and thus, exemplifying 'judicial' rhetoric. Medea reminds him that every Greek knows that at the time he was trying to get hold of the Golden Fleece, she saved his life. Jason argues that it was not Medea, but Cypris who helped him and saved his life: "My view is that Cypris was alone responsible/ Of men and gods for the preserving

---

[55] Medea lays out the situation and role of women in Ancient times. She indicates that women have to get a husband to control them:

> We women are the most unfortunate creatures.
> Firstly, with an excess of wealth it is required
> For us to buy a husband and take for our bodies
> A master; for not to take one is even worse.
> And now the question is serious whether we take
> A good or bad one; for there is no easy escape
> For woman, nor can she say no to her marriage. (229-235)

Furthermore, she points out that men have the liberty to seek comfort elsewhere when they are bored at home, while women are deprived of the same rights. Also, she criticizes the general belief that women have a "peaceful time" living at home while men fight in war, underlining that she would prefer fighting in war rather than bearing children:

> A man, when he's tired of the company in his home,
> Goes out of the house and puts an end to his boredom
> And turn to a friend or companion of his own age.
> But we are forced to keep our eyes on one alone.
> What they say of us is that we have a peaceful time
> Living at home, while they do the fighting in war.
> How wrong they are! I would very much rather stand
> Three times in the front of battle than bear one child. (242-249)

[56] Insinuation is an address which by dissimulation and indirection unobtrusively steals into mind of the auditor."(Cicero, 1993: 43).

of my life." (515-516). He moves on to the next argument by suggesting that Medea, by coming to Greece, was fortunate and actually gained a lot more than she gave: "inhabit a Greek land and understand our ways/How to live by law instead of sweet will of force." (523-525). Here a contrast is drawn between 'barbarians' and civil Greek land, and by "our ways" he praises the law that enables him to act out his heart's desire –taking a second wife– while it prevents Medea from acting out hers.

After the 'exordium', he continues with an 'introduction' presenting the aim of his case as if he were under trial. He sets out the points which he aims to make, such as proving that taking a new bride was "first" a "clever move", "second[ly]" "wise" and finally, that it was for the best interest of both Medea and the children: "Here I will prove that, first, it was a clever move,/Secondly, a wise one, and, finally, that I made it/In your best interests and the children's." (536-538). He clearly implies that his case is misunderstood. He emphasizes that his decision to marry Creon's daughter was not motivated by his lack of sexual interest in Medea or a desire to have more children. It was instead a sacrifice that had to be made to bring the two families together by producing more brothers for their two sons:

> It was not–the point that upsets you– that I
> Grew tired of you bed and felt the need of a new bride;
> Nor with any wish to outdo your number of children.
> We have enough already. I am quite content.
> [...]
> By producing more of them
> To be brothers of yours, we would draw the families
> Together and all be happy. You need no children. (539-544)

Then he asks her whether or not it is a good plan, finishing off by diminishing Medea's sacrifice for him and marriage to a mere 'love question': "Do you think this a bad plan?/ You wouldn't if the love question hadn't upset you" (555-556). Thus, Jason tries to conceal the fact that he is betraying Medea by the employment of sophisticated rhetoric. However, a member of the Chorus notes that "Jason, though you have made this speech of yours look well,/Still I think, even though others do not agree,/You have betrayed your wife and are acting badly." (564-566). Additionally, Medea, in a soliloquy, stresses the dangers of good rhetoricians who are evil, pointing out that such rhetoricians deserve the greatest punishment because their confidence in their skills as a rhetorician gives them the power to do evil:

> [...] I think that the plausible speaker
> Who is a villain deserves that greatest punishment.
> Confident in his tongue's power to adorn evil,
> He stops at nothing. Yet he is not really wise.
> As in your case. There is no need to put on the airs
> Of a clever speaker, for one word will lay you flat. (568-571)

As for Roman playwrights that may be beneficial to the student of rhetoric, Quintilian indicates that Accius and Pacuvius are the most remarkable "for the force of their general reflections", "the weight of their words" and the "dignity of their character", but claims that that they lack polish, and have failed to put the finishing touches on their works (*Books X-XII*, 1998: 57). Among the tragic writers that he "has seen", he lists Pomponius Secundus, "as the best" (*Books X-XII*, 1998: 57).

Although Quintilian argues that "comedy" is the Roman's weakest point, he still cannot deny the perfection in Plautus' use of language. He quotes Aelius Stilo who says that if the muses wished to speak Latin, they would use the language of Plautus. He also mentions Afranius and Seneca in particular (*Books X-XII*, 1998: 57). The last Roman playwright Quintilian mentions is Seneca. Quintilian states that Seneca's style is weakened by "every kind of terror" and for this reason "the young men loved him rather than imitated him, and fell as far below him as he fell below the ancients." (*Books X-XII*, 1998: 71-73). However, he continues by indicating that Seneca had many excellent qualities such as "a quick and fertile intelligence with great industry and wide knowledge" and dealt with almost every department of knowledge such as for speeches, poems, letters and dialogues (*Books X-XII*, 1998: 71- 73). Generally, Quintilian stresses that Seneca's style "is for the most part corrupt and exceedingly dangerous, for the very reason that its vices are so many and attractive" (*Books X-XII*, 1998:73). He indicates that Seneca would have won the approval of the "learned" instead of the enthusiasm of boys, if "he had despised all unnatural expressions and had not been so passionately fond of all that was incorrect, if he had not felt such affection for all that was his own, and had not impaired the solidity of his matter by striving after epigrammatic brevity" (*Books X-XII*, 1998: 75). Nevertheless, it is underlined that there is much in Seneca's work to be admired and for this reason deserves to be read by those students who have acquired the "critical faculties in distinguishing between his merits and his defects". (*Books X-XII*, 1998: 75).

It is not clearly known whether Seneca's plays were closet dramas, intended to be read rather than recited, or whether his plays were staged during his lifetime. Boyle states that:

> Recent analyses of Seneca's stage techniques reveal theatrical mastery in the shaping of dramatic action, the structural unfolding of dramatic language and imagery, the blocking of scenes and acts, the disposition of roles, the handling of actors and of the chorus, the interrelationship of chorus and act, the use of ghosts, messengers, extras, mutes, the dramatic and thematic use of stage setting and props, the employment of implicit stage directions in the text itself (especially entrance and exit cues, and implicit directions for stage business) and in Senecan tragedy's manipulation of pace, movement, violence, spectacle and closure. (1997: 12)

Seneca's eight tragedies; *Hercules Furens, Troades, Medea, Phaedra, Oedipus, Agamemnon, Thyestes*, and *Phoenissae*[57] are all marked by vivid and powerful verse, psychological insight, highly effective staging, an intellectually demanding verbal and conceptual framework, and preoccupation with theatricality (Boyle, 1997: 15).

Quintilian praises Euripides while he criticizes Seneca, both of whom he praises for their eloquence of style. It is also interesting to note that they each composed a tragedy out of the 'Medea' story. The difference between the two versions is that, compared to Euripides, Seneca's version includes more explicit representations of violence on the stage. Seneca's "many and attractive vices", mentioned earlier by Quintilian can be observed in a scene that does not exist in Euripides' version. Medea, in distress, calls on Hecate, the goddess of witches (such a connection is not underlined in Euripides' version) and seeks her support in the process of her revenge:

> [...] to thee on the altars bloody turf we perform thy solemn rites; to thee a torch caught up from the midst of a funeral has illumed the night;

[57] Although the exact dates of the plays are not known, they are predicted to have been composed in 41-9 A.D.

> to thee, tossing my head and with bended neck, I have uttered my magic words; for thee a fillet, lying in funeral fashion, binds my flowing locks; to thee is brandished the gloomy branch of cypress from the Stygian stream; to thee with bared breast will I as a maenad smite my arms with the sacrificial knife. Let my blood flow upon the altars; accustom thyself, my hand, to draw the sword and endure the sight of beloved blood. (She slashes her arm and lets the blood flow upon the altar.) Self-smitten have I poured forth the sacred stream. (Seneca, 1964: 370)

It was the scenes that Seneca's excellence of style was combined by visual violence and especially the scene of the murder of the two sons on stage that caused Seneca's works to be criticized by Quintilian. It follows that in Quintilian's opinion, Seneca's work serves as an example for those experienced students who may study his diction, but not the 'violence' or 'terror' he chooses to display on stage.

The playwrights of the Renaissance were greatly influenced by Greek and Roman playwrights. As already mentioned earlier in this chapter, as a result of the revival of ancient texts, training in rhetoric had become an important part of elementary and advanced education in the Renaissance period. Both the playwrights and the audience had knowledge of and enjoyed the use of rhetorical devices in drama.

One of the outstanding features of the drama of this period was "a tendency toward richness and copiousness of language." (Prior, 1964: 21). While the dramatists of contemporary drama rely on technical elements on the staging process, in Elizabethan drama, the "emphasis necessarily fell wholly on the spoken line, which had to sustain nearly the entire burden of whatever effects needed to be made. Dialogue was given the "highest possible importance" in Elizabethan drama (Prior, 1964: 21). There was a high tendency towards the employment of "ornateness" and "lavishness" (Prior, 1964:22). In terms of style, the preoccupation with rhetoric was the "cultivation of point", "of patterned artifice", and "of figurative ornament." (Prior, 1964: 25). McDonald claims that the popular texts instructing the use of rhetoric emphasized teaching certain devices for effect, including such uses as "irony" and "hyperbole" to enhance the language. Prior states that nearly all dramatists from Marlowe to Shirley share a capacity for the use of imaginative language, arresting and revealing metaphors and brilliant images (in Fowler, 1987: 206).

The practice of blank verse as the accepted verse medium of Elizabethan drama also served as a vehicle for the attainment of excellence in style. The metrical scheme of the blank verse line, had "sufficient flexibility to permit its use either for the easy interchange of dramatic dialogue or of the demands of impassioned eloquence." (Prior, 1964: 30). The original formality of blank verse was in part due to its having been made subject to the ends of rhetoric[58].

Christopher Marlowe was the first great English poet to employ drama "as a medium of poetic expression" (Parrott and Ball, 1958: 91). Although others such as Peele and Kyd used it to a certain extent, they were not Marlowe's "peer as a poet" (Parrott and Ball, 1958: 91). Marlowe had mastered blank verse. Parrot and Ball also indicate that Shakespeare learned the secret of blank verse from Marlowe and he was to expand its range (Parrott and Ball, 1958: 91). Elizabethan drama as a whole is essentially poetic drama, and all the best of Elizabethan dramatic poetry is in Marlowe's measure, in blank verse (Parrott and Ball, 1958: 91). Thus, Parrot and Ball indicate that poetry of power and of passion, was Marlowe's greatest gift to Elizabethan drama (1958: 92). Prior seems in agreement with Parrot and Ball when he points out that if the tragedies of "Shakespeare and of the ancients had not been poetic tragedies, the impression of depth and vividness which their characters convey would have been impossible (Prior, 1964: 13).

The year 1587-8 highlighted by Marlowe's *Tamburlaine* together with Kyd's *Spanish Tragedy*, marks a critical point. Although each play represents in its own way a radical reorganization in the matter of diction, *Tamburlaine* has enjoyed a greater fame, probably because in this play the celebrated "mighty line" of Marlowe made its first appearance (Prior, 1964: 33). *Tamburlaine, Part I* will be dealt with in the following chapter of this book.

It was Shakespeare, however, who reached perfection in both poetic language and form. Prior indicates that no English dramatist equals Shakespeare in virtuosity and imagination with which he uses language (Prior, 1964: 59). He adds that other than Shakespeare's, there was no genius among his contemporaries or successors which proved a catalyst strong enough to effect an organization of the possibilities of

[58] In infrequency of run-on lines and the general regularity of the iambic meter in early dramatic blank verse merely rendered it more suitable as a mould for such devices as balance accentuated by assonance and alliteration, patterned antithesis within the line and between separate lines, stichomythia, and the like (Prior, 1964: 31).

the Elizabethan tragic style on the same scale and with the same wholeness (Prior, 1964: 93)

Shakespeare knew and used over two hundred different figures in his plays, both to express powerful feelings of his characters and to hide them. Shakespeare's working vocabulary of twenty thousand words and his complex rhetoric did not dissuade readers but instead ignited their curiosity and wonder of language (Crane, 1937: 204-205). Additionally, as Crane indicates, the "banter with rhetorical terms and expressions in the early plays of Shakespeare argues familiarity with such matters on the part of the audience (1937: 204-205). His puns and ambiguous phrases show what a master of rhetoric, and grammar Shakespeare was, but most important to Shakespeare's work was his love and perhaps addiction to language (1937: 204-205). In the final chapter of Part I, Shakespeare's *Richard III* will be examined for its perfection of rhetorical usage.

Since both *Tamburlaine, Part I* and *King Richard III* involve rulers and wars, both of the plays draw a parallel between rhetorical skill and the art of war craft. In fact, Machiavelli himself points out the important place of rhetoric in his work *The Art of War.* In "Book IV", Zanobi and Fabrizio discuss the role of "haranguing" (attempt to persuade someone that you are right with a long and angry speech) in making soldiers and officers fight. Fabrizio states that "it is necessary that a general should be an orator as well as a soldier; for if he does not know how to address himself to the whole army, he will sometimes find that it is no easy task to mold it [the army] to his purposes." (1965: 128). He points out that "haranguing" the soldiers functions to "dispel their fears, inflame their courage, confirm their resolution, point out the snares laid for them, promise them rewards, inform them of danger and the way to escape it;" and the general may "rebuke, entreat, threaten, praise, reproach, or fill them with hopes" (1965: 128). He also indicates that 'religion' can be used in service of controlling soldiers:

> Religion too, and the oath soldiers took when they were enlisted, greatly contributes to making them do their duty in ancient times; for upon any default, they were threatened not only with human punishments, but the vengeance of the gods. (1965: 128)

To this end, he gives the example of Sertorious:

> Sertorious[59], the last major Marian leader, knew this [the use of religion] well; he used to have consultations with a hind that he said was sent by the gods to assure him of victory. Sulla pretended to converse with an image he had taken out of the temple of Apollo, and several generals have given out that some god or other has appeared to them in dreams an visions and commanded them to fight the enemy. In the days of our ancestors, when Charles VII of France was at war with the English, he pretended to be advised in everything by a virgin sent from heaven, commonly called the virgin of France, who won him many a victory. (1965: 128-129)

Christian prudence articulates without equating intensions and results. Thus, it is presented as a technical skill of deliberation that can be used well or badly and that is governed by rhetorical considerations of circumstance, place, and audience (Kahn, 1994: 91).

In terms of using rhetoric, the thoughts of Machiavelli have been influential in the works of Elizabethan playwrights[60]. Victoria Kahn in *Machiavellian Rhetoric* states that in the Renaissance, the stage Machiavel was a "figure of force and fraud, coercion and deceit, and-related to these-rhetorical skills" (1994: 7). He was typically a powerful rhetorician, which registers the anxiety about the power of rhetoric or illusion to persuade to evil (1994: 91). The association of the Machiavel with hypocrisy and dissembling suggests, brought with it anxiety about the political and religious abuse of rhetoric (Kahn, 1994: 88)

Kahn suggests that the Machiavel was well known in England before his appearance in Elizabethan, and the theatrical Machiavel provides further evidence that contemporaries recognized the contribution of rhetoric and theatrical representation to the "subversion –or maintenance– of" the political and religious quo. To this end, in *Henry VI, Part* 3, the duke of Gloucester (later Richard III) boasts about the use of rhetoric to gain political power:

[59] The last major Marian leader.

[60] Shakespeare and other writers understood that the rhetorical dimension of Machiavelli's political thought "embraced the stereotypical Machiavel as well as the neutral political analyst, the dissembling rhetorician of politic necessity as well as the historian of tyranny. They understood, too, the distinction was often, for all practical political purposes, hard to obtain" (Kahn, 1994: 130).

> I'll play the orator as well as Nestor; Deceive more slily than Ulysses could; And, like a Sinon, take another Troy; I can add colours to the chameleon;
> Change shapes with Proteus for advantages; And set the murdrous Machiavel to school.
> Can I do this and cannot get a crown? (III. ii, 188-193)

Richard III assumes the connection between rhetoric, protean flexibility, and the crown. “Proteus” in line 191 better illustrates the traits of a Machiavel. In Greek mythology, Proteus is an early sea-god who can foretell the future. However, he will change his shape to avoid having to and will answer only to someone who is capable of capturing him. From this feature of Proteus comes the adjective “protean”, with the general meaning of "versatile", "mutable" and "capable of assuming many forms" as many Machiavellian orators do.

CHAPTER 2
'WORDS AS SWORDS': VERBAL BATTLES IN CHRISTOPHER MARLOWE'S *TAMBURLAINE, PART ONE*

Christopher Marlowe's *Tamburlaine* is a two-part tragedy written in blank verse. *Part I* was first performed in 1587 and published in 1590[61]. The play deals with the rise of Timur Khan (Tamburlaine), originally a Scythian shepherd-robber, to a powerful ruler who left the world in awe. A century after his defeat of Sultan Bayezid I[62] (Bajazeth) in the battle of Angora (Ankara) in 1402, Tamburlaine, as a historical figure, became a subject for the study of power structures by European scholars. Thomas and Tydeman point out the work of Petrus Perondinus and the translated works of Pedro Mexia[63] as the major sources of Marlowe's *Tamburlaine* (Thomas and Tydeman: 1994, 69-123).

Tamburlaine, Part I, depicts the early process of Tamburlaine's rise to power. Tamburlaine first helps Cosroe to overthrow his brother, the Persian king Mycetes, but then seizes the Persian crown for himself. He next conquers the forces of Soldan Bajazeth, imprisons him and his wife Zabina and humiliates them to the point of leading them to suicide. Lastly, he captures the city of Damascus, and defeats the 'Soldan of Egypt', and crowns Zenocrate, the Soldan's daughter, as his empress[64].

In the article "The Rhetoric of Marlowe's Orations", J. W. Van Hook indicates that the protagonists in Marlowe's plays distinguish themselves by the vigor of their orations (1988: 49)[65]. Marlowe generally employs a great deal of rhetoric in his

---

[61] There are four early editions of *Tamburlaine*, published in 1590, 1593, 1597, and 1605-6 (Cunnigham, 1981, 85).

[62] One of the earliest examples of the representation of Bayezid I (1389-1402), the Turkish Sultan, is in Christopher Marlowe's *Tamburlaine the Great, Part I.* Contrary to the label 'Bayazeth the Emperor', Bayezid I was not an emperor. The Ottoman rulers were not conceived as 'Emperor' until the time after Istanbul was conquered by Sultan Mehmed the Conqueror (1432-1481). The most commonly used forms of the Turkish Sultan Beyazid I in English are 'Beyazeth' 'Bayazeth'. 'Bayazith' and 'Bajazeth'. Throughout this study the 'Bajazeth' spelling has been used when referred to Marlowe's character.

[63] Mexia's works have been translated by Thomas Fortescue and George Whetson (Thomas and Tydeman: 1994, 69-123)

[64] *Part II* continues the story of Tamburlaine's conquests, which reach their peak when his carriage is drawn to Babylon by the captured kings.

[65] Van Hook states that the protagonists in Marlowe's plays distinguish themselves by the vigor of their orations, and questions why their speeches have not been widely studied (Van Hook, 1988: 49).

dramatic works; *Tamburlaine,* however, is considered the most rhetorical (Ousby: 1998, 910). The intensity of rhetoric employed in the play[66] is effective in creating a world in which Tamburlaine, through his mastery of rhetoric, terrorizes and holds control over everyone on the stage. The 'prologue' to the play indicates that a parallel exists between Tamburlaine's display of power through his use of language and the power he possesses as a military conqueror: "[...] you shall hear the Scythian Tamburlaine/Threat'ning the world with high astounding terms/And scourging kingdoms with his conquering sword." (Prologue, 4-6) It is interesting to note that in the opening lines, the spectators will 'hear' Tamburlaine "threatening the world with his high astounding terms". Ian McAdam claims that the spectators shall not 'see' him scourging kingdoms, pointing out that these lines imply that the play will be based on 'talk' rather than action (1999: 78).

Tamburlaine, Part I, exhibits powerful rhetorical language, and while the physical warfare takes place off stage, the verbal battles are fought on the stage. In fact, the only time we see Tamburlaine in physical action is in the battle with Bajazeth in Act III, scene iii. In verbal confrontations, power is reflected through the command of language and words are used as 'swords' to persuade, manipulate, trick, mock, demoralize, degrade, humiliate and insult the other characters. In addition, the exercise of verbal skill in *Tamburlaine, Part I* is closely connected to authority, and the characters' degree of competence in oratory is matched with their political strength or weakness. Tamburlaine, in particular, is able to control and exploit everyone who is less competent than he is in verbal combat. It follows that the focus on the rhetorical skills the characters have been endowed with, serves as a proper means for bringing out the dynamics of this particular play by Marlowe.

Act I, scene i of the play introduces a monarch, Mycetes, the king of Persia, who is about to lose his throne, and his brother Cosroe, who plans to replace him. Mycetes, lacking the ability to act or speak in line with his position as king, has no hold over his commanders or his people, and is mocked and degraded by others including his brother Cosroe, who turns out to be the more intelligent of the two. At the very beginning of the play, Cosroe accuses Mycetes of having lost control over Persia, once the land of mighty kings, and having stooped to the Turks and the Tartars. He continues to humiliate Mycetes by stating, through the use of good many

[66] Ian McAdam states that the "language in the play transforms the material into art and generates a willing enthusiasm for the quest for an earthly crown, in the audience." (1999: 76)

rhetorical devices that at the time he was born, the gods had denied having a positive influence on his brain, thus calling him 'stupid':

> Unhappy Persia[67], that in former age
> Hast been the seat of mighty conquerors[68]
> [...]
> Now to be ruled and governed by a man
> At whose birth-day Cynthia with Saturn joined,
> And Jove, the Sun, and Mercury denied[69]
> To shed their influence in his fickle brain!
> Now Turks and Tartars shake their swords at thee [Persia], (I.i, 6-17)

Mycetes can only challenge Cosroe's verbal attacks by false threats[70]: "I might command you [Cosroe] to be slain for this [insulting him]"; and seeks confirmation from Meander, one of his lords: "Meander might I not? [have him slain]" (I.i, 23-24). In fact, in the opening scene observe a melancholic Mycetes grieved because he is not able to make a 'thund'ring' speech that would motivate his troops before the battle against Tamburlaine who "[...]like a fox[71] in midst of harvest time/Doth prey upon my [his] flocks of passengers" (I.i, 31-32). As Mycetes is so conspicuously unable to find a rhetoric that matches his position, his briefing to Theridamas, who has been given the job of exterminating the 'Scythian thief' becomes highly ironic: "Go, stout Theridamas, thy words are swords,/ And with thy looks thou conquerest all thy foes." (I. i, 74-5). When later Cosroe challenges his authority as a king, Mycetes doesn't know how to be revenged for his "contemptuous words" (I.i, 100) and once again

---

[67] Persia is personified in line 6 and 17.

[68] Cosroe employs 'Insultatio': "Derisive ironical abuse of a person to his face" (Lanham, 1991: 187) by using 'Anamnesis': "Recalling ideas, events, or persons of the past" (Lanham, 1991:188).'By 'mighty conquerors', Cosroe invokes the memory of Cyrus the Great; who founded the Persian Empire and established its boundaries from the Indus and the Jaxartes to the Aegean and the borders of Eqypt, and Darius his successor, who encountered the freezing 'bounds of Europe' in war against the Scythians (Cunningham, 1981: footnote, 155).

[69]Cosroe uses 'Argumentum ad hominem': "1) Abuse of opponent's character: 2) Basing your argument on what you know of the opponent's character" (Lanham, 1991:191) to indicate Mycetes' lack of intelligence. Saturn, "the most powerful of the malefic planets", joins Luna's vacillation. Jupiter "would have mitigated more than any other planet the evil influence of the malignant conjunction" and the lack of beneficence from Sol and Mercury robs Mycetes of kingly stature and of wise eloquence (Parr quoted in Cunnigham, 1981: footnote 116).

[70] 'Cataplexies': "Threatening punishment, infortune, or disaster". (Lanham, 1991: 186)

[71] Mycetes is endeavoring, by the use of two 'simile's, to make an explicit comparison between the 'fox' and Tamburlaine, and 'flock' and his own army.

turns to Meander like an injured child: "That darest presume thy sovereign for to mock./ Meander, come, I am abused, Meander" (I.i, 105-106).

In line with his inability to speak effectively, Mycetes has lost most of his authority as early as Act I, scene i. Mycetes' lack of verbal skill is later shown in another instance, when on the battle ground Mycetes once again abstains from playing the part of the orator giving this task to Meander:

> And 'tis a pretty toy to be a poet.
> Well, well, Meander, thou art deeply read,
> And having thee I have a jewel sure.
> Go on, my lord, and give you charge I say,
> Thy wit will make us conquerors today. (II. ii, 54-58)

Through the character of Mycetes, who falls short of being a match for his opponents in either speech or orations, Marlowe has made it quite clear that verbal eloquence and military power go hand in hand.

Compared to Mycetes, Cosroe is a better rhetorician, and appears to be a more competent warrior and politician. He is presented with the Persian crown by other lords, in the name of other 'Persian states' and declared the monarch of the East, Emperor of Asia and of Persia. Although Cosroe has, in fact, made plans to overthrow his brother and get hold of the crown, he stages a public performance in which he allows himself to be persuaded by the Persian lords into accepting the crown:

> Well, since I see the state of Persia droop
> And languish in my brother's government[72],
> I willingly receive th' imperial crown
> And vow to wear it for my country's good,
> In spite of them shall malice my estates[73]. (I.i,155-159)

With such a 'noble' speech, Cosroe masks his ambition to be king with the rhetoric of duty and service[74].

---

[72] Cosroe uses the art of 'Aetiologia': "Giving cause or reason [...]" (Lanham, 1991:3)
[73] Here is an instance of 'Exuscitatio': "Emotional utterance that seeks to move hearers to a similar feeling" (Lanham, 1991: 77)

After the presentation of the two brothers, one who holds the crown and the other pursuing it, Marlowe presents Tamburlaine, in Act I, scene ii, as a "gigantic and energetic man lusting for military dominion, believing his own power" (Parr, 1991: 114). In Marlowe's play, this energy is generated through Tamburlaine's rhetorical skills and mastery in oration. In fact, the majority of the rhetoric in *Tamburlaine* is employed by the protagonist himself. Even though his enemies consider him a devilish thief and a barbaric villain, he verbally sounds, as Sales coins it, like a "Renaissance prince" (Sales: 1991, 54) and demonstrates his verbal superiority in every situation that necessitates it. He uses rhetoric in order to convince, persuade, mislead, manipulate, and to convince the audience of his omnipotence and to justify this power, to gain the support of rulers, and give courage to his troops.

Tamburlaine establishes himself as a skilled rhetorician and orator at his very first appearance in the play. From his first utterance, it is apparent that rhetoric, for Tamburlaine, is to be more than a cold and weak vice of style (Van Hook, 1988: 51). While still a shepherd, commanding only a gang of highwaymen who are about to be attacked by the combined might of the Persian army in Act I, scene ii, he woos Zenocrate, the daughter of the Soldan of Egypt, with an overwhelming display of clever metaphors and comparisons, arranged into several different types of

[74] In Shakespeare's *Hamlet* Claudius' speech at his first enterance as king resembles that of Cosroe's:

> Though yet of Hamlet our dear brother's death
> The memory be green, and that it us befitted
> To bear our hearts in grief, and our whole kingdom
> To be contracted in one brow of woe,
> Yet so far hath discretion fought with nature
> That we with wisest sorrow think on him
> Together with rememberance of ourselves.
> Therefore our sometime sister, now our Queen,
> Th'imperial jointress to the warlike state,
> Have we, as 'twere with a defeated joy,
> With an auspicious and a dropping eye,
> With mirth in funural and with dirge in marriage,
> In equal scale weighing delight and dole,
> Taken to wife. Nor have we herein barred
> Your better wisdoms, which have freely gone
> With this affair along. For all, our thanks. (I.ii, 1-16)

Although his murder of his brother the king is revealed later on in the play, in the above extract, Claudius plays the mourning brother, who is 'humbly' accepting the crown for the good of the kingdom.

'amplification'[75] (Van Hook, 1988: 51-52). Tamburlaine uses both 'merismus', stressing the importance of a subject by analyzing it into its components and dwelling on each of them separately, and 'synathroesmus' (aiming to stress the importance of a subject by stating a single proposition in several different ways), in his appeal (Van Hook, 1988: 51-52).

In Act I, scene ii, Zenocrate, her followers and her treasure are denied the right of passage by Tamburlaine, despite the Soldan's letter that authorizes them to free travel. When Agydas, a lord attending Zenocrate, forwards his hope that their treasures may serve to ransom their liberties, he makes it clear that he has fallen in love with Zenocrate and means to keep her. Tamburlaine addresses both Zenocrate and her followers with the first amplification concerning Zenocrate's high worth and beauty[76]:

> Disdains Zenocrate to live with me?
> Or you, my lords, to be my followers?
> Think you I weigh this treasure more than you?[77]
> Not all the gold in India's wealthy arms
> Shall buy the meanest soldier in my train.
> Zenocrate, lovelier than the love of Jove,
> Brighter than is the silver Rhodope[78]
> Fairer than whitest snow on Scythian hills,
> Thy person is more worth to Tamburlaine
> Than the possession of the Persian crown,
> Which gracious stars have promised at my birth. (I.ii, 82-92)

In this speech, Tamburlaine personifies India, stating that the gold she holds in her "wealthy" arms, or the "possession of the Persian crown" is not more valuable to him

---

[75]'Amplification': "A device in which language is used to extend or magnify or emphasize." (Cuddon, 1999: 32)
In chapter 9 of *Poetics,* Aristotle states that amplification best suits demonstrative oratory, because the orator takes the actions for granted and thus remains only to invest them with greatness and beauty (Aristotle, 1995 :66).

[76] Tamburlaine's description of Zenocrate is an example of 'icon', a painting resemblance by imagery.

[77] Here is an example of 'Hypophora': "Asking questions and answering them" (Lanham, 1991:87). 'Epiplexis': "Asking a question in order to reproach or uphaid, rather to elicit information [...]" (Lanham, 1991: 69) is also used here.

[78] Mount of Rhodope, where silver mines are found.

than Zenocrate herself. Then he continues with a comparison of her beauty to "silver", "snow" and the "love of Jove", which altogether comprise a 'synathroesmus' by glorifying her beauty in several different ways through the use of similes (comparison to Juno, silver, and snow). Also, the speaking stars who have promised him the Persian crown make up a 'metonymy'[79] which domesticates them as dispensers of grace and connects Tamburlaine's invincibility with the impelling power of the stars. This passage also emphasizes the fact that he attaches more importance to Zenocrate than any earthly possessions or power, such as gold and the Persian crown.

At this point Janet Clare remarks that Tamburlaine's plea to Zenocrate's beauty, which seems in another context to be a display of "decorous and courtly rhetoric" expressive of inner feelings, conceals the violence that is the real basis of the speaker's power (2000: 78). In reality, Tamburlaine woes Zenocrate for political reasons. Although he is only a shepherd, he aims to take a royal princess as his wife so as to hint his potential rise in the future.

The second amplification augments Tamburlaine's offer to Zenocrate:

> A hundred Tartars shall attend on thee,
> Mounted on steeds swifter than Pegasus;
> Thy garments shall be made of Median silk,
> Enchased with precious jewels of mine own,
> More rich and valurous [valuable] than Zenocrate's;
> With milk-white harts upon an ivory sled
> Thou shalt be drawn amidst the frozen pools
> And scale the icy mountains' lofty tops,
> Which with thy beauty will be soon resolved;
> My martial prizes, with five hundred men,
> Won on the fifty-headed Volga's waves,
> Shall all we offer to Zenocrate,
> And then my self to fair Zenocrate. (I.ii, 93-105)

Here the amplification is made through a 'merismus' (stressing the importance of a subject by dividing it into its fragments and dwelling on each of them separately) by

[79] 'Metonymy': "Substitution of cause for effect. effect for cause. Proper name for one of its qualities. Or vice versa" (Lanham, 1991: 189).

detailing the future state that she will enjoy as his 'empress'. He emphasizes aspects that would appeal to a young princess such as a "hundred Tartars" attending her, garments made of "Median silks" and precious jewels, and sexuality as in the ice and peaks [I. ii, 98-105] that seem emblematic of her present virginity (Van Hook, 1988: 52).

Tamburlaine also uses 'auxesis'[80], placing items in an ascending order of importance. The intended wedding gifts –power, wealth, sexuality– are mentioned in such an order that the ultimate prize she evidently is to consider –that of "my selfe" (Tamburlaine himself to fair Zenocrate)– is left to the last.

When Theridamas, who is carrying on a champagne against Tamburlaine upon the orders of Mycetes, arrives the audience is confronted with another "surprising revelation of the hero" Tamburlaine (Brown, 1991: 89). Tamburlaine, who has been in the guise of a lover in the first part of the scene, is now to turn into an orator. The Persian army is composed of a thousand well-armored horsemen while Tamburlaine has only five hundred men on foot. Tamburlaine asks Techelles, one of his followers, whether they should go fighting in the battlefield or play the orator: "Then shall we fight courageously with them,/Or look you I should play the orator?" (I.ii, 128-129), to which Techelles answers: "No: cowards and faint-hearted runaways/Look for orations when the foe is near./Our swords shall play the orators for us" (I. ii, 130-132). Tamburlaine, however, is not planning to listen to this advice; he chooses to play the orator rather than the soldier (Sales, 1991: 61).

Tamburlaine first addresses Theridamas and argues against the competence of the present Persian King:

> In thee, thou valiant man of Persia,
> I see the folly of thy emperor:
> Art thou but captain of a thousand horse,
> That by characters graven in thy brows,
> And by thy martial face and stout aspect,
> Deservest to have the leading of a host?
> Forsake thy king and do but join with me,
> And we will triumph over all the world. (I.ii, 165-72)

[80] 'Auxesis': "Placing items in an ascending order of importance" (Lanham, 1991: 183).

Tamburlaine's second argument is that he is a chosen leader guarded by heavens in military affairs:

> See how he [Jove] rains down heaps of gold showers
> As if he meant to give my soldiers pay;
> And as a sure and grounded argument
> That I shall be the monarch of the East,
> He sends this Soldan's daughter rich and brave[81]
> To be my queen and portly emperess. (I.ii, 181-186)

Moreover, Tamburlaine has an immense skill in verbal portraiture of himself as a man highly favored by gods[82]. He allows himself a superior position among men by linking himself to Jove[83], the god of gods. He states that he is destined to be the monarch of the East, and for this reason Jove has sent him the daughter of the Soldan of Egypt to have as his queen and "emperess". The "heaps of golden showers" that she has brought with her, is regarded as a gift from Jove. Thus, through his verbal skills Tamburlaine succeeds in creating the impression that his encounter with Zenocrate is associated with the will of divine powers[84].

Through Tamburlaine's brilliantly successful oration, Theridamas is won by his "words" and conquered by his "looks", and, becoming a traitor against Mycetes, joins forces with Tamburlaine:

> *Theridamas* : But shall I prove a traitor to my king?
> *Tamburlaine* : No, but the trusty friend of Tamburlaine.
> *Theridamas* : Won with thy words and conquered with thy looks,
> I yield myself, my men and horse to thee:
> To be partaker of thy good or ill
> As long as life maintains Theridamas. (I. ii, 225-230)

---

[81] Fine, splended (Cunnigham, 1981: footnote 132)
[82] Waith states that the "effect of the speech is double, for though it displays the hero as an orator, it also presents, as by means of eloquence, his self-portrait as conqueror of the world and even as demigod." (1991: 90)
[83] Jove (Roman equivalent of Zeus, the king of the Gods) was regarded as the sky-god, the god of light, of the day and of the seasons which he created, as well as thunder and lightning.
[84] Sales indicates that Tamburlaine uses Zenocrate as a useful ladder to the Persian crown, since her silent presence in Act I, scene ii, helps to persuade Theridamas to change sides and join forces with Tamburlaine (1991:72-73).

When Theridamas asks whether he is a traitor to his king, Tamburlaine makes use of 'peristrophe'[85], thus converting Theridamas' argument to his own use by replacing an unfavorable aspect with a favorable one. Thus, Tamburlaine's first actual battle, towards which the play has built up a great deal of suspense, is postponed. The battle is replaced by verbal persuasion and Theridamas is won by words instead of military force. Waith believes that Tamburlaine's image of himself as a hero in full control of his fate, and his comparison of himself to Jove as "conqueror of the world and even demigod, doubles the effect of the speech". Waith also states that "such self-praise might be taken as Marlowe's way of portraying a man who will say anything to get ahead" (1991: 90).

After Theridamas, Cosroe comes to join forces with Tamburlaine against Mycetes' troops (II. iii). On his arrival, Cosroe indicates that he attaches all his hope in Tamburlaine's fortunes:

> Now, worthy Tamburlaine, have I reposed
> In thy approved fortunes all my hope.
> What thinkest thou, man, shall come of our attempts?
> For even as from assured oracle,
> I take thy doom[86] for satisfaction. (II. iii, 1-5)

Tamburlaine answers Cosroe's question by indicating that Cosroe's faith in his powers is not without sufficient ground:

> And so mistake you not a whit, my lord,
> For fates and oracles of heaven have sword
> To royalise[87] the deeds of Tamburlaine
> And make them blest that share in his attempts.
> And doubt you not but, if you favour me
> And let my fortunes and my valour sway
> To some direction in your martial deeds,
> The word will strive with hosts of men at arms
> To swarm unto the ensign I support.

---

[85]'Peristrophe': "Converting an opponent's argument to one's own use." (Lanham, 1991: 114)
[86] Doom: Judgement, opinion -though these synonyms lack the appropriate portentousness. (Cunningham, 1998: 142)
[87] Render famous, celebrate (Cunnigham, 1981: 143)

[...]
And bullets like Jove's dreadful thunderbolts
Enrolled in flames and fiery smouldering mists
Shall threat the gods more than Cyclopian wars;
And with our sun-bright armour as we march
We'll chase the stars from heaven and dim their eyes
That stand and muse at our admired arms. (II.iii, 6-24)

These lines, which are an example of 'demonstrative' speech, display reasons why Cosroe is not mistaken in his choice. Since, "fates" and "oracles of heaven" have sworn to "royalise" his deeds, the people who join with him will also be awarded. Additionally, Tamburlaine uses a 'metonymy'[88]; substituting the personified 'stars' for 'fate', and indicating that if the stars get in the way of their destiny, they will chase the stars from heaven and dim their eyes. Thus, he stresses their invincibility.

Following Tamburlaine's speech, Theridamas addresses Cosroe so as to emphasize and praise Tamburlaine's verbal skill, which also implies the potential for great military skill: "You see, my lord, what working words he hath,/But when you see his actions top his speech,/Your speech will stay, or so extol his worth" (II, iii, 25-7). Theridamas, by 'working words' underlines the effectiveness of Tamburlaine's rhetoric, stating that when Cosroe sees that his military competence exceeds his speech, there will be nothing left but to highly praise him.

Later in the act, a messenger arrives and notifies them that the Mycetes' army is ready for battle. The lofty language Cosroe uses in addressing Tamburlaine just before the battle is significant in that it demonstrates Tamburlaine's power of speech has maneuvered him into a firm belief in his military powers:

Come, Tamburlaine, now whet thy winged sword
And lift thy lofty arm into the clouds,
That it may reach the king of Persia's crown
And set it safe on my victorious head. (II. iii, 51-54)

[88] Metonymy: "Substitution of cause for effect, effect for cause, proper name for one of its qualities, or vice versa" (Lanham, 1991: 189).

Cosroe, by combining 'winged' and 'sword' alludes to the heavenly powers supporting Tamburlaine's 'sword', a 'metonymy' for military power. He wants Tamburlaine to lift his arms to the skies until they reach the sky, and set the crown given by the heavens on Cosroe's 'victorious' head.

The battle is concluded with Mycetes' defeat and Cosroe replacing him as the new Persian king. When Cosroe goes to ride through Persepolis in celebration of his kingship, Tamburlaine immediately begins to play on the thoughts and desires of the Persian lords in order to provoke them against Cosroe, their new king:

Tamburlaine: And ride in triumph through Persepolis!
Is it not brave to be a king, Techelles?
Usumcasane and Theridamas,
Is it not passing brave[89] to be king,
And ride in, triumph through Persepolis?[90]
Techelles: O my lord, 'tis sweet and full of pomp.
Usumcasane: To be a king is half to be a god.
Theridamas: A god is not so glorious as a king.
I think the pleasure they enjoy in heaven
Cannot compare with kingly joys in earth: (II. v, 50-59)

The above passage, which includes short dialogues between four characters, is a beautiful example of 'amplification', which Marlowe maintains through appealing first one by one to the innermost desires of the three Persian lords and then proceeding to the comments each makes. The rest of the dialogue demonstrates the result of his act of manipulation. Techelles, speaking first, hails the idea of kingship as "sweet and full of pomp"; in turn, Usumcasane, amplifies the idea of being a king to being superhuman; and finally Theridamas raises the position of a king above that of a god, finally commenting that the pleasures enjoyed in heaven cannot be compared with kingly pleasures on earth. Then Tamburlaine goes on manipulating the Persian lords by offering them kingships, telling them that he will first seek the Persian crown for himself and the crowns of lands such as Scythia and Media for them. As a result, he persuades them to turn against Cosroe.

[89] Glorious
[90] Here, Tamburlaine makes use of 'Anacoenosis': "Communication", "[...] asking the opinion of one's readers or hearers." (Lanham, 1991: 9-10).

Cosroe is perfectly familiar with the rules of the game of politics, where the betrayal of a Mycetes is "venial" and "competence" has its modest reward. All the same, he will not be able to escape the shock of the betrayal directed towards him, when after the defeat of Mycetes, Tamburlaine gains the support of the other Persian lords and seizes the Persian crown for himself (Waith, 1991: 95). Cosroe's cry of pain when Tamburlaine betrays him: "Barbarous and bloody Tamburlaine" (II. vii, 1) expresses the outrage of one who finds that Tamburlaine's strategy is so much more daring and his treachery so much more preposterous that they are beyond the imagination of Cosroe (Waith, 1991: 95). By the end of Act II, Tamburlaine has been able to defeat both Mycetes and Cosroe and gain the Persian crown thanks to his skills of persuasion and political manipulation and tactics. Tamburlaine's next opponent, Bajazeth, however, is going to turn out to be a better match for him.

Bajazeth, Tamburlaine's third antagonist, is not only a successful king, but is also a proud ruler who is used to be served by kings and obeyed by thousands of subjects. According to Waith, Bajazeth is what Mycetes would have liked to be and what Cosroe might have become in time if he had been fortunate. So, Bajazeth is a kind of "final term or the ultimate monarch in mathematical progression, and in himself sums up others" (Waith, 1991:96). Thus, the fact that even a monarch so great should fall (as Bajazeth soon will) so easily, defines the limitations of the species and sets Tamburlaine in a world apart (Waith, 1991: 96).

In Act III, scene i, Bajazeth first sends one of his followers to order Tamburlaine to back down from such an unequal contest, but Tamburlaine refuses to be daunted by the large size of Bajazeth's army and declares that as the scourge and wrath of god, he will defeat the Turks and liberate Christians. Tamburlaine and Bajazeth confront each other face to face for the first time in Act III, scene iii. This scene in Act III is considered to be the most important verbal confrontation in *Tamburlaine, Part I,* which takes place on the meeting of Bajazeth and Tamburlaine before the battle between their troops. Talking with Roger Warren[91] about *Tamburlaine* in general, J. S. Cunnigham, the editor of the Revels edition of the play, tells him that Marlowe's structuring in Act III, scene iii, is strictly symmetrical:

> Bajazeth is accompanied by the queen Zabina, her maid, and his three contributory kings, Tamburlaine by Zenocrate, her maid, and his three

[91] Roger Warren is a lecturer in English at the University of Leicester, the editor of several volumes in the Oxford Shakespeare and a dramaturge.

lieutenants; after the antithetical ''And dars't thou bluntly call me Bajazeth?'...'And dar'st thou call me Tamburlaine?', the three contributory kings have speeches which are then exactly paralleled by the three lieutenants; Bajazeth seats Zabina and gives her his crown to wear; Tamburlaine echoes the process with Zenocrate; the rivals fight off-stage, while Zabina and Zenocrate engage in balanced mutual recrimination onstage. (Cunnigham and Warren, 1982:130)

In the relevant scene, the use of 'isocolon'[92], phrases of equal length and (usually) corresponding structure creates a balance in the play, and is used by the two rulers to crush each other. Both Bajazeth and Tamburlaine believe that they are the superior side and deserve victory. 'Amplification' is used by each ruler to highlight the reasons why they will win; their superiority, confidence in their victory, pride in their women and troops.

They first start with each other, trying to establish themselves a superior position by insulting each other. Tamburlaine gains an advantage by verbally degrading Bajazeth with the employment of 'litotes'[93], a figure of speech which contains an understatement for emphasis (the opposite of hyperbole) by addressing him as merely "Bajazeth" without adding his royal titles: "Techelles and the rest, prepare your swords:/I mean t'encounter with that Bajazeth" (III. iii. 64-65). Bajazeth shows his contempt by stressing the fact that Tamburlaine "this Scythian slave" makes another move and dares to call him by his name while kings respect him and call him their lord. Bajazeth insults Tamburlaine by stating that even the persons in charge of his horses have "titles of dignity":

Kings of Fesse[94], Moroccus, and Argier,
He calls me Bajazeth, whom you call lord!
Note the presumption of this Scythian slave.
I tell thee, villain, those that lead my horse
Have to their names titles of dignity–
And darest thou bluntly call me Bajazeth?[95] (III. iii, 66-71)

---

[92] 'Isocolon': "Phrases of approximately equal lenght and corresponding structure." (Lanham, 1991: 93)

[93] 'Litotes': "Danial of contrary; understatement that intensifies [...]" (Lanham, 1991: 95).

[94] Fez

[95] 'Argumentum ex concessi': "Reasoning from the premises of one's opponent." (Lanham, 1991: 192)

To this, Tamburlaine skillfully replies that the persons leading his horses will lead Bajazeth as a captive to Africa, repeating Bajazeth's lines by replacing "Tamburlaine" with "Bajazeth": "And know thou, Turk, that those which lead my horse/Shall lead thee captive thorough Africa–/And darest thou bluntly call me Tamburlaine?" (III. iii, 72-74). With the last line, Tamburlaine returns Bajazeth's insult by pointing out that Bajazeth won't be able to bluntly call him Tamburlaine when Bajazeth is defeated by him and those which lead Tamburlaine's horse shall lead him as captive through Africa.

In the above mentioned dialogue between Bajazeth and Tamburlaine, Tamburlaine repeats many of the phrases Bajazeth has employed in his verbal attack: "those which lead my horse", "And darest to bluntly call me", "know thou" and Tamburlaine also imitates the style in which Bajazeth has insulted him:

Bajazeth: "I tell thee, villain, [...]" (III. iii. 69)
Tamburlaine: "And know thou, Turk, [...]" (III. iii. 72)

Bajazeth: "And darest thou bluntly call me Bajazeth" (III. iii. 71)
Tamburlaine: "And darest thou bluntly call me Tamburlaine" (III. iii. 74)

It is interesting to note in these examples that Bajazeth relies on his "present" status, while Tamburlaine is pointing at the status he is sure to attain in the future.

Tamburlaine and Bajazeth carry on an argument by using similar expressions to declaring what they will do to each other after their victory. The two opponents employ similar artistic devices of argument when they proceed further and begin threatening each other. Bajazeth, swearing by 'Mahomet' and 'the holy Alcoran' announces that Tamburlaine will be transformed into a "lustless" eunuch to attend his concubines and his captains will draw the chariot of his "empress":

By Mahomet my kinsman's sepulchre
And by the holy Alcoran I swear
He shall be made a chaste and lustless eunuch
And in my sarell [seraglio] tend my concubines;
And all his captains that thus stoutly stand

Shall draw the chariot of my emperess [Zabina][96],
Whom I have brought to see their overthrow. (III. iii. 75-81)

Swearing by his 'sword', Tamburlaine, in turn, asserts that Bajazeth will soon find himself in such a terrible state that Tamburlaine's soldiers will laugh at him:

By this my sword that conquered Persia,
Thy fall shall make me famous through the world.
I will not tell thee how I'll handle thee,
But every common soldier of my camp
Shall simile to see thy miserable state. (III. iii, 82-86)

Then, they address their lords. Bajazeth proudly indicates that they shall "swallow up" the base-born Persians (III. iii, 95), while Tamburlaine's self-confidence takes him to the point of claiming that his "words are oracles" ("Fight all courageously and be you [his lords] kings:/I speak it, and my words are oracles") (III. iii, 101-102).

The two rulers next continue with praising their women, Zabina and Zenocrate. Bajazeth praises his empress Zabina for bringing three brave boys into the world, who will "batter turrets" with their "manly fists" and wear the "imperial crown":

Zabina, mother of three braver boys
Than Hercules,
[…]
Who, when they come unto their father's age,
Will batter turrets with their father's age,
Will batter turrets with their manly fists–
Sit here upon this royal chair of state
And on thy head wear my imperial crown,
Until I bring this sturdy Tamburlaine
And all his captains bound in captive chains. (III. iii, 103-115)

Bajazeth's stand in this speech appears to be much firmer than that of Tamburlaine, who does not yet own a family (a wife and sons) and has not yet established for

[96] 'Ara': "Curse or imprecation [...]" (Lanham, 1991: 20)

himself a secure position as ruler. After the speech, Zabina his empress wishes Bajazeth good luck.

Tamburlaine, in turn, confronts Bajazeth's scorn by simply praising Zenocrate's beauty, personality and her skills in speech through a detailed 'icon'[97] of his concubine:

> Zenocrate, the loveliest maid alive,
> Fairer than rocks of pearl and precious stone,
> The only paragon[98] of Tamburlaine,
> Whose eyes are brighter than the lamps of heaven,
> And speech more pleasant than sweet harmony;
> That with thy looks canst clear the darkened sky
> And calm the rage of thund'ring Jupiter[99]–
> Sit down by her, adorned with my crown,
> As if thou wert the empress of the world.
> [...]
> Till then, take thou my crown, vaunt of[100] my worth,
> And manage words with her as we will arms. (III. iii, 117-131)

As also seen in his very first address to her in Act I, scene ii, Tamburlaine compares Zenocrate's beauty to "rocks of pearl and precious stone", the only companion worthy of him; her eyes are compared to stars, "the lamp of heavens", her speech is considered to be more pleasant than "sweet harmony", and her appearance is described as one that clears the darkest sky and calms the thundering rage of Jupiter. At the end of his speech, Tamburlaine entrusts his crown with her and asks her to wait for him as if she were the empress of the world. He continues his address to Zenocrate by asking her to "manage words" with Zabina, as he and Bajazeth will employ weapons. Like Zabina, Zenocrate sends him to the battlefield with her blessings.

Bajazeth goes on praising himself by stating that he has under his rule enough Turks, Arabs, Moors and Jews to cover the whole of 'Bithynia'[101]:

---

[97] 'Icon': "Painting resemblance by imagery [...]" (Lanham, 1991: 89).
[98] Consort
[99] 'Encomium': "Praise of a person or thing by extolling inherent qualities". (Lanham, 1991: 187)
[100] 'vaunt of' proclaim proudly, extol (Cunnigham, 1981: footnote 169)
[101] An ancient region, kingdom and Roman Province in the northwest of Asia Minor, adjoining Propontis, the Thracian Bosporus and the Euxine (Black Sea).

Now shalt thou feel the force of Turkish arms
Which lately made all Europe quake for fear.
I have of Turks, Arabians, Moors and Jews,
Enough to cover all Bithynia: (III. iii, 134-137)

Bajazeth continues his speech by producing a striking picture of the prospective battle between the two forces:

Let thousands die, their slaughtered carcasses [bodies]
Shall serve for walls and bulwarks [defensive wall] to the rest;
And as the heads of Hydra[102], so my power,
Subdued, shall stand as mighty as before.
If they should yield their necks unto the sword,
Thy soldiers' arms could not endure to strike
So many blows as I have heads for thee.
Thou knowest not, foolish-hardy Tamburlaine,
What 'tis to meet me in the open field,
That leave no ground for thee to march upon. (III. iii, 138-147)

There is once again the use of 'amplification': Bajazeth amplifies his large army to the point of exaggeration. The slaughtered bodies will serve as defense walls, and even if Bajazeth's soldiers do yield themselves to Tamburlaine's soldiers, it will not be possible for them to kill all the soldiers in Bajazeth's army, because they are too many. Additionally, Bajazeth warns Tamburlaine that he does not realize what kind of devastating experience it is to fight with him in battle that will be filled with his soldiers, and will leave no ground for Tamburlaine to march upon.

Tamburlaine, in turn, takes up the scenes of battle Bajazeth has envisaged and elaborates upon how his forces would confront the attack of Bajazeth's army. In reply to Bajazeth's claim that his soldiers will leave no ground "for thee to march upon" he starts by saying "Our conquering swords shall marshall [guide] us the way" and goes on:

We use to march upon the slaughtered foe,
Trampling their bowels with our horses' hoofs–

[102] A Greek island in the Aegean.

Brave horses, bred on the white Tartarian hills.
My camp is like Julius Caesar's host,
That never fought but had the victory;
Nor in Pharsalia was there such hot war
As these my followers willingly would have.
Legions of spirits fleeting in the air
Direct our bullets and our weapons' points
And make your strokes to wound the senseless air;
And when she sees our bloody colours spread,
Then Victory[103] begins to take her flight,
Resting herself upon my milk-white tent. (III. iii, 149-161)

Tamburlaine finishes his speech by addressing his lords and inviting them to battle: "But come, my lords, to weapon let us fall./The field is ours, the Turk, his wife and all." (III. Iii, 162-163) and exits with his followers. Bajazeth also addresses the soldiers and the kings that are supporting him with their army: "Come, kings and bassoes, let us glut our swords/That thirst to drink the feeble Persians' blood." (III. iii, 164-165).

Tamburlaine and Bajazeth having departed for the battlefield, Zabina and Zenocrate are left behind to guard their crowns. Zenocrate and Zabina, together with their maids, continue the battle of 'words':

Zabina: Base concubine, must thou be placed by me
That am the empress of the mighty Turk?
Zenocrate: Disdainful Turkess and unreverend boss[104],
Callest thou me concubine that am betrothed
Unto the great and mighty Tamburlaine?
Zabina: To Tamburlaine the great Tartarian thief!
Zenocrate: Thou wilt repent these lavish words of thine
When thy great basso-master and thyself
Must plead for mercy at his kingly feet
And sue to me to be your advocates. (III.iii,166-175)

[103] Victory is personified
[104] 'Boss' probably meaning "fat" or "bloated". (Sales: 1991, 74)

In this exchange of insults, Zabina, like Bajazeth, assumes a scornful attitude, while Zenocrate magnifies her state as well as Tamburlaine's. While Zabina gradually increases her insults against Tamburlaine, Zenocrate, like Tamburlaine, warns her against their 'fall' in the near future. Roger Sales indicates that they are like dummies who echo their masters' voices (Sales, 1991: 74). Zabina, disdainful as before, says that she will make Zenocrate the maid of her waiting-maid. Zenocrate, in turn, states that she will make Zabina do the work that Zenocrate's waiting-maid's chambermaid disdains.

When they both pray for the victory of their lords, however, both women employ an imaginative style worthy of their royal upbringing. Zenocrate addresses the "gods and powers that govern Persia":

Zenocrate: Ye gods and powers that govern Persia
And made my lordly love her worthy king,
Now strengthen him against the Turkish Bajazeth
And let his foes, like flocks of fearful roes
Pursued by hunters, fly his angry looks,
That I may see him issue conqueror.
Zabina: Now, Mahomet, solicit God himself,
And make him rain down murd'ring shot from heaven
To dash the Scythians' brains, and strike them dead
That dare to manage arms with him
That offered jewels to thy sacred shrine
When first he warred against Christians. (III. iii, 189-200)

As the battle advances Zenocrate says that by this time the Turks lie in their blood and Tamburlaine is lord of Africa, while Zabina says that she is deceived and that she should prepare herself to live and die as her slave. Zenocrate says that she would not be persuaded to believe that her royal lord is slain or conquered, even if Mohamet should come from heaven and swear it. At the end, Zenocrate proves to be true and the battle ends with Tamburlaine's victory

Act III, scene iii, is a richly entertaining climax in the absorbing process of Tamburlaine's discovery of his own power, which blends wit, opportunism, and confidence (Cunningham and Warren, 1982: 130) Tamburlaine's defeat of such a powerful monarch as Bajazeth, who equals Tamburlaine in both physical and rhetorical skill, sets Tamburlaine in "a world apart" (Waith, 1991: 96). Bajazeth loses because of his excessive pride connected to his great success in the past, while Tamburlaine is confidant and talks about his success in the future events to come.

When the spectators next see Tamburlaine and Bajazeth in Act IV, scene ii, Bajazeth is in a cage and is followed by Zabina. Tamburlaine's refusal of a ransom for Bajazeth, which he expresses in Act III, scene iii, is motivated primarily on an impulse to inflict humiliation on him. Tamburlaine constructs a sight of power by stepping on Bajazeth's back in order to ascend his throne (Sales, 1991: 65). Furthermore, Tamburlaine uses the words, employed by Bajazeth to insult Tamburlaine in their rhetorical battle:

> Base villain, vassal, slave to Tamburlaine,
> Unworthy to embrace or touch the ground
> That bears the honour of my royal weight,
> Stoop, villain, stoop, Stoop, for so he bids
> That may command thee piecemeal to be torn,
> Or scattered like the lofty cedartrees
> Struck with the voice of thumd'ring Jupiter. (IV.ii,19-25)

Tamburlaine employs the very insults such as "slave" and "villain" used by Bajazeth in Act III, scene iii. Thus, by the use of 'metastasis'[105], turning back an insult or objection against the person who made it, Bajazeth is defeated, not only on the battlefield but also in verbal battle.

Bajazeth's final reaction to his situation has a prophetic ring to them:

> Great Tamburlaine, great in my overthrow,
> Ambitious pride shall make thee fall as low
> For treading on the back of Bajazeth
> That should be horsed on four mighty kings. (IV.ii,75-8)

[105] 'Metastasis': Passing over an issue quickly, or turning back an insult or objection against the person who made it (Lanham, 1991: 101).

Here, Bajazeth employs 'prolepsis'[106], speaking as if a future event has taken place, to declare that Tamburlaine will not be able to control Fortune's wheel forever. Within the body of the play, this prophesy turns out to be merely wishful thinking.

Having lost his political power as well as his verbal mastery, Bajazeth who was previously very powerful has become a 'jester' entertaining the court with his curses and rejection of eating leftovers. Zabina and Bajazeth call on Mahomet to intervene against Tamburlaine and yet nothing happens. The apparent silence of the gods drives Zabina to despair:

> Then is there left no Mahomet, no God,
> No fiend, no future, nor no hope of end
> To our infamous, monstrous slaveries?
> Gape earth, and let the fiends infernal view
> A hell as hopeless and as full of fear
> As are the blasted banks of Erebus,
> Where shaking ghosts with ever-howling groans
> Hover about the ugly ferryman
> To get a passage to Elysium! [Heaven] (V.i, 239-46)

Bajazeth, not being able to bear Tamburlaine's insults any longer, kills himself by smashing his head on the bars of the cage in which he is kept. When Zabina finds his body, it becomes a sight of Tamburlaine's uncontrollable power in a world the gods seem to have forgotten. Her language disintegrates as she prepares to run at the cage and beats out her own brains (Sales, 1991: 75):

> The sun was down. Streamers white, red, black, here, here, here. Fling the meat in his face. Tamburlaine, Tamburlaine! Let the soldiers be buried. Hell, death, Tamburlaine, hell! Make ready my coach, my chair, my jewels, I come, I come, I come! (V.i, 314-16)

Empress Zabina's speech becomes crazed, when she sees the corpse of her husband. The disempowering effects of brutality can be seen through an individual's use or

---

[106] 'Prolepsis': "Foreseeing and forestalling objections in various ways" (Lanham, 1991: 120)

loss of language. Parallel with brutality is the distortion or suppression of speech (Clare, 2000: 78).

Tamburlaine does not see the corpses of Zabina and Bajazeth until he is half through his speech designed to affirm to himself and the Soldan that he is now the general of the world. When he does notice them, he skillfully and effortlessly incorporates their presence into the rhetorical elaboration on his martial exploits (Sales, 1991: 53):

> And see, my lord, a sight of strange import–
> Emperors and kings lie breathless at my feet:
> The Turk and his great empress as it seems,
> Left to themselves while we were at the fight,
> Have desperately despatched their slavish lives;
> With them Arabia too hath left his life–
> All sights of power to grace my victory;
> And such are objects fit for Tamburlaine,
> Wherein as in a mirror may be seen
> His honour, that consists in shedding blood
> When men presume to manage arms with him. (V.i, 469-79)

Thus, Act V, scene i, concludes the major demonstrative rhetoric in *Tamburlaine, Part I* that reflect verbal violence. The rest of the play continues with Tamburlaine's capture of Damascus, defeat of the Soldan of Egypt, and killing everyone in Damascus including the virgins, except for the Soldan, Zenocrate's father, and crowning of Zenocrate as his 'empress'.

In *Tamburlaine, Part I*, Christopher Marlowe portrays some of the episodes in the life of Timur Lang (Tamburlaine). Although Timur Lang is not a Christian, history books alluded to him as the 'scourge of god' for defeating Bajazeth, the Ottoman Sultan, representative of the common enemy of Christians. Similarly, Marlowe's portrayal of Tamburlaine resembles that which is reflected in Christian historiography[107]. Some historical details with the purpose of portraying Tamburlaine

---

[107] In Richard Knolles' *The Generall Historie of the Turkes* (1603), the description of the capture of Bajazeth by Tamerlane is reflected as God's will:

> And so causing him [Bajazeth] to be taken out of his [Tamerlane] presence, turning unto his followers said, behold a proud and cruell man, he deserveth to be chastised accordingly, and

as the 'scourge of god' with the power of a supernatural demigod. The most evident alteration is the one made to Tamburlaine's physical feature; the name 'Tamerlane' is a European deformed version of the name Timur Lang (Timur the Lame) given to him because his left side was physically disabled, but Marlowe's Tamburlaine does not have any trace of such a disability. Marlowe's preference to eliminate Tamburlaine's well-known disability might be explained as Marlowe's effort to create a hero resembling a demigod. Also, Tamburlaine's numerous references to 'Jove' (Jupiter) allude to Tamburlaine as Hercules (the son of the mortal Alcmere and Jove) who is half mortal and famous for his extraordinary strength and courage. This attitude assumed by Marlowe explains why Tamburlaine in *Tamburlaine, Part I*, does not have any physical defects. The second alteration in the play is Timur Lang's age and the size of his army at the time of Battle of Angora. Timur Lang was born in 1336, and was 65 years old and at the peak of his power when he fought with Bayezid I in the Battle of Angora in 1402. However, in *Tamburlaine, Part I,* Tamburlaine is still young, almost at the beginning of his career, and has a relatively small army compared to Bajazeth's. Marlowe's alteration of such historical facts emphasize Tamburlaine's power and invincibility and helps to portray him as an unbeatable demigod who was able to beat such a legendary ruler as Bajazeth, at a young age with a much smaller army.

Language plays an important role in *Tamburlaine, Part I*, because Christopher Marlowe glorifies rhetorical skill, and draws a parallel between the 'word' and the 'sword'. Tamburlaine, the protagonist, is highly skilled in the management of both words and arms. Through his mastery of oration, he displays his power and authority to both Zenocrate and his followers. He persuades both the Persian lords and Cosroe to join him against Mycetes, and then the Persian lords against Cosroe. In case of Bajazeth and Tamburlaine, rhetorical skills are used for boasting, insulting as well as degrading the opponent.

> to be made an example to all the proud and cruell man of the world of the just wrath of God against them. I acknowledge that God hath this day delivered into my hands a great enemy; to whom we must give thanks. (1603: 220)

Thus, Tamerlane's victory over Bajazeth is seen as a manifestation of provincial justice. Knolles published this chronicle almost 16 years after Tamburlaine, Part I was first staged (1587) and for this reason, Marlowe could not have read it. However, Knolles' text is the first chronicle about the Ottoman Turks written in English, and one that has used many Latin Chronicles as sources. Therefore, it is a reflection of the attitude of Christians towards the Ottoman Turks.

Most of Tamburlaine's battles are fought verbally, rather than physically. The battle between the Persian forces in charge of Theridamas and Tamburlaine's troop which does not take place at all is replaced by verbal skill. Furthermore, when a battle does take place, it is fought off stage, is rather short and through verbal bragging, language continues to be the focal point of the action. Thus, the word is truly mightier than the sword. Language is used to persuade, manipulate, trick, mock, demoralize, degrade, humiliate and insult the other.

The style that Marlowe employs in *Tamburlaine, Part I*, is a specialized and heightened verbal rhetoric. Almost all of the characters use a rhetorical style, to a certain extent. The diction used by the characters is full of ornate elements composed of gods of classical mythology, principally Jove (Jupiter); jewels, treasures, precious stones and metals (silver); stars, planets (Saturn), and other heavenly bodies, elemental forces of nature, features of the classical underground, historical and geographical references such as Persia and India scattered to establish a more elevated, noticeable and impressive style.

Although all the characters speak in an ornate style, they do not all have the same degree of rhetorical skill. The rulers who are more competent rhetoricians, get the upper hand, and destroy the unskillful speakers. Tamburlaine is singled out as having an extensive ability for rhetoric to the point of beating an opponent like Bajazeth, well-equipped with both verbal skills and military power. It follows that Tamburlaine is able to defeat all his allies through his mastery of words as well as warfare.

CHAPTER 3

RHETORIC IN THE HANDS OF MACHIAVELLLIAN MANOEUVRERS: WILLIAM SHAKESPEARE'S *RICHARD III*

Richard III, one of the most attractive history plays composed by William Shakespeare was first performed in 1594 and published in 1597. The primary sources for the play are Edward Hall and Raphael Holinshed's *Chronicles* (Hammond, 2006: 73). The play is the forth and last of the First tetralogy dealing with the civil war between the houses of Lancaster and York before the ascension of the Tudor dynasty to the English throne (Tillyard, 1999, 117). The first three plays of this tetralogy are *Henry VI, Part 1, Part 2* and *Part 3.*

The War of the Roses was fought by King Henry VI and his wife Margaret of Anjou of the House of Lancaster, and representatives of the House of York led by Richard, Duke of York and the Earl of Warwick between 1455 and 1487. Both houses were branches of the Plantagenet royal house, tracing their descent from King Edward III.

The rivalry between the House of York and the House of Lancaster started when King Richard II was overthrown by his cousin Henry Bolingbroke, Duke of Lancaster. However, the civil war began with the First Battle of St. Albans in 1455 and was followed by Battle of Northampton (1460), Battle of Wakefield (1460), Battle of Barnet (1471), Battle of Tewkesbury (1471) and Battle of Bosworth Field (1485). The last battle ended both the Plantagenet dynasty and the War of the Roses, and heralded the Tudor dynasty represented by King Henry VII[108].

---

[108] *Henry VI* plays are significant sources that serve as the background for the relationships in *Richard III.* Therefore, a brief summary of each play is included below.

Henry VI, Part 1 begins after the death of King Henry V. King Henry V's son, King Henry VI, has become the king of England. Duke of York (Edward, Clarence and Richard's father) exerts his claim to the throne. Richard, Duke of York quarrels with John Beaufort, 1st Duke of Somerset and the lords select red or white roses to indicate whose claim they believe is correct. King Henry selects a red rose, aligning himself with Somerset and setting in motion the Wars of the Roses between the House of Lancaster, represented by the red rose, and the House of York, represented by the white.

In *Henry VI, Part 2,* Henry VI marries the French princess Margaret of Anjou, through whom William de la Pole, 4th Earl of Suffolk aims to influence the king. The major obstacle for them is the regent of the crown, Duke Humphrey (Humphrey, Duke of Gloucester). Duke of Gloucester is accused of treason, imprisoned and assassinated by agents of Suffolk and the Queen.

In *Richard III,* the War of the Roses has ended with the victory of the House of York and the accession of Edward IV. However, King Edward is sick, and his brother Richard, Duke of Gloucester is determined to force his way to the throne by eliminating a number of rivals by murder or execution. Richard plays the part of an honest and honourable man, but secretly contrives against those who stand in his way such as his brother Clarence, Queen's relatives Rivers, Grey and Vaughan, Lord Hastings, the two young sons of Edward IV, Lady Anne and Buckingham. Richard eventually does become king and continues scheming in order to secure his position. To this end, he orders King Edward's children, and his wife Lady Anne to death, and insists on marrying his niece Elizabeth (daughter of King Edward) for political necessity.

Henry, Earl of Richmond, who has claim to the throne through the Lancaster line, lands with an army in South Whales, and is joined by many who are discontented with Richard. The armies of Richard and Richmond meet near Market Bosworth (the Battle of Bosworth Field), where Richard is killed in single combat by the Earl of Richmond. The play ends with the establishment of the Tudor dynasty in

---

Meanwhile, Duke of York exerts his claim to the throne, supported by his sons, Edward (the future King Edward IV of England) and Richard (the future King Richard III of England). The English nobility now takes sides (with the House of Lancaster or the House of York), and the Battle of St. Albans is fought.

In Henry VI, Part 3 King Henry VI, threatened with physical violence by the Earl of Warwick (Richard Neville), declares the Duke of York as his heir. However, Queen Margaret, with the assistance of Lord Clifford (whose father was killed by the Duke of York), her son Edward, Prince of Wales and others, declares war on the Yorkists and defeats them at the Battle of Wakefield. Also, Lord Clifford murders York's young son, the Earl of Rutland, and together with Queen Margaret taunts the Duke of York before killing him.

At the Battle of Towton, the Earl of Warwick and Edward (later King Edward IV of England) take revenge on Margaret's army, and Clifford is killed. Following the battle, Edward is proclaimed king, and his two brothers, George and Richard respectively become Dukes of Clarence and Gloucester. However, Warwick turns against Edward when he marries Lady Grey (Elizabeth Woodville) while Warwick is in France courting the French king's sister on Edward's behalf.

Queen Margaret gets military aid from France and as a result of an invasion Edward IV is taken prisoner and King Henry is restored to the throne until Edward is rescued by his brother Richard and Lord Hastings. Meanwhile, the young Earl of Richmond (the future King Henry VII of England), a descendant of John of Gaunt and therefore a potential Lancastrian heir, is shipped into exile in France for safekeeping.

Edward defeats and kills Warwick at the Battle of Barnet and in the subsequent Battle of Tewkesbury, he kills the Prince of Wales and captures Queen Margaret. After the death of King Henry VI and, with all the Lancastrians dead or exiled, the play ends with the establishment of the House of York and the birth of Edward's son.

England by Richmond, who is hailed as King Henry VII. Richmond declares that he will marry Princess Elizabeth and unite the houses of York and Lancaster.

Although Shakespeare employed rhetoric in all his plays, Anthony Hammond[109] indicates that *Richard III* stands out as the most dependent on a rhetorical style (1981; 2006:114). Power and identity in the play depend heavily on the possession of a powerful verbal style. Shakespeare endows Richard with Machiavellian qualities[110] complying with the rhetorical dimension of Machiavelli's political thought. In his works such as *The Prince* and *The Discourses*, Machiavelli establishes a new set of priorities unconstrained by ethical norms in the domain of politics. Naturally, this view encompasses the abuse of rhetoric for personal gain[111] and moves the focal point of rhetoric from 'representation' to 'misrepresentation', 'persuasion' to 'coercion', 'means' to 'ends', 'intention' to 'effect' where it becomes an instrument of force and fraud, violence and misrepresentation[112].

The fact that Richard is fully aware of the connection between 'rhetoric' and 'power' is explicitly expressed in *Henry VI, Part* 3[113], the third play of the tetralogy:

> I'll play the orator as well as Nestor;
> Deceive more slily than Ulysses could,
> And, like a Sinon, take another Troy.
> I can add colours to the chameleon[114],
> Change shapes with Proteus[115] for advantages,

[109] The editor of *Richard III*'s Arden edition.

[110] The rhetorical foundations of political power and its role in subversion and maintaining political and religious power were recognized by Renaissance playwrights. The stage Machiavellian in the Renaissance is typically a hypocrite, cunning, a figure of "force and fraud, coercion and deceit" (Kahn, 1994: 7) and a powerful rhetorician (Kahn, 1994: 91).

[111] In her book *Machiavellian Rhetoric* Victoria Kahn defines 'rhetoric' as a repertoire of means of persuasion ranging from the figurative language and formal organization of a text to the ethos (G. disposition, character) and pathos (G. emotion, experience) of the speaker, which are available for the service of both good and evil (1994: 5).

[112] For this reason Machiavelli is generally identified with the political and religious abuse of rhetoric (Kahn, 1994: 10) Cardinal Pole provided a sketch of the Machiavel in his *Apologia ad Caralum Quintum* (1539). He tells us that Machiavelli's works "stink of the malice of Satan" and that *The Prince* was written "by Satan's hand". He condemns Machiavelli's divorce of ethics from politics and his merely instrumental use of the virtues as immoral cunning (in Kahn, 1994: 87).

[113] Shakespeare, William. "*Henry VI, Part* 3". In *The Complete Works of William Shakespeare*. Edited by W. J. Craig. London: Pordes, 1914. 609-644.

[114] A member of the lizard family that can change color.

And set the murd'rous Machiavel to school.
Can I do this, and cannot get a crown?
Tut! Were it further off, I'Il pluck it down. (III. ii, 188-95)

In this soliloquy, Richard, the Duke of Gloucester claims that it is impossible for him not to gain the crown by being a Machiavel. He indicates that he will be an orator as wise as "Nestor"[116], as deceitful as "Ulysses" and "Sinon"[117]. He then indicates that he has the ability to transform into different roles by making reference to a "chameleon", known for its ability to change colours, and "Proteus", a sea-god who had the ability to change to any form he wishes. He believes that by such means, he will be so successful that he will surpass the discourses of Machiavelli and send the evil Machiavel back to "school".

To this end the rhetoric used by Richard in his strife to attain kingship in *Richard III* is highly motivated, powerful and effective. Moreover, just as Marlowe had done in *Tamburlaine, Part I,* Shakespeare has chosen to associate verbal skill with political power. It follows that in the course of this historical drama, King Richard, who proves to be a master rhetorician and schemer during his rise to power, becomes –after he has attained his goal– so obsessed with the fear of losing his crown that his mental strength (along with his rhetorical skills) starts to decline.

Unlike Marlowe's *Tamburlaine, Part I,* in which the instances of physical violence are hardly ever expressed in the dialogues, Richard in his rhetorical discourse includes frequent references to physical violence that has taken place off stage. Thus, verbal violence not only manifests itself in Richard's effective use of rhetoric, but also functions as a powerful representation of the terrible dimensions of the off-stage action. According to Russ Mcdonald "words speak louder than actions" for Richard, who is bestowed with an unparalleled gift for language, carries out his evil deeds through his verbal skill and at no point is he shown killing anyone (1996: 199). For the purpose of tracing the relationship between language and power, the discussion here will specifically concentrate on the scenes in which Richard uses a

[115] Proteus, an early sea-god in Greek mythology, who had the power to foretell the future. He, however, only answered those who were able to capture him and changed shape in order to avoid getting caught. For this reason, he symbolizes 'flexibility', 'versatility' and 'adaptability'.
[116] The oldest and wisest of the Greeks in the Trojan War and the king of Pylos.
[117] In Greek mythology, Sinon or the crafty Sisyphus was a Greek warrior who tricked the Trojans to accepting the giant wooden horse left by the Greeks, telling them that it was intended as a gift to the gods to ensue their safe voyage home. For this reason, he is thought to be deceitful and treacherous.

vast amount of rhetoric -namely his opening soliloquy (Act I, scene 1), his wooing of Lady Anne (Act I, scene ii) and Act II, scene iv, in which Richard is persuaded to accept the crown. As Richard's rise to the throne is seen through Act I, Act II and most of Act III, while Act IV and V illustrate his downfall, the above mentioned scenes which depict Richard's rise to power and mastery of rhetoric are paralleled with those scenes that reflect his loss of power and intellectual superiority along with his rhetorical effectiveness. These scenes include Richard's attempt to persuade Elizabeth to arrange his marriage with her daughter in Act IV, scene iv (Richard's second wooing scene) his soliloquy after his nightmare on the eve of the battle, and finally Richmond and Richard's consecutive orations to their armies in Act V, scene iii.

The opening soliloquy of Richard in Act I, scene i, serves as a kind of prologue to the entire action of the play. With this monologue, Richard establishes a close relationship with the audience and provides information about the historical background, about his own state (his deformity and his attitude towards it), as well as his schemes and the role he is going to play in the scenarios he has created. It also initially shows Richard's skill in using language and sets up a platform for him to perform in.

The first thirteen lines of Richard's soliloquy illustrate the initial situation after the war and the position of the new King, Edward IV:

> Now is the winter of our discontent
> Made glorious summer by this son[118] of York;
> And all the clouds that lour'd upon our House
> In deep bosom of the ocean buried.
> Now are our brows bound with victorious wreaths,
> Our bruised arms hung up for monuments,
> Our stern alarums charge'd to merry meetings,
> Our[119] dreadful marches to delightful measures[120].
> Grim-visag'd War hath smooth'd his wrinkled front[121]:

[118] Edward IV assumed the device of a sun as his emblem in consequence of the vision of three suns which appeared to him during the battle of Mortimer's Cross (Hammond, 2006: 125). There is a 'pun'[118] on 'sun'/'son', the humorous use of different words that sound the same, in which the word 'sun' in the badge of the house of York is changed to 'son'.

[119] Lines 6-8 are an example of 'anaphora': "Repetition of the same word in successive lines or verses". (Lanham, 1991: 11).

[120] Stately dances, tunes and melodies.

And now, instead of mounting barber[122] steeds
To fright the souls of fearful adversaries,
He capers nimbly in a lady's chamber,
To the lascivious pleasing of a lute. (I. i, 1-13)

The War of the Roses has ended with the victory of the House of York, and the accession of Edward IV, Richard's eldest brother. The past and present situations are depicted through conjoining contrasting metaphors such as images of war put next to images of peace. The difficult time of the civil war between the houses of York and Lancaster is indicated by 'winter' connoting hardships while the present situation is depicted throughout an atmosphere of peace symbolized by 'summer' with the victory of the house of York represented by Edward 'the son of York'. The clouds that had roamed over the house of York have been buried into the 'personified' ocean's deep "bosom". Since the war is now over, their "bruised arms" are hung for exhibition and war "capers nimbly in a lady's chamber,/To the lascivious pleasing of a lute" instead riding armed horses to fright the "souls of fearful adversaries". By using the word "capers", moving playfully, Richard scornfully makes fun of the lover's role and underlines his low opinion of a warrior's unmanly behaviour in peace-time. In this part of Richard's soliloquy opening the play, the physical violence inherent in warfare is expressed through rhetorical artistry by which the conditions of war and peace are contrasted.

After sarcastically presenting this pleasant portrait of present times, Richard positions himself within this 'picture' of the reign of the house of York, by moving from the possessive pronoun "our" dominant in the first section, to the pronoun "I":

But I, that am not shap'd for sportive tricks [love games],
Nor made to court an amorous looking-glass;
I, that am rudely stamp'd, and want love's majesty
To strut before a wanton ambling nymph:
I, that am curtail'd of this fair proportion,
Cheated of feature by dissembling Nature,
Deform'd, unfinish'd, sent before my time
Into this breathing world scarce half made up–

[121] Forehead
[122] Armed for war.

And that so lamely and unfashionable
That dogs bark at me, as I halt by them–
Why, I, in this weak piping time of peace,
Have no delight to pass away the time,
Unless to spy my shadow in the sun,
And descant on mine own deformity.
And therefore, since I cannot prove a lover
To entertain these fair well-spoken days,
I am determined to prove a villain,
And hate the idle pleasures of these days. (I. i, 14-31)

The above lines draw an 'icon' or picture description of Richard as "rudely stamped", cheated by "nature" (not in proper proportions), "deformed" (hunchbacked) and sent unfinished (born prematurely). By emphasizing such characteristics relating to his deformity, Richard stresses the role that his deformity plays in motivating him to carry out evil plans. Since he is not handsome or "fair proportioned", he is not made to court ladies, to take part in "sportive tricks" (love games), or to pass the time admiring himself in the mirror and thus, he has nothing to do in times of peace but to watch the shadow of his deformed body. Such images, including the mention of dogs barking upon his appearance are examples of 'commiseratio'[123] designed to evoke pity and sympathy in the spectator and also to provide justification for the character's planned course of action depicted in the lines that are to follow. Richard's physical features do not enable Richard to take on the role of the lover, so he is determined to become a false and treacherous villain and "hate the idle pleasures of these days".

After creating a sense of pity and attempting to justify his evil tendencies by his physical deformity, Richard goes on to explain the 'plots' he has engineered:

Plots have I laid, inductions[124] dangerous,
By drunken prophecies, libels, and dreams,
To set my brother Clarence and the King
In deadly hate, the one against the other:
And if King Edward be as true and just
As I am subtle, false, and treacherous[125],

[123] 'Commiseratio': To evoke pity and sympathy in the audience (Lanham, 1991: 37).
[124] Preperation, first steps.

This day should Clarence closely be mew'd up
About a prophesy, which says that 'G'
Of Edward's heirs the murderer shall be– (I. i. 32- 40)

He is determined to set his two brothers, Edward and Clarence against each other. King Edward has been told through a prophesy that 'G', one of the heirs to the throne shall be his murderer and believes that it is Clarence because his name is 'George'.

The closing lines of his "self-address"[126]: "Dive, thoughts, down to my soul/ Here Clarence comes" (I. i, 41-42) is a reminder that Richard's secret thoughts, though revealed to the spectator, must remain unknown to the other characters in the play (Clemen, 1999: 67).

Richard then encounters his brother Clarence, who is being sent to the Tower (of London) by the order of King Edward. Although Richard appears to be upset while he is talking to his brother, he remarks after Clarence departs, that he 'loves' Clarence so much that he will shortly send his soul to Heaven ("Go, tread the path that thou shalt ne'er return;/Simple, plain Clarence, I do love thee so/That I will shortly send thy soul to Heaven" [I. i, 118-120]). Here, Richard uses 'euphemism', substituting a mild and pleasant expression for a harsh and blunt one. Richard then sees Hastings, just released from imprisonment, who tells him that King Edward is sick. Richard appears to be sad about this bit of bad news but reveals his true intent when Hastings leaves:

He [Edward] cannot live, I hope, and must not die
Till George be pack'd with post-horse[127] up to Heaven.
I'll in to urge his hatred more to Clarence,
With lies well-steel'd with weighty arguments;
And if I fail not in my deep intent,
Clarence hath not another day to live:
Which done, God take King Edward to his mercy,
And leave the world for me to bustle in.
For then I'll marry Warwick's youngest daughter[128]–

---

[125] Line 36-37 are an example of 'Contrarium'; "One of two opposite statements is used to emphasize the truth of the other". (Lanham, 1991: 41)
[126] A rhetorical device also used by Seneca.
[127] In great speed
[128] Anne Neville is the widow of Edward, Prince of Whales (son of Henry VI)

What though I kill'd her husband and her father? (I.i, 145-154)

So Richard's plan is clear. He will get Clarence out of the way before Edward dies. He then plans to marry Lady Anne, widow of Edward, the Lancastrian Prince of Wales, in order to divert any residual sympathy for the Lancastrian cause.

Act I, scene ii moves straight to Richard's first wooing scene. Gloucester's conversation with Lady Anne is probably one of the best examples of persuasion and manipulation in Shakespearean drama, because at the beginning of the scene, all the odds are against Richard. There are several reasons why Lady Anne should hate Richard; he is a member of the house of York while she is a member of the house of Lancaster. He has killed both her father-in-law (King Henry the Sixth), and her husband Edward (Prince of Wales)[129]. Lady Anne knows that Richard is the murderer of those near and dear to her and therefore hates him.

The scene is quite extraordinary. It begins with the entrance of King Henry's corpse carried by guards followed by Lady Anne. She starts by cursing the murderer of her father-in-law by employing 'anaphora'[130], the repetition of the word 'cursed' at the beginning of successive lines: "O! cursed be the hand that made these holes!/Cursed the heart that had the heart to do it!/ Cursed the blood that let this blood from hence!"[131] (I. ii, 14-16). She curses the murderer's "hand", "heart" and "blood" for killing her father-in-law. Here, then, physical violence that has caused her misery is reflected in her rhetorical use of language. Her employment of verbal violence continues with curses that the murderer's future child be "prodigious, and untimely brought to light,/Whose ugly and unnatural aspect" may "fright the hopeful mother at the view;" (I. ii, 22-24) and that his wife be "more miserable" by the murderer's death (I. ii, 26-27). The words "prodigious", "untimely", "ugly" and "unnatural" used for the future child seem to be direct references to the physical characteristics of Richard, the murderer.

Richard then enters the stage and asks the soldiers to put down the corpse in the name of "Saint Paul" (I. ii, 36), threatens them with death if they act otherwise. The soldiers put down the corpse and Lady Anne becomes irritated by their obedience but does not blame them for fearing him because of his diabolical

[129] He is also Queen Margaret's son.
[130] 'Anaphora': "Repetition of the same word at the beginning of successive clauses or verses" (Lanham, 1991: 11).
[131] By the repetition of "heart" and "blood", Lady Anne uses 'Antanaclasis', repeating a word while shifting from one meaning to another (Vickers, 1987: 397).

qualities: "mortal eyes cannot endure the devil." (I. ii, 45).

The scene then continues with an extended example of 'stichomythia' between Richard and Lady Anne. The arguments proceed with the employment of parallel structures that include the use of antonyms and binary opposition that go back and forth between extremities, good-evil, holy-unsacred and saint-devil.

Despite Anne's earlier reference to Richard as "minister of hell" (Satan, devil) in line 43, he turns 'the other cheek' and asks her not to curse: "Sweet saint, for charity be not so curst" (I. ii, 49) to which Anne continues by drawing a portrait of Richard as the "devil" who has made the "unhappy" earth his hell and filled it with "cursing cries and deep exclaims" through his "butcheries":

> Foul devil, for God's sake hence, and trouble us not;
> For thou hast made the unhappy earth thy hell,
> Fill'd it with cursing cries and deep exclaims.
> If thou delight to view thy heinous [wicked] deeds,
> Behold this pattern of thy butcheries.
> O gentlemen! See, see dead Henry's wounds
> Open their congeal'd mouths and bleed afresh.
> Blush, blush, thou lump of foul deformity,
> For 'tis thy presence that exhales this blood
> From cold and empty veins where no blood dwells:
> Thy deed inhuman and unnatural
> Provokes this deluge most unnatural.
> O God! which this blood mad'st, revenge his death;
> O earth! which this blood drink'st, revenge his death;
> Either heav'n with lighting strike the murderer dead,
> Or earth gape open wide and eat him quick,
> As thou dost swallow up this good King's blood
> Which his hell-govern'd arm hath butchered. (I. ii, 50-67)

In her long speech, Anne also employs 'anamnesis'[132] by drawing a disturbing picture of Henry's lifeless corpse bleeding afresh in the presence of Richard (his murderer), in lines 55-6. Here verbal violence employed by Anne turns out to be more impressive than an actual description of Henry being stabbed by Richard.

The use of 'stichomythia' is dominant in the lines that follow. As a response to

[132] 'Anamnesis': "Recalling ideas, events, or persons of the past". (Lanham, 1991: 11).

her curses, Richard in turn employs religious imagery as he woos Anne. He asks her whether she does not know the rules of charity which teaches people to respond to curses by blessings (as he is in fact doing):

Richard: **Lady, you know no rules of charity**[133],
Which renders good for bad, blessings for curses.
Anne: **Villain, thou know'st no law of God nor man.**
No beast so fierce but **knows** some touch of pity.
Richard: But I **know** none, and therefore am **no beast**. (I. ii, 68-72)

He displays himself as a 'repenter' who has repented exercising charity:

Anne: **O wonderful, when devils tell the truth**!
Richard: **More wonderful, when angels are so angry**.
Vouchsafe, divine perfection of a woman,
Of these supposed crimes, to give me leave,
By circumstancesing, but to acquit myself.
Anne: **Vouchsafe, diffus'd infection of a man,**
Of these known evils, but to give me leave,
By circumstance, t'accuse thy cursed self. (I. ii, 73-80)

While Richard speaks to her as a lover, he also implies that she should be forgiving, charitable and show him pity (as an angel would):

Richard: **Fairer than tongue can name thee, let me have**
Some patient leisure to excuse myself.
Anne: **Fouler than heart can think thee, thou canst make**
No excuse current but to hang thyself.
Richard: By such despair I should **accuse** myself.
Anne: And by despairing shalt thou stand **excus'd** (I. ii, 81-86)

[133] The instances of 'stichomythia' in the passages quoted on pages 13-15 have been shown in bold letters so that they may be pinpointed more easily.

Then, quite by surprise, Richard accepts the fact that he has killed her husband, but states that he was provoked by Queen Margaret's "sland'rous tongue" (I. ii, 99). Anne comments that Richard was not provoked by anyone, but his own "bloody mind" (I. ii, 101) and the 'stichomythia' develops as follows:

Anne: [...]
O he was gentle, mild, and virtuous.
Richard: The better for the King of **Heaven** that hath him.
Anne: He is in **Heaven**, where thou shalt never come.
Richard: Let him thank me that help to send him thither,
For he was **fitter for that place that earth**.
Anne: And thou **unfit for any place but hell.**
Richard: Yes, one **place** else, if you will hear me name it.
Anne: **Some dungeon**?
Richard: **Your bed-chamber**. (I. ii, 106-114)

In the above lines, Richard uses 'antanagoge'[134], balancing an unfavourable aspect with a favourable one. Richard agrees to her husband Edward's, having been gentle, mild and virtuous, and adds that he, being such a gentle soul, is "fitter" to be with God "the King of heaven" in Heaven than on earth. When Anne replies that Richard is "unfit" for any place but hell, Richard shocks her by saying that he is fit to be in her "bed-chamber" too, thus hinting that he desires her sexually.

The next part of Richard's argument is designed to change Anne's mind about the circumstances that led to the death of her husband. Richard makes his final move by pleading to her as a stubborn lover who has sacrificed everything for her. He uses "amplification" to elaborate on her beauty as "aetiologia"[135], the "causer of the timeless deaths" (I. ii, 121) and the hope of spending one hour in her sweet bosom which "haunted" him to commit such a terrifying task:

Your beauty was the cause of that effect [murder];
Your beauty that did haunt me in my sleep
To undertake the death of all the world,
So I might live one hour in your sweet bosom. (I. ii, 125-128)

[134] 'Antanagoge': "Ameliorating a fault or difficulty implicitly admitted by balancing an unfavorable aspect with a favorable one" (Lanham, 1991: 13).
[135] 'Aetiologia': "Giving a cause or reason." (Lanham, 1991: 3).

Richard argues that his aim was to give her a 'better' husband, one who loved her more than her former husband: "He that bereft thee, lady, of thy husband,/Did it to help thee to a better husband." (I. ii, 142-143). The use of 'stichomythia' reaches its peak when Anne spits at him at him as he is attempting to present himself as the "better husband":

Richard: Why dost thou **spit** at me?
Anne: Would it were mortal **poison**, for thy sake.
Richard: Never came **poison** from so sweet a place.
Anne: Never hung **poison** on a fouler toad.
Out of my sight! Thou dost **infect mine eyes**.
Richard: Thine **eyes**, sweet lady, have **infected mine**. (I. ii, 148-153)

Richard goes through the act of persuading Lady Anne to favour him by re-defining her understanding of the situation. Richard is no longer a devil and a murderer, but instead a man so madly in love with her that he has even killed a man whom he considered virtuous. By killing Anne's husband, he has sent him to a place more fit for such a virtuous man, and also offers her a chance to have a better husband, thus implying that he did those unspeakable acts for Lady Anne's welfare.

When Richard states that it was her "eyes" that "infected" him, she wishes that her eyes were "basilisks" so that they would strike him dead. Richard replies that he also wishes they were "basilisks" so that they would kill him right away, because at present her eyes have sentenced him to a living death and have "drawn salt tears" from his eyes due to his misery (I. ii, 157). He emphasizes the importance of shedding tears and continues to illustrate his transformation by pointing out that he had not felt more miserable even when his young cousin Rutland was killed or when Lady Anne's "warlike" father told him of the death of his father. His intentional and casual drop of "warlike father" seems to point out that her family fought and murdered as well. Thus, he amplifies the extent of the pain he could endure; yet, her eyes have made him a different man and planted the feeling of sorrow in his heart:

My manly eyes did scorn a humble tear;
And what these sorrows could not thence exhale,
Thy beauty hath, and made them blind with weeping.

> I never sued to friend nor enemy:
> My tongue could never learn sweet smoothing word;
> But now thy beauty is propos'd my fee,
> My proud heart sues, and prompts my tongue to speak. (I. ii, 168-174)

And if her "revengeful heart" cannot forgive him, she might as well kill him. Richard gives her a sword and pretends to urge her to kill him (I. ii, 177-182):

> Nay, do not pause, for I did kill King Henry–
> But 'twas thy beauty that provoked me.
> Nay, now dispatch:'twas I that stabb'd young Edward–
> But 'twas thy heavenly face that set me on. (I. ii, 183-186)

Richard's emphasis on her beauty as the provocateur of his crimes causes Lady Anne's guard to fall. With reference to this situation, Samuel Johnson has humorously indicated that Shakespeare "countenances the observation that no woman can ever be offended with the mention of her beauty" (In Woudhuysen, 1989: 215). As a result of Richard's brilliant manoeuvre, the mood changes to the advantage of the wooer:

> *Anne*: I would I knew thy heart.
> *Richard*: 'Tis figured in my tongue.
> *Anne*: I fear me both are false.
> *Richard*: Then never was man true. (I. ii, 196-199)

Lady Anne defeated in the rhetorical contest, remarks that she wishes that she "knew thy [his] heart", that is, his true feelings. Lady Anne's desire seems to indicate her awareness of Richard's 'sophistries', but nevertheless, she wears his ring expressing the joy that his transformation has brought her: "With all my heart, and much it joys to me too/ To see you are become so penitent." (I. ii, 223-224)

In his first wooing scene, Richard constructs his arguments in response to Anne's insults mainly by using holy images like "saint" and "angel" to suit his role as 'repentant' reborn into this world with the love of Lady Anne. Lady Anne's last remark and acceptance of his ring proves that Richard's rhetorical plea has been a success. Despite all the circumstances working against Richard, not to mention his physical deformity and insincere intentions, he woos her and achieves the impossible by changing her impression of him through his rhetorical skill. Richard persuades Lady Anne through pleading to her charity, appearing to be honest, sincere and repentant and by accepting that he is the murderer of her husband and father-in-law. He thus leads her to believe that it was not his hatred but her angelic beauty which made him commit the unforgivable crimes (murder of Henry and Edward).

This scene is a spectacle of persuasion, brilliantly played out by Richard. He later comments on his performance as follows: "Was ever woman in this humour woo'd?/Was ever woman in this humour won?" (I. ii, 232-233). These lines pinpoint the rhetorical performance he has just given as a parody of proper wooing, and the point is enforced by the immediate switch to direct speech which follows:

> I'll have her, but I will not keep her long.
> What, I that kill'd her husband and his father:
> To take her in her heart's extremest hate,
> With curses in her mouth, tears in her eyes,
> The bleeding witness of her hatred by,
> Having God, her conscience, and these bars against me–
> And I, no friends to back my suit at all
> But the plain devil and dissembling looks–
> And yet to win her, all the world to nothing!
> Ha! (I. ii, 234-243).

Richard's skilled use of rhetoric, in contrast to his villainous intentions indicates the splendour and falsity of rhetoric in the hands of manoeuvrers such as Richard.

Richard continues to do mischief in the court in Act I, Scene iii. He creates hostility between the older nobility and the relatives of the Queen Elizabeth (Edward IV's wife). In this case, Richard uses 'judicial oratory', in which he employs past tense and goes over the events that took place before the final victory of the house of York[136]. Richard makes use of 'amplification'[137] to point out that Queen Elizabeth

---

[136] In Act I, scene iii, Richard approaches Lord Rivers, Lord Grey and Queen Elizabeth about the rumors that have been spread about him concerning his lack of love for Queen Elizabeth and her allies because he can't "flatter, and look fair," (I. iii, 42- 59). Richard, apart from accusing Queen Elizabeth of influencing the king for imprisoning Clarence (I.iii, 78) and Hastings, and promoting her 'milieu', he adds another point which might cause antipathy for the Queen; her potential to remarry another king (one that is an enemy of the house of York) after King Edward's death (I. iii, 98-100).

and her allies have been promoted while people like Richard, Clarence and Lord Hastings who have helped King Edward gain the throne are being falsely accused or imprisoned. This scene (III, iii) is also significant due to Queen Margaret's appearance. Richard attacks the ex-queen the Lancaster on the stage by reminding her of the harm done to his family, his words bringing out more violence than that done in the past:

> The curse my noble father laid on thee
> When thou didst crown his warlike brows with paper,
> And with thy scorns drew'st rivers from his eyes,
> And then to dry them, gav'st the Duke a clout [cloth]
> Steep'd in the faultless blood of pretty Rutland–
> His curses then, from bitterness of soul
> Denounc'd against thee, are all fall'n upon thee,
> And God, not we, hath plagu'd thy bloody deed. (I.iii, 174-181)

Margaret, in turn, addresses the assembly of the Yorkists as murderers and curses each of them for their individual part in the violence exerted on her family. The verbal violence employed in her curses turns out to be more horrifying then the actual deeds of physical violence performed by the Yorkists:

> Why then, give way, dull clouds, to my quick[138] curses:
> Though not by war, by surfeit die your King,
> As ours by murder, to make him a king.
> Edward thy son, that now is Prince of Whales,
> For Edward my son, that was the Prince of Whales,
> Die in his youth, by like untimely violence.

Richard then moves on to present which side Queen Elizabeth, Clarence and he supported during the War of the Roses, with reference to present condition or position of each. Richard indicates that while "Ere you were queen, ay, or your husband king,/I was a pack-horse in his great affairs;" who spent his own blood to "royalize" Edward's (I. iii, 121-125). He further indicates that during the War of the Roses, Queen Elizabeth, her husband Sir John Grey (who was killed at the Battle of St Albans fighting on the Lancaster side) and Lord Rivers were factions for the House of Lancaster, and thus, the enemy of the house of York (I. iii, 127-133). Here, Richard amplifies Queen Elizabeth and her allies' advancement in a comparison to the situation of Clarence and himself, who have helped King Edward gain the throne are being punished.

[137] 'Amplification': A device in which language is used to extend or magnify or emphasize. (Cuddon, 1999: 32)

[138] Full of vigor and energy.

Thyself, a queen, for me that was a queen, (I. iii, 196-202)

Through such rhetorical figures, Richard aims to create a negative attitude towards Queen Elizabeth by accusing her of influencing the King into imprisoning Clarence's and Hastings, and promoting her friends and relatives. By accusing her, thus, he prevents any accusations (Clarence's imprisonment and death) to be made against him. Act I is concluded with the murder of Clarence in the tower by two murderers sent by Richard (Act I, scene iv). When, in Act II, scene ii, Edward, hearing of Clarence's death, indicates that the order for Clarence's execution was reversed, Richard points out that Clarence was killed by the king's first order, and that his change of heart came too late.

As a result of his manoeuvring through rhetoric, Richard manages to direct the accusations concerning Clarence's death at Queen Elizabeth. In addition, by stating that he only carried out Edward's orders, he holds Edward responsible for the deed. His success in manipulating others is illustrated by the conversation between Clarence children and their grandmother the Duchess (mother of King Edward, Clarence and Richard) about Clarence's death. It is apparent that the children believe Richard's version of events:

Boy: [...] my good uncle Gloucester
Told me the King [Edward], provok'd to't by the Queen [Elizabeth],
Devis'd impeachments to imprison him [Clarence];
And when my uncle told me so he wept,
And pitied me, and kindly kiss'd my cheek;
Bade me rely on him as on my father,
And he would love me dearly as a child. (II. ii, 20-26)

However, the Duchess of York knows her son too well. When Elizabeth informs them that King Edward is dead, the Duchess of York expresses her grief by stating that after her husband's death, she continued living on his images (sons), but now two mirrors of his "princely semblance" are cracked (death of Clarence and Edward) and she is left with "one false glass [Richard]" (II. ii, 50-53)[139]. The joint lamentation (II.

[139] Also, when Richard proceeds to get the Duchess' blessings and kneels, she says: "God bless thee, and put meekness in thy breast;/Love, charity, obedience, and true duty" (II.ii,107-108) making him, in Richard's words, the "butt-end of a mother's blessings" (II. ii, 110).

ii, 70-79) of Elizabeth, the Duchess and Clarence's children that follows is broken up with the entrance of Richard, Buckingham, Stanley, Hastings and Ratcliffe. Richard tells them that although they all have reason to "wail the dimming" of their "shining star", crying will not improve their condition (II. ii, 101-3). To this, Buckingham adds; "Though we have spent our harvest of this king,/We are to reap[140] the harvest of his son." (II. ii, 115-116) He then suggests that a small party should be sent to Ludlow to fetch the young Edward Prince of Wales (King Edward's elder son) and bring him to London for his coronation. Alone with Richard on the stage, Buckingham, the latter suggests that they should also follow the party and part the Queen's kindred from the Prince, to which Richard 'humbly' consents.

In Act II, scene iv, the Archbishop of York, Queen Elizabeth, the Duchess of York and the young Duke of York await the arrival of Prince Edward, but a messenger brings news that Lord Rivers, Lord Grey and Sir Thomas Vaughan accompanying the young prince have been sent by Gloucester and Buckingham to the Castle of Pomfret as prisoners. At this point, Queen Elizabeth, seeing the ruin that has befallen her family, decides to go into sanctuary with young York and is accompanied by the Duchess of York. However, Richard is determined to eliminate both of the sons of the deceased king. When, on his arrival to London, Prince Edward is informed that his mother and brother were not able to welcome him due to her entrance to sanctuary, Richard prevails on the Archbishop of Canterbury to break the sanctuary in order to unite the two brothers. Richard's plan proves to be a success. The younger prince comes to London and the two princes are sent to the Tower of London by Richard as 'a safety precaution'. Richard's wicked intention to murder the princes' is forwarded to Buckingham in private in the form of 'antisagoge'[141]: in return for the fulfilment of the task, Richard promises to present him with "The earldom of Hereford, and all the moveables/Whereof the King my brother was possess'd." when he has become king (III. i, 195-200).

Besides planning to kill the princes, Richard continues with his plots to eliminate others who might constitute an obstacle in his path towards kingship. To this end, he not only sends Queen Elizabeth's relatives Rivers, Grey and Vaughan to

[140] This is an example of "Adianoeta", an expression that has an obvious meaning and an unsuspected secret one beneath. (Lanham, 1991: 2) When Buckingham says "Though we have spent our harvest of this king/We are to reap the harvest of his son" (II. ii, 115-116), the literal meaning is that they are going to "reap" what belongs to Edward's son.

[141] 'Antisagoga': "Assuring a reward to those who possess a virtue, or a punishment to those who hold it in contempt." (Lanham, 1991: 15).

death (Act III, scene iii) but he also, on discovering that Lord Hastings stands in opposition to his kingship, he also accuses him of being a traitor[142] and has him executed without a trial. In order to justify the executions and convince the Lord Mayor of London that there has been a plot against their lives, Richard and Buckingham rehearse their parts before they actually present their performance in front of company:

Richard: Come, cousin, canst thou quake and change thy colour,
Murder thy breath in middle of a word,
And then again begin, and stop again,
As if thou were distraught and mad with terror?
Buckingham: Tut, I can counterfeit the deep tragedian,
Speak, and look back, and pry on every side,
Tremble and start at wagging of a straw,
Intending deep suspicion. Ghastly looks
Are at my service like enforced smiles,
And both are ready in their offices (III. v, 1-10)

When it is time to 'perform' so as to persuade the Mayor that he had no evil intents towards Hastings, Richard indicates that he loved Hastings and took him "for the plainest harmless creature/That breath'd upon the earth a Christian;" (III. v, 25-6) but that "subtle traitor" had plotted to murder him and the Lord of Gloucester at thc

---

[142] In Act III, scene iv, at the council, Richard claims that his arm has been deformed through witchcraft, when in reality it had been in that condition since his birth:

Richard: Then be your eyes the witness of their evil.
See how I am bewitch'd! Behold, mine arm
Is like a blasted sapling wither'd up!
And this is Edward's wife, that monstrous witch,
Consorted with that harlot, strumpet Shore,
That by their witchcraft thus have marked me.
Hastings: If they have done this deed, my noble lord-
Richard: If? Thou protector of this damned strumpet,
Talk'st thou to me of ifs! Thou art a traitor:
Off with his head! [...] (III. iv, 67-76)

He says that people supporting Elizabeth are using witchcraft to deform him, acting paranoid, and when Hasting uses "if" to indicate that it might be true, which Richard accepts as a sign of doubt about the truth of what Richard has just announced and uses this answer as a chance to accuse him of conspiring against him by witchcraft and executes Hastings' at once.

council-house (III. v, 35-37).

Richard's next step is the elimination of the two princes' claims to the throne. He sends Buckingham to address the assembled citizens so as to convince them of his right to the crown. To this end, Buckingham promises to use his oratory skills: "Doubt not, my lord: I'll play the orator/As if the golden fee for which I plead/Were for myself; [...]" (III. v, 94-95)[143], but cannot create the desired effect on the audience during the assembly. He returns in Act III, scene vii and informs Richard that he talked of King Edward and his children's 'bastardry', Richard's "discipline in war", "wisdom in peace", "bounty", "virtue" and "fair humility", but when he bid those who love their country to cry "'God save Richard, England's royal King." no one spoke a word (III. vii, 5-22). The only support Richard got was from a group of ten persons made up of Buckingham's own men.

Although Richard does not get much support in the assembly, the Mayor, contrived by Buckingham, nevertheless comes to persuade Richard to accept the English crown in Act III, scene vii. In this scene, Richard employs visual religious images[144] and religious rhetoric. On their arrival, Lord Major and Buckingham are told by Catesby, acting as intermediary, that Richard is praying.

Catesby informs Lord Mayor and Buckingham that Richard is praying and does not wish to be disturbed, but after a while Richard enters between two Bishops holding a prayer book. The Mayor is impressed at this sight, while Buckingham comments that the bishops and the prayer book Richard holds are "[t]rue ornaments to know a holy man." (III. vii, 98). Buckingham apologizes for interrupting him in devotion and Richard, in response, asks them to pardon him "[w]ho-earnest in the service of my [his] God-" has "[d]eferr'd the visitation" of his friends and does not waste any time in coming to the point: "But leaving this, what is your Grace's pleasure" (III. vii, 104-107). Richard inquires whether they have come to notify about some offence he has done. Buckingham uses this opportunity to forward their proposal. The following passage illustrates Buckingham's pretension to persuade Richard to accept the crown by using impressive rhetoric:

Buckingham: Know then, it is your fault that you resign

143 'Argumentum ad Populum': "Appealing to the crowd." (Lanham, 1991: 21).

144 Buckingham advices Richard to get a prayer-book, stand between two churchmen over a "build a holy descant" and "Play the maid's part: still answer nay, and take it [the English crown]."(III. vii, 44-50)

The supreme seat, the throne majestical,
The sceptred office of your ancestors,
Your state of fortune, and your due of birth,
The lineal glory of your royal House,
To the corruption of a blemish'd stock; [King Edward's children]
[…]
The noble isle doth want her proper limbs;
Her face defac'd with scars of infamy,
Her royal stock graft with ignoble plants,
And almost shoulder'd in the swallowing gulf
Of dark forgetfulness and deep oblivion; (III. vii, 116-128)

In this speech, Buckingham elaborates England's situation through the use of verbal violence by 'personifying' her as a trapped woman seeking her "proper limbs", faced with "scars of infamy" due to her "royal stock" filled with illegitimate "ignoble plants [the princes]" (III. vii, 124-126)[145]. Then he comes to the reason of their visit and asks Richard to become their king (III. vii, 129-135)[146]. Richard thanks them warmly for their faithful love but rejects their proposal by the use of 'Antirrhesis'[147] :

Your love deserves my thanks, but my desert
Unmeritable shuns your high request.
First, if all obstacles were cut away,
And that my path were even to the crown
As the ripe revenue and due of birth,
Yet so much is my poverty of spirit,
So mighty and so many my defects, (III. vii, 153-159)

Richard indicates that there is no need of him since Edward has left a heir, using two metaphors (one for Edward, one for his son): "The royal tree [Edward] hath left us royal fruit [his son, the prince]," (III. vii, 166), praying that "God defend" that he should take away what "fortune of his stars" bestowed on the prince (III. vii, 170-172).

---

[145] 'Chorographia': "Description of a nation". (Lanham, 1991: 34) By such a personification, Buckingham draws a 'Chorographia' of England.
[146] 'Aporia': "true or feigned" (to represent by false appearance, pretend). (Lanham, 1991: 19)
[147] 'Antirrhesis': "Rejecting an argument because of its insignificance, error, or wickedness." (Lanham, 1991: 15)

Buckingham's next argument is connected to the princes' legitimacy. Although Richard states that young Edward is his brother's son, Buckingham argues that he is a 'bastard' because he is not from "Edward's wife", since Edward IV was first "contract[ed] to Lady Lucy" and then to the sister of the King of France (represented in *Henry VI, Part 3*). He claims that Queen Elizabeth, "mother to a many sons", seduced Edward even as a distressed widow to "base declension and loath'd bigamy" and in "unlawful bed" got "[t]his Edward, whom our manners call the Prince" (III. vii, 175-190). After his elaborate presentation of the case, Buckingham implores Richard to "draw forth" his "noble ancestry" from "the corruption of abusing times/Unto a lineal, true-derived course" (III. vii, 197-199).

Buckingham's arguments coupled with Richard's 'holy' appearance and assumed humility turn out to be highly impressive. As a result, the Mayor supported by Catesby, tries to persuade Richard into accepting the crown (III. vii, 200-202). Richard, however, continues to appear as if to withdraw from accepting such a 'responsibility' because he is "unfit for state and majesty." (III. vii, 204). At this point, the Mayor and Buckingham start to leave and Catesby implores him to accept the crown and Richard, no longer able to reject their pleas, accepts their proposal: "[...] I am not made of stones,/But penetrable to your kind entreaties,/Albeit against my conscience and my soul." (III. vii, 223-5) In Act III, scene vii, Richard proves to be a great religious hypocrite. There is nothing that Richard will not use or 'abuse' in order to gain power. As a result, Richard becomes king and Anne his queen.

After becoming the king of England, Richard now works to secure his position by getting rid of the other possible heirs to the throne. To this end, Richard tells Buckingham that he wants the "bastards [princes] dead" (IV. ii, 18), orders Catesby to spread a rumour that his wife Lady Anne is sick and is likely to die, and asks him to find "a mean poor gentleman" to marry Clarence's daughter in order to "stop all hopes whose growth may damage" him (IV. ii, 59). Richard also states his desire to marry young Elizabeth (Kind Edward's daughter) after the death of her two brothers (and death of Lady Anne), or else his kingdom "stands on brittle glass." (IV. ii, 61). When Buckingham hesitates about Richard's plan to murder the two young princes in the tower, Richard sends Tyrrell to fulfil the task.

Act IV, scene ii, also marks the point where Buckingham and Richard begin to draw apart. Now that Richard is King, Buckingham asks him to grant the promises he had made earlier ("Earldom of Hereford, and the moveables" belonging to Edward IV) [III. i, 194-197]), but Richard turns him down by saying that he is not in the "giving vein" (IV. ii, 116) that day[148]. This is due to Buckingham's hesitation about the murder of the two young princes. Although Buckingham feels deceived for not being delivered with what was initially promised by Richard, he nevertheless remembers Hastings' terrible fate and flees. Thus, Richard has lost his partner in crime. The two princes are murdered by Tyrrel who notifies Richard of the act in Act IV, Scene iii. Following the news King Richard outlines his evil deeds and updates his plan:

> The son of Clarence have I pent up close;
> His daughter meanly have I match'd in marriage;
> The sons of Edward sleep in Abraham's bosom,
> And Anne my wife hath bid this world good night.
> Now, for I know the Breton Richmond aims
> At young Elizabeth, my brother's daughter,
> And by that knot looks proudly on the crown–
> To her go I, a jolly thriving wooer. (IV. iii, 36-43)

Having taken care of Clarence, his daughter and his sons, and Lady Anne, Richard now aims to have Edward's daughter young Elizabeth as his Queen. This marks the point where his verbal powers begin to fail him and he no longer processes the talent to deceive people through rhetoric. His talents of employing rhetoric begin to decline the moment he has gained full power over England. For, now he feels his power is at stake and is overcome by the fear of losing his hard-attained power.

The second wooing scene in Act VI, scene iv, starts in a melancholic atmosphere in which (Queen) Elizabeth and the Duchess of York are mourning the princes' deaths. They are joined by Queen Margaret who reminds Elizabeth about her loss of loved ones, power and position (IV. iv, 92-97). Soon after Margaret leaves them to return to France, Richard enters with his train. The Duchess of York and Elizabeth confront King Richard with his crimes[149]. Here Richard uses 'apophasis' and pretends to deny what is really affirmed. The Duchess, not being able to get through to him, employs 'ara'[150] and sets on him a curse so that on the battle day

[148] Richard seems to be distracted by Henry the Sixth's prophesy that Richmond will be king, and that he will not live long after he saw "Richmond".
[149] This is an instance of 'Categoria': "Reproaching a person with his wickedness to his face." (Lanham, 1991: 32)
[150] 'Ara': "Curse or imprecation". (Lanham, 1991: 20)

"little souls of Edward's children" promise his enemies "success and victory" and that his end be "bloody" to which (Queen) Elizabeth says "Amen" (IV. iv, 189-198).

Although it is obvious that (Queen) Elizabeth dislikes him Richard still has the nerve to ask her to persuade her daughter (young) Elizabeth to marry him. Similar to the first wooing scene between Richard and Lady Anne, Richard and (Queen) Elizabeth employs "stichomythia" extensively in their dispute.

King Richard uses 'diallage', which means bringing several arguments to establish a single point[151]. He aims to persuade (Queen) Elizabeth to consent to the marriage by presenting several propositions such as the England's welfare, advancement of her child, making up for (Queen) Elizabeth's loses and the love he feels for her daughter.

(Queen) Elizabeth reminding him that he has killed her children, Richard replies by claiming that he intends to do her and her family more good than she thinks instead of talking about the death of her sons, uses 'apoplenesis'[152]: "As I intend more good to you and yours/ Than ever you or yours by me were harm'd." (IV. iv, 238-9)

Richard then moves on to his pleas concerning how the marriage will affect (Queen) Elizabeth. He indicates that the advancement of her child will help her forget the miseries, which she thinks he has caused:

> Will I withal endow a child of thine;
> So in the Lethe of thy angry soul
> Thou drown the sad remembrance of those wrongs
> Which thou supposest I have done to thee (IV. iv, 250-253).

He then confesses his love for young Elizabeth and indicates his wish to make her the Queen of England, but (Queen) Elizabeth mockingly replies: "Well then, who dost thou mean shall be her king?" (IV. iv, 265). When Richard asks her to advise him on how to woo young Elizabeth, she sarcastically proposes, again, that he should send her a "pair of bleeding hearts" engraved with 'Edward' and 'York' presented by their murderer (IV. iv, 271-273), or to present her a handkerchief drained with her brother's blood and if they do not work, she mockingly suggests that if they do not

[151] 'Diallage': "Bringing several arguments to establish a single point." (Lanham, 1991: 51)
[152] 'Apoplenesis': "Evading the issue by digressing; irrelevant answer to distract attention from a difficult point". (Lanham, 1991: 19)

work, he should send her a letter presenting his "noble deeds" (IV. iv, 276-280). With reference to his wicked deeds in the past, (Queen) Elizabeth stresses the impossibility of their marriage unless Richard: "put[s] on some other shape/And not be Richard" (IV. iv, 286-7).

To Elizabeth's opposition to the marriage, Richard brings on a line of arguments by employing 'alloiosis'[153] resembling the ones addressed to Lady Anne, but at this point, it sounds ridiculous. Richard asks Elizabeth to tell her daughter that he did "all this for love of her?" (IV. iv, 288) his words cannot create the same effect as it once did on Lady Anne. Elizabeth simply exclaims: "[…] then indeed she cannot chose but hate thee,/Having bought love with such a bloody spoil." (IV. iv, 289-290). Richard's strongest argument is that this marriage will restore the things that have, supposedly, been taken away from Queen Elizabeth by Richard (IV. iv, 290-320).

Elizabeth asks him how she should present him, the possibilities being her "father's brother", "uncle" or as "he that slew her brothers and uncles" (IV. iv, 337-339). Then the conversation between King Richard and Elizabeth is summarized in the form of 'stichomythia', organized in the pattern of 'suggestion' and 'rejection':

King Richard:	Infer fair England's peace by this alliance.
Elizabeth:	Which she shall purchase with still-lasting war.
King Richard:	Tell her the King, that command, entreats.
Elizabeth:	That, at her hands, which the King's King forbids[154].
King Richard:	Say she shall be high and mighty queen.
Elizabeth:	To vail the title, as her mother doth. (IV. iv, 343-348)

Then King Richard takes up the topic of his 'love' for young Elizabeth, as he did with Lady Anne:

King Richard:	Say I will love her everlastingly.
Elizabeth:	But how long shall that title 'ever' last?
King Richard:	Sweetly in force, until her fair life's end.
Elizabeth:	But how long fairly shall her sweet life last?
King Richard:	As long as heaven and nature lengthens it.
Elizabeth:	As long as hell and Richard likes of it.

[153] 'Alloiosis': Breaking down a subject into alternatives. (Lanham, 1991: 7)
[154] 'Eidolopoeia': "Presenting a dead person as speaker, or he speech thus assigned". (Lanham, 1991: 193)

King Richard:	Say I, her sovereign, am her subject low.
Elizabeth:	But she, your subject, loathes such sovereignty.

(IV. iv, 349-356)

King Richard claims that he will love (young) Elizabeth "everlastingly" to which (Queen) Elizabeth, implying Lady Anne's destiny asks how long "ever" will last. When he indicates that her life shall last "as long as" 'heaven' and nature "lengthens it" and Elizabeth bitterly corrects him with "[a]s long as hell and Richard "likes of it" (IV. iv, 349-354). All these variations of 'forever' put forth by Elizabeth is a direct reference to his merciful dealings with Lady Anne.

The next topic that Richard emphasizes is 'eloquence', which is, as indicated in Part I, chapter 1 of this study, an important element of rhetoric:

King Richard:	Be eloquent in my behalf to her.
Elizabeth:	An honest tale speeds best being plainly told.
King Richard:	Then plainly to her tell my loving tale[155].
Elizabeth:	Plain and not honest is too harsh a style. (IV. iv, 357-360)

Richard wishes Elizabeth to forward his wish to young Elizabeth with an eloquent style, but Elizabeth says that 'truth' does not need 'eloquence', because it can be best told 'plainly'. To this, Richard suggests that she should tell his "loving tale" plainly, to which Elizabeth says that a style that lacks both truth and eloquence will be "too harsh", thus indicating that he is a liar. Richard swears by "George", his "Garter"[156] and his crown that his feelings are true, but Elizabeth cuts him off and, step by step, illustrates that there is nothing he can swear by, neither honour, nor self, nor religion, and be believed:

Queen Elizabeth:	Swear then by something that thou hast not wrong'd.
Richard:	Now, by the world–
Queen Elizabeth:	'Tis full of they foul wrongs.
Richard:	My father's death–
Queen Elizabeth:	Thy life hath it dishonour'd.

[155] All these suggestions that Richard makes are examples of 'dilemma': Argument that offers an opponent only unacceptable choices. (Lanham, 1991: 184)

[156] Emblems of chivalry; the Order of the Garter was augmented by the pendant image of St.George in Tudor times (Hammond, 1981: 291)

Richard:	Then, by myself–
Queen Elizabeth:	Thyself is self-misus'd.
Richard:	Why then, by God–
Queen Elizabeth:	God's wrong is most of all: (IV.iv,373-80)

With these responses Elizabeth, employs 'chleuasmos'[157], sarcastic reply that mocks an opponent and leaves him no answer. This part of their argument highlights the connection between eloquence and verbal violence, and the hypocrisy of the eloquent attitude.

After a long debate, Elizabeth appears to have been persuaded and leaves to talk to her daughter with Richard calling her 'mother' and instructing her to "bear her my [his] true love's kiss;" (IV. iv, 430) but calling her "[r]elenting fool, and shallow, changing woman!" (IV. iv. 431) after she exits. While the first wooing scene was proof of Richard's verbal skills, the second one illustrates the diminishing of his intellectual and rhetorical power, as he has failed to trick (Queen) Elizabeth. Accordingly, this scene functions as a kind of foreshadowing to Richard's loss of political power.

After Elizabeth leaves, King Richard is informed that a powerful navy commanded by Richmond, is riding in the west coast, with Buckingham welcoming them ashore. Soon, however, Buckingham's army is dispersed and he is captured. Richard orders his army to march towards Salisbury to encounter Richmond, who has received a message from the Earl of Derby that (Queen) Elizabeth consents to his marriage to her daughter.

Richard's condition becomes worse with Richmond's arrival. He has lost most of his allies (Buckingham is led to execution in Act V, scene i). Furthermore, in Act V Richard must face Richmond, who is both a legitimate heir to the throne and believes that he fights in "God's name" against "tyranny" in order to "[t]o reap the harvest of perpetual peace/By this one bloody trial of sharp war." (V. ii, 1-16). In this respect, it is important to compare Richard and Richmond's use of rhetoric in Act V, scene iii, because it helps to illustrate Richard's rhetorical downfall.

In Act V, scene iii, the night before the battle of Bosworth, the ghosts of Richard's victims (Prince Edward [son of Henry VI], Henry VI, Clarence, Rivers,

[157] 'Chleuasmos': "A sarcastic reply that mocks an opponent and leaves him no answer." (Lanham, 1991: 34)

Grey and Vaughan, Hastings, the two young princes, Lady Anne and Buckingham) visit Richmond and Richard in their sleep. They wish Richmond success while cursing Richard and telling him to "despair and die" (V. iii, 121; 128; 136; 141; 144; 155; 164;173). Richard wakes up startled and much affected by the dream. His (last) soliloquy, after the dream, opens with three short exclamatory sentences conveying the transition from Richard's experience of the dream to wakefulness: "Give me another horse! Bind up my wounds!/Have mercy, Jesu! –Soft, I did but dream./O coward conscience, how dost thou afflict me!" (V. iii, 178-180)[158]. His mention of "coward conscience" followed with his interrogation of himself in the following lines illustrate that Richard is not only trying to cope with the effect of the dream, but also with his soul:

> The lights burn blue[159]; it is now dead midnight.
> Cold fearful drops stand on my trembling flesh.
> What do I fear? Myself? There's none else by;
> Richard loves Richard, that is, I and I.
> Is there a murdered here? No. Yes, I am!
> Then fly. What, from myself? Great reason why,
> Lest I revenge? What, myself upon myself?
> Alack, I love myself. Wherefore? For any good
> That I myself have done unto myself?
> O no, alas, I rather hate myself
> For hateful deeds committed by myself.
> I am a villain –yet I lie, I am not!
> Fool, of thyself speak well! Fool do not flatter[160].
> My conscience hath a thousand several tongues,
> And every tongue brings in a several tale,
> And every tale condemns me for a villain: (V. iii, 181-196)

---

[158] Richard's cry in the first line "Give me another horse!" (V. iii, 178) prefigures the last words of the king: "A horse! A horse! my kingdom for a horse!" (V. iv, 7). It evokes a foreshadowing of the actual circumstances of his final defeat on the battlefield, as does the demand "Bind up my wounds!" and "Have mercy, Jesu" (V. iii, 178-179).

[159] Blue light is also thought to indicate the presence of ghosts.

[160] In lines 193-5 the words "tongues" (193) and "tongue" (194), "tale" (194) and "tale" (195) are an example of "Anadiplosis", which gives the same word the last position in one clause and the first (or near the first) in the clause following it (Lanham, 1991: 10). Vickers, Brian. "Shakespeare's Use of Rhetoric". *In A Reader in the Language of Shakespearean Drama.* Essays collected by Vivian Salmon and Edwina Burness. Amsterdam: John Benjamins Publishing Company, 1987. 391-406. P.396

He admits, reluctantly, that he is afraid of himself "What do I fear? Myself? There's none else by;" (V. iii, 183). Conscience, a notion alien to Richard throughout the play has turned into a being with a "thousand several tongues" (V. iii, 194). He finally condemns himself as a "villain" and examines his evil deeds for the first time in the play:

> Perjury, perjury, in the highest degree;
> Murder, stern murder, in the direst degree;
> All several sins, all us'd in each degree,
> Throng to the bar, crying all, 'Guilty, guilty!'
> I shall despair. There is no creature loves me,
> And if I die, no soul will pity me–
> And wherefore should they, since that I myself
> Find in myself no pity to myself? (V. iii, 197-204)

His sins such as "perjury" and "murder" cry out "Guilty, guilty!" (V. iii, 200). Lines such as "I shall despair" (V. iii, 201) demonstrates that all attempts to justify his actions have failed and his despair is deepened by the admission of his complete isolation: "There is no creature loves me" (V. iii, 201). The soliloquy ends with what he has dreamt: "Methought the souls of all that I had murder'd/Came to my tent, and every one did threat/Tomorrow's vengeance on the head of Richard." (V. iii, 205-207) The souls of those he has "wronged" threaten Richard with "vengeance", thus foreshadowing his final downfall.

The contrast is complete between these faltering lines and the compact strength of the soliloquy with which the play opens. Richard's last soliloquy is significant in that its style and language distinguish itself from Richard's former planned, controlled, formal and well-constructed speech throughout Acts I-III reflecting his plans and thoughts. Wolfgang Clemen indicates that:

> It is effective at this point partly because its style and language distinguish it from the rest of the play, but also because of the sudden breakdown of Richard's complacent role-playing which he has sustained with much skill until this moment. As the nightmare makes its impact, the villain's cunning masquerade collapses and he stands before us, as plaintiff and defendant. (1987: 20)

This is a very different man from the bloodless Machiavellian who has done all those terrible deeds. He is now the victim of his horrible deeds and conscience.

Although Richard continues to use rhetorical figures in his monologue in Act V, it is uncontrolled and fragmented. The broken incoherent phrases in his self-address illustrate the breakdown of Richard's role-playing, which he has sustained until this moment. Much affected by the dream, he tells Ratcliffe that he had a dream that frightened him: "I fear, I fear!" (V. iii, 215).

Before the battle, both Richmond and King Richard present a 'war' oration to their armies in order to motivate them[161]. This scene, resembles in many ways the verbal battle between Bajazeth and Tamburlaine that took place in Act III, scene iii, in *Tamburlaine, Part I.* Both Richard and Richmond believe that they are the superior side, use 'amplification' to highlight their confidence in their victory. In these speeches, both in *Tamburlaine, Part I* and *Richard III,* the speakers start their address with insults directed at the opponent and end with emphasis on religious imagery. Another interesting coincidence is that Richard, like Bajazeth (in *Tamburlaine, Part I*), connects his high chance of victory to his past victories, while Richmond, similar to Tamburlaine, makes reference to the future.

Richmond, starts by reminding his soldiers that "God, and our [their] good cause" and the "prayers of holy saints and wronged souls," fight on their side (V. iii, 238-241) [162]. He claims that even those fighting beside Richard, "A bloody tyrant and

[161] In "Book IV" of Machiavelli's *The Arte of War* Zanobi and Fabrizio discuss the role of "haranguing" (attempt to persuade someone that you are right with a long and angry speech) in making soldiers and officers fight. Fabrizio states that "it is necessary that a general should be an orator as well as a soldier; for if he does not know how to address himself to the whole army, he will sometimes find that it no easy task to mold it [the army] to his purposes." (1965: 128). "Haranguing" the soldiers functions to "dispel their fears, inflame their courage, confirm their resolution, point out the snares laid for them, promise them rewards, inform them of danger and the way to escape it;" and the general may "rebuke, entreat, threaten, praise, reproach, or fill them with hopes" (1965: 128)

[162] In" Book IV" of Machiavelli's *The Arte of War* it is stated that "Religion too, and the oath soldiers took when they were enlisted, greatly contributes to making them do their duty in ancient times; for upon any default, they were threatened not only with human punishments, but the vengeance of the gods. (Machiavelli, 128). To this end, Sertorious who "used to have consultations with a hind that he said was sent by the gods to assure him of victory", Sulla who pretended to converse with an image he had taken out of the temple of Apollo, and several generals have given out that some god or other has appeared to them in dreams an visions and commanded them to fight the enemy are given as examples (Machiavelli, 1965: 128-9). Also, it is stated that when Charles VII of France was at war with the English, "he pretended to be advised in everything by a virgin

a homicide" (V. iii, 244- 246) would prefer that they should win the battle. Richmond "amplifies" Richard's character by referring to his "bloody" deeds through 'argumentum ad hominem', the abuse of your opponent's character:

> One rais'd in blood, and one in blood establish'd;
> One that made means to come by what he hath,
> And slaughter'd those that were the means to help him;
> A base foul stone, made precious by the foil
> Of England's chair, where he is falsely set;
> One that hath ever been God's enemy. (V. iii, 248-253)

With lines 247-252, Richmond draws a portrait of Richard as a tyrant "raised" and "establish'd" in blood, one who has "slaughter'd" those that helped him, and a God's enemy "falsely" "set" on the English throne. By employing 'contrarium'[163], and he uses the image of Richard as "God's enemy" to support his following statement. He indicates that anyone fighting against Richard will, naturally, become God's soldiers:

> Then, **if you** fight against God's enemy,
> God will, in justice, ward **you**[164] as his soldiers;
> **If you do** sweat to put a tyrant down,
> **You** sleep in peace, the tyrant being slain;
> **If you do** fight against your country's foes,
> **Your** country's fat shall pay your pains the hire;
> **If you do** fight in safeguard of your wives,
> **Your** wives shall welcome home the conquerors;
> **If you do** free your children from the sword,
> **Your** children's children quits in it your age. (V. iii, 254-263)

The rhetorical figure 'anaphora' [165], repetition of the same word at the beginning of successive verses, is used in the "if you" and "you"/"your" pattern create a cause and

---

sent from heaven , commonly called the virgin of France, who won him many a victory" (Machiavelli, 1965: 128-9)

[163] 'Contrarium': "One of the two opposite statements is used to prove the other". (Lanham, 1991: 41)

[164] Emphasis in bold character has been made to pinpoint the rhetorical techniques.

[165] 'Anaphora': "Repetition of the same word at the beginning of successive clauses or verses". (Lanham, 1991: 11).

effect chain, of actions and their rewards. This also illustrates that Richmond, similar to Tamburlaine in *Tamburlaine Part I*, employs the future tense in his speech. By the use of 'antisagoga'[166], he concentrates on the rewards awaiting them in their country, wives and children, "if" they choose to "fight against God's enemies", put an effort to "put a tyrant down" and fight against their "country's fows,". Richmond's last remarks to his soldier establish Richard as God's scourge on Richard:

> Then, in the name of God and all these rights,
> Advance your standards, draw your willing swords!
> For me, the ransom of my bold attempt
> Shall be this cold corpse on the earth's cold face;
> But if I thrive, the gain of my attempt
> The least of you shall share his part thereof.
> Sound, drums, and trumpets, boldly and cheerfully!
> God, and Saint George! Richmond and victory! (V. iii, 264-271)

In the lines above, Richmond is portrayed as a man with a noble cause standing up against King Richard, the 'tyrant'. Richmond's speech inspires his men, clarifies the values in question, and finally produces its intended result. In lines 254-259, Richmond attributes all his success to God, and indicates that his bold attempt will either end with his death or his victory, which will be shared with those around him. Through these lines, Richmond innovates God and their just cause, essential weapons in military oratory as indicated by Machiavelli in *The Art of War* (1965: 128).

Placed after Richmond's, Richard's speech presents a clear contrast of the two and to highlight the disappearance of his rhetorical power. While Richmond's oration involves reference to God and a just cause, Richard's is commonplace and thus unimpressive. He begins by drawing a 'chorographia'[167] of the French:

> What shall I say, more than I have inferr'd?
> Remember whom you are to cope withal:
> A sort of vagabonds, rascals, and runaways;
> A scum of Bretons and base lackey peasants,
> Whom their o'er-cloyed country vomits forth

[166] 'Antisagoga': "Assuring a reward to those who possess a virtue, or a punishment to those who hold it in contempt." (Lanham, 1991: 15)
[167] 'Chorographia': "Description of a nation". (Lanham, 1991: 34).

To desperate adventures and assur'd destruction.
You sleeping safe, they bring to you unrest;
You having lands, and bless'd with beauteous wives,
They would restrain the one, distain the other. (V. iii, 315-323)

He defines the French as "vagabonds", "rascals", "runaways", "A scum of Bretons" and "base lackey peasants" whom their country "vomits forth" to a desperate "adventure" with assured "destruction". Richard indicates that the reason the French are disturbing them in their "safe" sleep is because the English have lands and are "blessed" with "beauteous wives". Then Richard continues with insulting their commander Richmond. He claims that the French are lead by nothing but a "paltry fellow" kept in Britain at their cost, a "milksop" who has been well-kept but can't endure the bad conditions such as the cold (V.iii, 324-7).

Richard, like Bajazeth in *Tamburlaine, Part I*, makes reference to their past success against the French:

Let's whip these stragglers o'er the seas again,
Lash hence these overweening rags of France,
These famish'd beggars, weary of their lives–
Who, but for dreaming on this fond exploit,
For want of means, poor rats, had hang'd themselves. (V. iii, 328-332)

Lastly, Richard expresses that even if they are to be conquered, it should not be by the unmanly French, who their forefathers defeated in their own lands, but real men:

If we be conquer'd, let men conquer us!
And not these bastard Bretons, whom our fathers
Have in their own land beaten, bobb'd, and thump'd,
And in record left them the heirs of shame.
Shall these enjoy our lands? Lie with our wives?
Ravish our daughters? (V. iii, 333-8)

And lastly, Richard asks them to fight as the "gentlemen" of England:

Fight, gentlemen of England! Fight, bold yeomen!
Draw, arches, draw your arrows to the head!

Spur your proud horses hard, and ride in blood!
Amaze the welkin with your broken staves! (V. iii, 339-342)

This oration is a sign of Richard's downfall, as a rhetorician and the loss of his power as a king. Richard's oration addressed to his troops is composed of insults, downward comparisons and base epithets[168]:

> Shakespeare's Richard retains the insults, the "downward comparisons," "base epithets," and "unsavory similes" that are more appropriate to a tavern lord than to the king of England. Most of Richard's address to his troops contains insults, the desperate ad hominem assaults of a pathetic, nearly impotent foe. (Hassel, 1987: 39)

Instead of motivating his soldiers to protect their country, wives and daughters, he prefers to only degrade their enemy. He insults the French and their commander Richmond with petty qualities. He expresses that if they are to be conquered, it should be by real men instead of the 'unmanly' French formerly defeated by their forefathers. And lastly, he advocates that such men should not enjoy their lands, lie with their wives and ravish their daughters, as if it would be acceptable if performed by others. Compared to Richmond, Richard's speech lacks truth, sincerity and genuine confidence. His oration is full of base remarks that do not suit a king. As Hassel also remarks, Richard seems to become "pettier", "duller" and "base if bustling in his colloquialism, repetitive and unimaginative in his oratorical strategies (Hassel: 1987, 45). Richard's oration does not display the wit and audacity that was present in his earlier speeches in Act I-III. Richard's final address to his troops is:

A thousand hearts are great within my bosom.
Advance, our standards! Set upon our foes!
Our ancient word of courage, fair Saint George,
Inspire us with the spleen of fiery dragons!
Upon them! Victory sits on our helms. (V.iii, 348-352)

He orders them to march and asks Saint George to inspire them with the "spleen of fiery dragons" –an invocation to absolute violence.

---

[168] Attributions

In Act V, scene iv, on the field of Bosworth Richard is totally isolated, unhorsed and trapped. His final despairing cry that is repeated on lines 7 and 13 of Act V, scene iv is: "A horse, a horse! My kingdom for a horse!" (V. iv, 7). At this point, Richard is ready to give up the kingdom for which thousands of men fought in exchange for a horse.

In Act V, scene v, Richmond kills Richard on the battlefield. He has won over Richard in both political and rhetorical power. His marriage to young Elizabeth, sister of the murdered princes, will unite the houses of York and Lancaster.

The study of rhetoric employed in the two chapters make up Part I of this book. *Tamburlaine I, Part I* and Richard III, two English Renaissance plays (blank-verse), each employing an actual phase in history as its subject matter, illustrate the same concept of power and language. In both of these plays the rhetorical skill of characters serve as a metaphor for political power. In both of these plays that have been constructed on dialogue rather than physical action, verbal violence is employed as a substitute for physical violence on the stage.

PART II:
VERBAL VIOLENCE AS A MEANS OF CONSTRUCTING AND DECONSTRUCTING AUTHORITY IN CONTEMPORARY DRAMATIC DIALOGUE

CHAPTER 1
MANIFESTING POWER THROUGH CONTEMPORARY FORMS OF DRAMATIC LANGUAGE

The language employed by contemporary dramatists has changed a great deal since the time of the English Renaissance during which Marlowe and Shakespeare produced their dramatic works. McDonald indicates that even though characters in modern plays seem to speak more 'naturally' than their Shakespearean counterparts, who employed an excessively ornamented style in their dialogues, this conclusion may be misleading, since

> modern forms of theatrical language are no more real than those spoken by the characters in *Hamlet.* Both styles of speech are arranged and artificial, the difference arises from their author's dependence on different conventions. The practices of sixteenth-century dramatic language were developed and refined by playwrights who were committed to the value of eloquence [...] (1996: 186)

The poetic and ornamental language of blank verse employed in English Renaissance drama by playwrights like Christopher Marlowe and Shakespeare (studied in Part I of this book) has been largely replaced by prose and daily language in contemporary times. Although everyday language[169], at times, seems to be too far removed from rhetorical effect, it is not less influential. As Jacques Derrida has declared, "Now, everyday language is not innocent or neutral" (1981:19)[170]. It rather carries the value system of the dominant power and forms our conception of the world. Albert Einstein has rightly stated that the "greater part of our knowledge and beliefs has been communicated to us by other people through the medium of a language which others have created." (Einstein, 1986: 13). However, people use language without realizing the kind of ideology it supports.

---

[169] Mc Cormick defines 'everyday talk' as ordinary kinds of communication used by people at work, at home or friends, expressing that it is influenced by the more official patterns of discourse widely circulated in any given socio-cultural context (McCormick: 2003:109).

[170] Derrida concentrates on how logocentric language reinforces established power structures by introducing the critical theory of deconstruction.

Ideological power[171], projection of one's practices as universal and 'common sense', is a significant contributor in establishing and maintaining power, which is exercised through discourse. The system, through ideology and language (discourse), defines what is 'normal' and sets acceptable norms or forms of 'standardization' to make individuals "normal" with values concerning how they should live or act (being good citizens, being patriotic and serving the state). Furthermore, the persons who do not comply with this order are constantly under threat and eventually converted or destroyed. These standards begin to shape individuals' perceptions of people, events and ideas with their awareness of language (Galbraith, 1985: 9).

Much of the contemporary debate about power[172] is related to the works of the French philosopher Michel Foucault. He conveys a view of power as a social force that is present everywhere, but especially in social institutions. He points out that the idea of 'state', emerging in the sixteenth century, is a kind of political power that only considers the interests of the majority, a certain class or group and ignores individuals (1991: 14). He further states that institutions such as prisons, schools and hospitals, which appear to be neutral and independent, are in fact a means of political violence employed by the state (1991: 6). Violence is exerted by such social institutions which are used to normalize people by 'oppression', 'domination', 'exclusion', 'censorship' and 'concealment' (Foucault, 1995: 194).

The state does not only use institutions to construct authority, but also makes use of discourse. Foucault stresses that language inflicts violence through knowledge

[171] Fairclough indicates that ideology is closely linked to language, because using language is the "commonest form of social behavior" on which we rely on. But despite its importance for language, the concept of 'ideology' has very "rarely figured in discussions of language and power within linguistics, which is itself symptomatic of their limitations" (Fairclough, 2001: 2)

[172] In terms of recent social theory, Fairclough mentions that three contributors who have explored the "role of language in the exercise, maintenance and change of power are Bourdieu, Foucault and Habermas. "The first [Bourdieu's] work is on the theory of ideology, which on the other hand has pointed to the increasing relative importance of ideology as a mechanism of power in modern society, as against the exercise of power through coercive means, and on the other hand has come to see language as a (or indeed the) major locus of ideology, and so of major significance with respect to power. The second is the influential work of Michel Foucault, which has ascribed a central role to discourse in the development of specifically modern forms of power. And the third is the equally influential work of Jurgen Habermas[172], whose 'theory of communication action' highlights the way in which our currently distorted communication nevertheless foreshadows communication without such constraints (Fairclough, 2001: 10). While acknowledging power, Jurgen Habermas insisted that a distinction should be made between legitimate and illegitimate uses of power. To make such distinctions, he introduces a theory of 'communicative action' within the idealizing presuppositions of discourse which are identified and justified through what he calls "discourse ethics." (Kelly, 1994: 1-2).

or discourse such as 'science' and 'truth' which define, categorize and set standards used by the state to widen the control. Foucault points out that categorizing people and problems in particular ways in which they should be handled and controlled:

> Generally speaking, all the authorities exercising individual control function according to a double mode; that of binary division and branding (mad/sane; dangerous/harmless; normal/abnormal;) and assignment of differential distribution, (who he is; where he must be; how he is to be characterized; how he is to be recognized; how a constant surveillance is to be exercised over him in an individual way, etc.) (1995: 199)

As more people accept such views as common knowledge, the ideas associated with that belief system gain power. Within such a belief system or 'discourse', the figures of authority[173] such as lawyers, teachers, doctors or priests present ideas (legislative, scientific, religious etc.) that are considered to be undeniable 'truths'. As a result, a particular way of seeing the world associated with such 'truths' is viewed as 'normal'. Thus, discourses such as law or religion are constructed as a standardized system, by which people will be evaluated and judged legally or morally.

Contemporary English drama abounds in dramatic discourse that echoes Foucault's theories about the connection between power and social institutions. Tom Stoppard's *Every Good Boy Deserves Favor* (1977) is a play directly illustrating Foucault's theory about power exerted through social institutions such as hospitals, prisons, schools and related discourse. In the play, Alexander Ivanov is put into the mental institution by the KGB[174] for writing to various people about an imprisoned friend. He shares his warden or cell with another patient with the same name Ivanov, who hears an orchestra that apparently does not exist. The dialogues between the

---

[173] Authority is "legitimized" political capacity or influence (Pfeffer in Macmillan, 1986, 18). If an organization allows a person to "induce, coerce, persuade, and obligate others, it means that person has legitimate power and influence and hence legitimate formal authority. People in an organization who are being induced, coerced, persuaded, and obligated by an individual consider these to be legitimate. The individual has legitimate power and influence and hence legitimate informal authority" (Macmillan, 1986: 19). Authority in a situation "gives rise to opportunities for developing a power base. An individual usually is given authority to accomplish some purpose. The fact that an individual has the authority to do it confers on him a mantle of formal legitimacy that the targets may not have. In such situations, the individual has an edge over anyone who is not regarded as having formal authority" (Macmillan, 1986: 19)

[174] KGB: Committee for State Security

doctor and his two patients "Alexander Ivanov" and "Ivanov" are noteworthy examples displaying Foucault's ideas. One of the conversations between the doctor and Ivanov is as follows:

Doctor:	Now look, *there is no orchestra.* We cannot make progress until we agree that there is no orchestra.
Ivanov:	Or until we agree that there is.
Doctor:	*(Slapping the violin, which is on the table) But there is no orchestra.*
	(Ivanov glances at the violin.)
	I have an orchestra, but you do not.
Ivanov:	Does that seem reasonable to you?
Doctor:	It just happens to be so. I play in an orchestra occasionally. It is my hobby. It is a real orchestra. Yours is not. I am a doctor. You are a patient. If I tell you you do not have an orchestra, it follows that you do not have an orchestra. (21)

In the dialogue, the doctor justifies his claim that Ivanov does not have an orchestra simply because he, as a "doctor", says so. In this case, the doctor represents authority, while Ivanov must be the obedient subject.

This kind of view is further clarified in the conversation between Alexander Ivanov and the doctor. The doctor tells him that he has been put in the "lunatic's hospital" for his views because Alexander Ivanov believes that sane people are put in mental hospitals, which are his symptoms:

Doctor:	Your behaviour is causing alarm. I'm beginning to think you're off your head. Quite apart from being a paranoid schizophrenic. I have to consider seriously whether an Ordinary Hospital can deal with your symptoms.
Alexander:	I have no symptoms, I have opinions.
Doctor:	Your opinions are your symptoms. Your disease is dissent. Your kind of schizophrenia does not presuppose changes of personality noticeable to others. (30)

As their dialogue proceeds, the doctor asks him whether the pills he gave helped him, meaning whether Alexander has accepted their views:

Doctor:	Did the pills help at all?
Alexander:	I don't know.
Doctor:	Do you believe that sane people are put in mental hospitals?
Alexander:	Yes.
Doctor:	They didn't help. (32)

So, it is apparent that in the play, mental institutions function to spread the views of the State and 'treat' those who hold 'false beliefs'.

Another institution tackled in Stoppard's play is education. Alexander Ivanov's son Sache's teacher tries to manipulate him into believing that the present situation (system of government) is better than the past:

Teacher:	Things have changed since the bad old days. When I was a girl there were terrible excesses. A man accused like your father might well have been blameless. Now things are different. The Constitution guarantees freedom of conscience, freedom of the press, freedom of speech, of assembly, of worship, and many other freedoms. The Soviet Constitution has always been the most liberal in the world, ever since the first Constitution was written after the Revolution.
Sache:	Who wrote it?
Teacher:	(*Hesitates*) His name was Nikolai Bukharin.
Sache:	Can we ask Nikolai Bukharin about papa?
Teacher:	Unfortunately he was shot soon after he wrote the Constitution. Everything was different in those days. Terrible things happened. (29-30)

The teacher's account of the "bad" "old" days is manipulative and provides a good example of how the state uses education to hold its control on children and strengthen their own authority and power.

In John Whiting's *The Devils* (1961), the State's values gain momentum by being taught, preached and being accepted by the subjects. In this play, the church, another social institution representing not only the values of the State but also the authority of God, need the voluntary obedience of its subjects to continue its power as illustrated in Grandier's final persecution scene. In the play, Grandier, the vicar of St. Peter's Church, is accused by the hunchback Sister Jeanne of 'possessing' demons and sending them to copulate with the Sisters of St Ursula's Convent. Grandier, having had sexual liaisons with Phillipe (the Public Prosecutor's daughter) admits to indulgence in sexual desire but denies to ever having met the sisters, of possessing demons or being a sorcerer. He is physically tortured and his knees are crushed in order to make him confess to something that he did not do, without any success, and finally Laubardemont, the King's Special Commissioner to Loudun, pleads to Grandier to confess so that the church might continue its power:

> *Laubardemont*: [...] Tell me, Do you love the Church?
>
> *Grandier*: With all my heart.
>
> *Laubardemont*: Do you want to see it grow more powerful, more benevolent, until it embraces every human soul on this earth?
>
> *Grandier*: That would be my wish.
>
> *Laubardemont*: Then help us to achieve this great purpose. Go to the market place a penitent man. Confess, and by confessing, proclaim to these thousands that you have returned to the Church's arms. By going to the stake unrepentant you do God a disservice. You give hope to the sceptics and unbelievers. You make them glad. Such an act can mine the very foundations of the Church. Think. You are no longer important. Are you any longer important?
>
> *Grandier*: No.
>
> *Laubardemont*: Then make a last supreme gesture for the Catholic faith.
>
> [...]
>
> *Grandier*: This is sophistry, Laubardemont, and you're too intelligent not to know it. Pay me the same compliment. (121-122)

Although Grandier loves the church and would like it to gain power, he does not "make a last supreme gesture for the Catholic faith" and instead "gives hope" to "unbelievers" as Laubardemont puts it. He is thus tortured and hanged without confessing or signing the confession prepared for him.

Caryl Churchill's *Vinegar Tom* (1976) questions the validity of the State's values in a patriarchal order in which discourses such as science and religion are controlled by the male. In such a system, it is most often women who are subjected to violence. In the play, poor, unmarried and lonely women not fitting the norms of the patriarchal society are accused of serving the devil as witches, because they happen to have birthmarks, and are hanged according to the book *The Hammer of Witches* written by Kramer and Sprenger. The injustice and irrationality of such witch hunts supported by the church are reflected in the song "If You Float" in the play (170)[175].

Irrational as they may sound, dominant ideas put forth by 'the State' are vital for maintaining authority, and the power of the authority depends also on its ability to control such ideas. And although the ruling class, valid ideologies or 'universal truths' might change, the means by which they are expressed is language, whether in the form of rhetoric or colloquial usage.

Norman Fairclough, who sees power as a social force[176] like Foucault, fully concentrates on the connection between power and language in his work *Language and Power (1989)*. Fairclough states that "the exercise of power, in modern society,

---

175 If you float you're a witch.
If you scream you're a witch
If you sink, then you're dead anyway.
If you cure you're a witch
Or impure you're a witch
Whatever you do, you must pay.
Fingers are pointed, a knock at the door,
You may be a mother, a child or a whore.
If you complain you're a witch
Or you're lame you're a witch
Any marks or deviations count for more.
Got big tits you're a witch
Fall to bits you're a witch.
He likes them young, concupiscent and poor. (170)

176 Linguistic phenomena are social in the sense that whenever people speak or listen or write or read, they do so in ways which are determined socially and have social effects. Even when people are most conscious of their own individuality and think themselves to be most cut off from social influences –'in the bosom of the family'- for example –they still use language in ways which are subject to social convention. And the ways in which people use language in the most intimate and private encounters are not only socially determined by the social relationships of the family, they also have social effects in the sense of helping to maintain (or, indeed, change) those relationships. (Fairclough, 2001: 19)

is increasingly achieved through ideology, and more particularly through the ideological workings of language", adding that we "live in a linguistic epoch" (2001: 2). Even though the concept of language with relation to power has always occupied an important position in discussions about authority, this correlation has become more focal as the use of linguistic skill has greatly replaced the use of physical force in the social and political area[177]. It is not only that language has become a primary medium of social control and power, but also because it has "grown dramatically in terms of the uses it is required to serve, in terms of the range of language varieties, and in terms of the complexity of the language capacities that are expected of the modern citizen." (Fairclough, 2001: 2). Thus, the manipulative use of language in establishing and legitimizing order plays a more vital role in contemporary discussions about power. As Fairclough has pointed out, "nobody who has an interest in relationships of power in modern society, can afford to ignore language" (2001: 3).

In contemporary English drama, language plays a central role in the exertion of power and violence. One of the few works on the use of verbal violence in drama is Jeanette R. Malkin's *Verbal Violence in Contemporary Drama: From Handke to Shepard.* It is indicated that after the World War II language moved to the forefront and not only reflected the world of drama but also became a central subject and object. This dramatic language employed in Pinter, Bond, Shepard, Ionesco, Havel, Kroetz, Mamet, and Albee's plays is "shown to be actively domineering and dangerous, a force which controls and manipulates man, becoming the essence of his being and the limit of his world" (Malkin, 2006: 3). Thus, the relationship between language and man has become one of torture, pain and coercion (Malkin, 1992: 10).

Although many English playwrights of the 20th century employed verbal and physical violence at different levels in their plays, those such as John Osborne, Edward Bond, Joe Orton, Martin McDonagh and Sarah Kane are some that stand out among them.

John Osborne's *Look Back in Anger* (1956) is described as the "bomb that would blow a hole in the old theatre and leave a nice-sized gap too big to be patched up" (Weintraub, 1982 (2): 272) due to its impact on the dramatists after the 1950s, employs a vast amount of verbal violence. Jimmy Porter, the "angry young man" the intellectual from the working class and his wife Alison, with upper middle class

[177] People use language without often thinking that it might embody ideas that directly or indirectly legitimize existing power relations (Fairclough, 2001: 27).

origin, live in a tiny flat in Midlands with a close friend Cliff Lewis in the 1950s setting. Throughout the play Alison, Cliff and Helena (Alison's friend who later comes to live with them) are subjected to verbal abuse and to a certain extent physical abuse, by Jimmy.

When Alison invites her friend Helena (whom Jimmy despises) to stay with them until she finds another place, he gets so angry that he calls his wife "Lady Pusillanimous":

> Pusillanimous, Adjective. Wanting of firmness of mind, of small courage, having a little mind, mean spirited, cowardly, timid of mind. From the Latin pusillus, very little, and animus, the mind. (*Slams the book shut.*) That's my wife! That's *her* isn't it? Behold the Lady Pusillanimous. (1956: 22)

In this example, Jimmy amplifies his opinion of Alison's 'small mindedness' by giving the etymology of the word "Pusillanimous" and then calling her "Lady Pusillanimous".

He verbally assaults Alison constantly in front of others. At one point, telling her that he wishes something terrible to happen to her, Jimmy resorts to cursing such as the death of her baby inside of her, so that she might wake up from her daydreaming. The verbal violence he employs is comparable to that of Queen Margaret in *Richard III*:

> Oh, my dear wife, you've got so much to learn. I only hope you learn it one day. If only something- something would happen to you, and wake you out of your beauty sleep! (*Coming close to her.*) If you could have a child, and it would die. Let it grow, let a recognisable human face emerge from that little mass of indiarubber and wrinkles (*she retreats away from him.*). Please- if only I could watch you face that. I wonder if you might even become a recognisable human being yourself. But I doubt it. (37)

This utterance by Jimmy is in the form of a curse. Later when Helena indicates that Alison is going to church, Jimmy gets angry claiming that he will write a story about them one day which will, unlike the Romantics, be "recollected in fire, and blood" instead of "tranquillity":

> One day, when I'm no longer spending my days running a sweet-stall, I may write a book about us all. It's all here (*Slapping his forehead.*) Written in flames a mile high. And it won't be recollected in tranquillity either, picking daffodils with Auntie Wordsworth. It'll be recollected in fire, and blood. My blood. (53-54)

Jimmy's outcry directed at the others illustrates the linguistic assault that he makes others go through due to his lack of hope in the future. In such scenes, Jimmy, who is an educated member of the lower social class, verbally assaults Alison and the others through eloquent and rhetorical speech. Although some instances of physical violence occur in the play, they fall short of comparison in the face of linguistic violence employed in the play.

When one mentions the subject of violence on the British stage, the first name that will definitely arise is Edward Bond[178]. Bond's works are among the most violent in British Drama before the 1990s. Bond has been especially preoccupied with the subject of violence as he himself stated in his preface to his play *Lear*: "I write about violence as naturally as Jane Austen wrote about manners" (1972: v). Thus, it is no surprise that violence constitutes an important aspect of his plays such as *Saved* (1965) and *Lear* (1971) in the form of both physical violence (torture) and linguistic violence (insult, harassment, verbal bullying etc.). For example, the degrading way Fred speaks to Pam, his girlfriend, in the play *Saved* is a form of verbal harassment through language:

> *Pam*: (*stops*). You're the kid's father! Yeh! Yer ain't wrigglin' out a that!
> *Fred*: Prove it.
> *Pam*: *I know!*
> *Fred*: You *know?*
> *Mike*: Chriss.
> *Fred*: 'Alf the bloody manor's bin through you.
> *Pam*: Rotten liar!

---

[178] Malkin indicates that Edward Bond's plays recreate the fragmented and radically restricted language of fringe or debased social groups and demonstrate the relationship between inarticulacy and brutality (1992: 9).

Fred:	Yeh?
	To Mike. Ain' you 'ad 'er?
Mike:	Not yet.
Fred:	Yer'll be next. (69)

Although there are many dialogues resembling the one above, physical violence is more focal in the play. At one point a baby is tortured (pulling of his hair, pinching, spitting, punching, shaking the baby carriage violently, throwing burning matches into the pram etc.) to death by Pete:

Colin:	There's no one about!
	PETE punches it.
	Ugh! Mind yer don't 'urt it.
Mike:	Yer can't.
Barry:	Not at that age.
Mike:	Course yer can't, no feelin's.
Pete:	Like animals. (77)

The same is true about the violence employed in Bond's *Lear*. King Lear's two daughters Fontanelle and Bodice marry his enemies North and Cornwall, and plot against their father. Warrington tells Lear that Fontanelle and Bodice each sent him a letter promising to make him the head of their army and bed, if he destroys the other sister's army. After it is evident that Warrington has betrayed both of the daughters, he is physically and verbally tortured by them in act I, scene iv:

Fontanelle:	Use the boot! (*Soldier A kicks him.*) Jump on him! (*She pushes Soldier A)* Jump on his head!
	[...]
Fontanelle:	Throw him up and drop him. I want to hear him drop.
	[...]
Fontanelle:	Do something! Don't let him get away with it. O Christ, why did I cut his tongue out? I want to hear him scream!
Soldier A:	(*jerks Warrington's head up*). Look at 'is eyes, Miss. Thass boney-fidey sufferin'.
Fontanelle:	O yes, tears and blood. I wish my father was here. I

wish I could see him. Look at his hands! Look at them going! What's he praying or clutching? Smash his hands!

Soldier A and Fontanelle jumps on Warrington's hands.

Kill his hands! Kill his feet! Jump on it– all of it! He can't his us now. Look at his hands like boiling crabs! Kill it! Kill all of it! Kill him inside! Make him dead! Father! Father! I want to sit on his lungs!

Bodice: (*knits*) Plain, pearl, plain. She was just the same at school. (14)

Such a scene in which actual physical violence is acted on the stage, was made even more disturbing with the language employed by the characters.

Contemporary plays not only display varieties of violence but also reflect the indifference of people towards it as in Joe Orton's *Entertaining Mr Sloane* (1964). As Banks states, there is a paradox between the sophisticated dialogues of the characters and the "grotesque" and "foul events" that they talk about such as sex and murder (Banks, 1986: 290). The play is set in a squalor, in which Mr. Sloane (a young man) comes to rent a room. The squalor is run by Kate, her father Kemp and her brother Ed (who does not live with them). Kate is a middle-aged woman who calls Mr. Sloane her boy, but seduces him and is impregnated. Ed is a seemingly macho homosexual, and Kemp is a man who used to work for a photographer killed by Sloane. When Kemp recognizes Sloane as the murderer, Sloane kicks him to death:

> You don't know what's good for you. [He knocks Kemp behind the settee. Kicks him.] You bring this on yourself. [He kicks him again.] All this could've been avoided. [Kemp half-rises, collapses again. Pause. Sloane kicks him gently with the toe of his boot.] Eh then. Wake up. [Pause.] Wakey, wakey. [Silence. He goes to the door and calls.] Ed! [Pause.] Ed! (216)

Ed and Kate's calm behaviour at their arrival at the 'scene of the crime' is noteworthy. The three characters are quite indifferent towards violence. They discuss the possibilities, and finally the two siblings agree to tell the police that Kemp died due to an accident in exchange for sharing Sloane (sexually as well) for six months at a time.

The British plays after 1990s become more violent, both in language and action, probably due to the increase of violence in the world and the general public's indifference towards it, and the decreasing control of censorship on the British stage[179]. The playwrights belonging to the Post-1990s British drama called "in-yer-face" generally employ violence, obscenity and verbal violence towards both the characters and the audience/reader. Some of these playwrights include Martin McDonagh, Sarah Kane and Anthony Neilson[180].

In Martin McDonagh's plays such as *The Queen of Leenane* (1996) and *The Cripple of Inishmaan* (1997), verbal violence is employed as part of the writer's dark humour. The individuals, families or the society in the plays use verbal violence as part of their daily colloquial language. In Martin McDonagh's *The Cripple of Inishmaan* (1997), there is an extreme level of verbal and psychological violence exerted by the folk of the island of Inishmaan towards Billy, a crippled orphan. Not only do people call him "Cripple Billy" to his face but also constantly make jokes about his 'defect'. For example, Bartley claims that Billy has not had his "arse groped by priests" because "I suppose they have to draw the line somewhere" (22). Helen, another 'friend' tells him that his parents drowned themselves when they "found out Billy was born a cripple-boy" (23). Such cruel remarks are directed at Billy throughout the play. People's indifference to Billy's feelings is further illustrated by the relationship between Johnny and Mammy, his mother. Johnny openly expresses that he wants his mother to drink herself to death: "Johnny: [...] I'd enjoy seeing you in your coffin the same as ya, if we can find a coffin big enough to squeeze your fat arse into. (52).

Blasted (1995) by Sarah Kane, however, lacks any kind of dark humour and is directed towards shocking the audience through obscenity accompanied by both physical and verbal violence. Written eight years before McDonagh's *The Cripple of Inishmaan,* the play includes scenes of physical violence such as cannibalism, inflicting pain on sexual organ, rape, torture and suicide.

---

[179] Stage-censorship was abolished in 1967

[180] Martin McDonagh's *The Cripple of Inishmaan* and Sarah Kane's *Blasted* will be briefly dealt with in this chapter while Antony Neilson's *The Censor* will be studied in detail in Part II, chapter 3.

The following quotations from *Blasted* would clearly show the extreme level of verbal violence Kane has employed in the play:

> *Soldier:* Went to a house just outside town. All gone. Apart from a small boy outside hiding in the corner. One of the others took him outside. Lay him on the ground and shot him through the legs. Hears crying in the basement. Went down. Three men and four women. Called the others. They held the men while I fucked the women. Youngest was twelve. Didn't cry, just lay there. Turned her over and– Then she cried. Made her lick me clean. Closed my eyes and thought of– Shot her father in the mouth. Brothers shouted. Hung them from the ceiling by their testicles. (43)

In the above passage, the soldier narrates what happened to his girlfriend to Ian, a sort of reporter. When Ian tells him that "This isn't a story anyone wants to hear" (48), the soldier violates Ian telling him that his "arse" is no different from anyone else's:

> It's nothing. Saw thousands of people packing into trucks like pigs trying to leave town. Women threw their babies on board hoping someone would look after them. Crushing each other to death. Insides of people's heads came out of their eyes. Saw a child most of his face blown off, young girl I fucked hand up inside her trying to claw my liquid out, starving man eating his dead wife's leg. Gun was born here and wont die. Can't get tragic about your arse. Don't think your Welsh arse is different to any other arse I fucked. Sure you haven't got any food, I'm starving. (50)

After an overview of contemporary English plays containing physical and/or linguistic violence, the following chapters will study linguistic violence in contemporary plays as a means towards the 'standardization' of the values imposed by the power structure, as well as in resisting such 'standardizations'.

The plays to be studied have been chosen from three different epochs of contemporary drama with the purpose of throwing light upon the dramatic use of verbal violence in the early 20th century, mid-century and the early 21st century. Chapter 2 will deal with the violent aspect of 'standardized' language (BBC English or the Queen's English) as a mark of social status in Bernard Shaw's *Pygmalion*

(1914). Chapter 3 will concentrate on the 'standardization' of citizens as true subjects of state power and its manifestation in the form of verbal abuse, verbal insult and verbal torture in Harold Pinter's *The Birthday Party* (1957). Lastly, in Chapter 4, the verbal violence as protest against the concept of censorship on language as state control over mental and artistic production will studied in Anthony Neilson's *The Censor* (1997). *Pygmalion, The Birthday Party* and *The Censor* all of which deal with structured linguistic violence have been particularly chosen because none of them include any particular acts of on-stage physical violence.

CHAPTER 2

"DONT LET THEM TAKE AWAY MY CHARACTER": LANGUAGE, EDUCATION AND CLASS IN BERNARD SHAW'S *PYGMALION*

George Bernard Shaw's *Pygmalion* was first produced in German in Vienna on October 16, 1913 and in English in London on April 11, 1914. *Pygmalion*, the title of the play, refers to the sculptor Pygmalion in Greek mythology, who carved an ivory statue of a maiden and fell in love with it. The statue, in response to his prayers, was brought to life by Aphrodite. Similar to this myth, in the play, Professor Higgins, a phonetician, undertakes the task of transforming Eliza Doolittle (a common flower girl) with a Cockney accent to an "artificial duchess" in Reynolds' words (1999: 15) by teaching her how to speak and behave according to 'standard' social norms. Eliza's educational process may be discussed as an illustration of Foucault's ideas concerning the employment of social institutions such as schools and discourse related to learning in order to standardize people according to the socially dominant idea of the 'normal' (1991: 26). Higgins, who represents education and authority in the play, educates Eliza in the field of etiquette and phonetics so as to render her socially acceptable in London in late Victorian times.

Jean Reynolds points out that Shaw, who has been recognized "as second only to Shakespeare in the British theatrical tradition", stood in a long tradition of rhetoricians who acknowledge the power of language (1999: 5). Thus, for Reynolds the Shavian style, its impressive wordplay, persuasiveness, fluency and eloquence originates in the "old speech" of ancient Greece and Rome (1999: 5). Similarly, *Pygmalion* is situated within the rhetorical tradition of the past by the importance attached to language, speech, eloquence, style, diction and dialect, but deals with such topics in a modern setting (early 20th century Britain) to better illustrate the connection between language and class.

It is true that, as Aristotle indicated in *Treatise on Rhetoric,* "a rustic and a man of education, will express themselves neither in the same words, nor in the same manner" and for this reason language has the effect of being characteristic (1995: 225), but this difference became highly significant during the early years of the 20th century. Speech and accent became the most visible and distinguishable marks of social class in England and, according to John Russell Brown, people "displayed their greatest prejudice through class consciousness, and differences in pronunciation and accent drove immense wedges between people [...]" (1985: xx). As Shaw also claims in his "Preface" to *Pygmalion,* it "is impossible for an Englishman to open his mouth without making another Englishman hate or despise him" (1957: 1). In this respect, *Pygmalion* examines the assumptions of social superiority and inferiority that underlie the class system, demonstrates speech differences as "hall-marks of class" (Morgan, 1982: 9) and illustrates how such social norms and values are imposed through education.

In both the United Kingdom and the United States, there are standard prestigious dialects (apart from regional dialects) preferred by particular social groups. Standard English, also termed as 'Queen's English', 'King's English', or 'BBC English' is often equated with 'proper' English. Although a standard pronunciation does not exist, the most prestigious accent is generally associated with broadcasting such as the BBC national news (Thomas and Wareing, 2002: 119). In contrast, the most common 'non-standard' regional British accents and dialects[181] are 'Cockney English' (spoken in the East End area of London), 'Geordie English' (spoken in the Newcastle-upon-Tyne area), and Glaswegian English (Honey, 1989: 2). The one presented in *Pygmalion*, is the rustic, less elevated 'non-standard' 'Cockney' accent generally linked with the lower social class.

According to their speech, speakers are not only associated with a certain position on the social scale or with particular social groups, but are also expected "to behave in linguistically appropriate ways" (Thomas and Wareing, 2002: 119). For example, it is assumed that professionals such as executives, politicians, and academicians, whom society associates with a high level of education and morals, will automatically speak the prestige variety while those employing an unrefined dialect and accent are associated with the lower class and immoral ways of behavior associated with that class. Consequently, persons who wish to be accepted in the 'higher milieu' are socially pressured to adopt the more prestigious styles, or are excluded or looked down upon.

Bernard Shaw attached a great deal of importance to phonetics, which is

[181] Honey indicates that 'dialect' refers to pronunciation, vocabulary, grammar and idiom while 'accent' signifies pronunciation and intonation (Honey, 1989: 2)

supported by his decision to partly base the character of Higgins on Henry Sweet[182], and his emphasis on the role of phoneticians (especially Henry Sweet) in the provision of a full, accurate and legible script for English (1914: Preface). He points out that phoneticians can help people move to higher class by changing their native dialect, which is evidently an obstacle:

> The modern concierge's daughter who fulfils her ambition by playing the Queen of Spain in Ruy Blas at the théatre Français is only one of the many thousands of men and women who have sloughed off their native dialects and acquired a new one. Our West End shop assistants and domestic servants are bi-lingual. But the thing has to be scientifically, or the last state of the aspirant may be worse than the first. [...] Ambitious lower girls must learn their alphabet from a phonetic expert. (9)

It is evident that Shaw enthusiastically applauds the new scientific approach to language by phoneticians, probably because it raised pronunciation "above the intense self-consciousness and class snobbery which had always bedeviled the subject in England" (Crompton, 1970: 142).

This chapter will consider the relationship between language (accent and dialect), social position and identity in *Pygmalion* and concentrate on the education (provided by Professor Higgins) as a tool for social 'standardization' in the Foucauldian sense. The process of educational standardization reveals also both the verbal violence (manipulation, insult, and abuse) directed by competent speakers of

---

[182] Eliza, the intelligent flower girl lacking an adequate education, is probably inspired by the miller described by Shaw in *The Intelligent Woman's Guide to Socialism and Capitalism*, who was excluded from the middle class by "speech and manners and dress":

> I [Shaw] remember wondering when I was a lad at a man who was in my father's employment as a miller. He could neither read nor write nor cipher (that is, do sums on paper): but his natural faculty for calculation was so great that he could solve instantly all the arithmetical problems that arose in the course of his work: for instance, if it were a question of so many sacks of floor at so much a sack, h could tell you the answer straight off without thinking, which was more than my father or his clerks could do. But because he did not know his alphabet, and could not put pen to paper, and had not the speech and manners and habits and dress without which he would not have been admitted into the company of merchants and manufacturers, or of lawyers, doctors, and clergymen, he lived and died a poor employee, without the slightest chance of rising into the middle class, or the faintest pretension to social equality with my father. (1928: 172-73).

English towards those that lack such a skill, and the power of language to discriminate, transform and destroy.

The opening Act of the play presents people from a variety of social classes in London with special emphasis on their dialectical differences and preconception about each other. A group of people composed of a not-so-well off middle-class family (Mrs. Eynsford-Hill, her son Freddy and daughter Clara), a flower girl (Eliza), a wealthy gentleman (Pickering) and a phonetician (Professor Higgins) are joined beneath the portico of St. Paul's Church in Covent Garden. The flower girl is trying to sell bunches of violets to the opera-goers who have just got out of a performance while they attempt to get cabs under the rain.

Mrs. Eynsford-Hill and Clara send Freddy to find a taxi. On the way, Freddy bumps into the flower girl, causing her basket of flowers to fall. Her first words, uttered in a cockney accent: "Nah then, Freddy: look wh'y' growin, deah. [look where you are going, dear]" (15) situate her among the lower social class, a view supported by her untidy physical appearance[183]. Mrs. Eynsford-Hill, noticing the flower girl calling Freddy familiarly by his first name, suspects that she is a prostitute and buys a bunch of flowers in to confirm her suspicion. The flower girl, however, indicates that she doesn't know her son: "I called him Freddy or Charlie same as you might yourself if you was talking to a stranger and wished to be pleasant." (17). In this case, Eliza is stereotyped as morally weak due to her accent and appearance, two hallmarks of social class.

The flower girl then tries to sell her flowers to another gentleman she calls "Captain" (Pickering) who gives her coins without demanding flowers. At that moment, a man in the crowd warns her that someone behind the pillar is noting down her words. Suspecting that he might be a police officer, he suggests that she present the "Captain" flowers in exchange for the coins he gave her. Fearful of being wrongly accused of something indecent such as prostitution, she denies having said anything of significance to the gentleman: "I aint done nothing wrong by speaking to the gentleman. Ive a right to sell flowers if I keep off the kerb. [*Hysterically*] I'm a respectable girl: so help me, I never spoke to him except to ask him to buy a flower off me." (19-20). She then asks the "Captain" for help: "Oh sir, dont let him charge

---

[183] She is described as an "unromantic figure around 18-20 years old" wearing a sailor's hat, with hair that needs "washing rather badly", wearing "a brown skirt with a course apron", worn boots and in need of a dentist. On comparison to the ladies, "she is very dirty" and her condition makes her undesirable (15).

me. You dunno what it means to me. Theyll take away my character and drive me on the street for speaking to gentlemen" (20). The flower girl's concern about her rights, her virtue and her arrest (punishment) are all due to her short dialogue with a gentleman.

Eventually, the note-taker reveals himself to be a phonetician taking down the flower girl's 'cockney' accent in phonetic script[184]. On being asked how she came so far from Lisson Grove (based on her accent), she answers in tears that Lisson Grove wasn't "fit for a pig to live in" (23) stressing that she is a "good girl" (24). Conscious of being viewed as morally weak, she will repeat that she is a "good girl" several times throughout Act I. A lower-class bystander, hearing their dialogue, remarks that the higher class view the lower class as scum: "You take us for dirt under your [their] feet, don't you? Catch you taking liberties with the gentleman!" (24). The note-taker continues to guess the persons' origin based on their accents, while the flower girl claims that "He's no right to take away" her "character" because her "character is" as important to her "as any lady's" (26).

Amused at the note-taker's talent, the Gentleman (referred to as "Captain" by the flower girl/later Colonel Pickering) asks the note-taker (Higgins) whether there is a good living in being a phonetician, and the note-taker's answer illustrates that his occupation resembles that of the ancient sophists:

> Oh yes. Quite a fat one. This is an age of upstarts. Men begin in Kentish Town with £ 80 a year, and end in Park Lane with a hundred thousand. They want to drop the Kentish Town; But they give themselves away every time they open their mouths. Now I can teach them. (27)

He teaches standard English to social upstarts, who are barred from the higher class due to their dialect.

From this point on, language becomes the focal point of Act I, in which the note-taker insults and bullies the flower girl due to her linguistic deficiencies,

[184] Hearing her protestations, the note-taker comes forth "There! there! there! there! who's hurting you, you silly girl? What do you take me for?" (20). A Bystander indicates that the note-taker is probably a "copper's nark". When the note-taker doesn't understand what the expression means, it is explained as "a sort of informer" (21). This example, together with the use of cliché names such as 'Freddy', 'Charlie' or 'Captain' by the flower girl in order to sound pleasant, is noteworthy because they signify that people living in the same city and speaking the same language actually live in different language communities. They also illustrate the gap and lack of accurate communication between different social classes.

regardless of her improper education. When the flower girl continues whining about being mistreated, the note-taker, referring to her speech, orders her to "cease this detestable boohooing instantly, or else seek the shelter of some other place of worship." (27) She claims that she has the right to be there as anyone else, but he thinks otherwise:

> A woman who utters such depressing and disgusting sounds has no right to be anywhere –no right to live. Remember that you are a human being with a soul and the divine gift of articulate speech: that your native language is the language of Shakespeare and Milton and The Bible; and don't sit there crooning like a bilious pigeon. (27)

The note-taker's (Higgins') exaggerated comment glorifying language as a superior entity shows that he has no tolerance for the abuse of the English language by its improper usage. Although he is soon to be observed as a not so typical representative of the Victorian upper-middle class in his thinking and behavior, he has, nevertheless, made use of all the privileges provided by the British education system offered to upper-middle classes.

Eliza's lack of proper language skills puts her at a disadvantage in her verbal dispute with the note-taker. His definition of her speech as "detestable", "depressing" and "disgusting" is highly offensive, but her lack of verbal skills leaves her no response except mumbling sounds that resemble physical pain: "Ah-ah-ah-ow-ow-ow-oo!" (27). As Berst has indicated, her feeling of "terror, rebelliousness, dismay, and indignation" are all expressed by a "howl" (1973: 209). Her employment of such mumbling sounds to express herself contributes to obscuring her thoughts and emotions instead of clarifying them. After the note-taker notes down her utterance exclaiming: "Heavens! what a sound!", he puts forth a claim illustrating the power of phonetics. He states that he can pass her off as a duchess at an Embassy garden party in three months by teaching her phonetics:

> You see this creature with her kerbstone English: the English that will keep her in the gutter to the end of her days. Well, sir, in three months I could pass that girl off as a duchess at an ambassador's garden party. I could even get her a place as lady's maid or shop assistant, which requires better English. (27)

The note-taker considers the proper use of English as an asset that would help a lower-class woman get a job as a lady's maid or shop assistant rather than enabling her to show off as a duchess. This is a stronger claim from passing her off as a duchess because the two jobs mentioned require the use of better English. It follows that, in this passage, the note-taker maintains quite a snobbish attitude towards both a duchess and a flower girl.

The flower girl shows a great interest and the note-taker confirms his claim through offensive metaphors: "Yes, you squashed cabbage leaf, you disgrace to the noble architecture of these columns, you incarnate insult to the English language. I could pass you off as the Queen of Sheba" (28). At this point, the gentleman that she calls "Captain" and the note-taker introduce themselves to each other. The Captain turns out to be Colonel Pickering, author of *Spoken Sanscrit* and expert in Indian dialects, while the note-taker reveals himself to be the phonetician Henry Higgins, author of *Higgins's Universal Grammar.* The two men depart together after Higgins throws a generous handful of coins to the flower-girl, who uses the money to take the cab finally brought by Freddy. In a pretentious manner, she first tells the driver to take her to "Buckham Pellis [Buckingham Palace]" (29) to show off to Freddy, but then changes the address to a poorer neighborhood on their departure.

The situation in Act I revolves around the connection between language and questions of social class, social roles and identity. On one hand, it shows how representatives of the higher class speaking 'standard' English can verbally offend and insult someone from the lower-class with 'non-standard' English without any regard for her living conditions or lack of education. On the other hand, it illustrates the position of a poor flower girl in fear of losing her "character" (reputation) by being labeled as a prostitute. It is evident that she might get in trouble with the police, one of the representatives of 'authority' in the play, and be easily labeled as immoral just for speaking to a gentleman or calling a member of the higher social class familiarly by his name. She has to endure insults directed at her by the representatives of the higher social class without the verbal power to duel with them.

Even though the flower girl can't speak in the 'proper' or 'standard' fashion, she is instinctively aware of the connection between language and power. She understands that she must speak 'properly' ('standard English') in order to improve her standard of living. To this end, in Act II, she visits Higgins' house the following day, to take lessons in phonetics. Higgins takes up an offensive attitude towards Eliza, continuing to insult her as he did the evening before. His employment of verbal violence aims at insult and abuse, and hardly suits a gentleman of his standing. He immediately tells her to "be off" (37). Upon learning the reason for her visit, he asks Pickering whether they should ask the "baggage to sit down" or "throw her out of the window?" (38). She is hurt, but is only able to say "Ah-ah-oh-ow-ow-ow-oo!" (38) to express herself. Although she cannot speak properly, she is aware of the connection between language and social advancement. She indicates that she wishes to take lessons in phonetics to get a respectable job as a lady in a flower shop (38) which grasps Higgins' attention. In order to get more information, Higgins thunders at her to be seated but she sits only after Pickering courteously asks her to do so. The flower girl, shaken by being badly treated, half-crying wipes her nose on her sleeve. Higgins hands her a handkerchief to wipe any part of the face that feels moist, stating that its function differs from that of a sleeve. When she indicates that her name is "[E]liza[185] Doolittle", the two men recite a rhyme about her name (39). Following their little fun, Eliza tells them not to be "silly", and Mrs. Pearce (the housekeeper) warns her not to speak to the "gentleman" in that manner (39). Eliza's question "Well, why wont he [Higgins] speak sensible to me?" is not answered (39). This example illustrates that Higgins and Pickering, two men of higher social standing and superior linguistic skills, are allowed to make fun of her while it is not socially acceptable for her, a woman of the working class, to tell them not to be "silly"

The two phoneticians are surprised but amused by her proposal to take lessons. Pickering, remembering Higgins' boasting remark in Act I, undertakes all the cost of the experiment claiming that Higgins cannot transform the flower girl into a convincing duchess in a period of six months. Wishing to prove his skill in phonetics, Higgins accepts his bet and declares that he "shall make a duchess of this draggletailed guttersnipe". In this statement, the word "guttersnipe" means "prostitute" (41). To his remarks, Eliza answers with a 'howl': "Ah-ah-ah-ah-ow-ow-oo!" (41). Higgins' use of verbal violence before and in the course of Eliza's education will function as a source of energy serving both to degrade (a superior's linguistic tyranny over his pupil) and to upgrade (a stimulating force in making his pupil work more completely towards her goal).

[185] The flower girl's name is spelled "Eliza" and "Liza" in different parts of the play. The version "Eliza" will be preferred in this study with the exception of quoted dialogues, in which case the original version will be given.

From this point on Eliza's education begins. Higgins first proceeds with her physical appearance by ordering Mrs. Pearce to throw out Eliza's clothes and give her a bath, instructing her to "wallop" and put her in the "dustbin" if she causes any trouble (41)[186]. When Mrs. Pearce asks him if they will pay Eliza any wages, Higgins' answer labels her as a drunkard: "She'll have her food and her clothes. She'll only drink if you give her money." (43). Pickering warns Higgins to be careful not to hurt her feelings with such insults, but Higgins indicates that she does not have any "feelings" that they should to worry about (43). At this point, Eliza –highly offended– gets up to leave, but Higgins tempts her with her favorite items in life: "Think of chocolates, and taxis" But when he adds "gold, and diamonds" to his list of assets, she immediately assumes that their experiment might include some kind of immodesty and refuses: "No: I don't want no gold and no diamonds, I'm a good girl, I am" (45). It is evident that words have different connotations for those two individuals from two different social classes. Chocolate", "taxis, "gold" and "diamonds" are used by Higgins to persuade Eliza towards a desirable life-style while they are conceived by Eliza as indicators of immorality.

Noticing that she has misinterpreted their intention, Pickering suggests that the situation be clarified to her. Higgins, on the other hand, claims that since "she's incapable of understanding anything" (45), it would be best to give her orders instead of explanations:

> There! Thats all youll get out of Eliza. Ah-ah-ow-oo! No use explaining. As a military man you ought to know that. Give her her orders: that's enough for her. Eliza: you are to live here for the next six months, learning how to speak beautifully, like a lady in a florist's shop. If youre good and do whatever youre told, you shall sleep in a proper bedroom, and have lots to eat, and money to buy chocolates and take rides in taxis. If youre naughty and idle you will sleep in the back kitchen among black beetles, and be walloped by Mrs Pearce with a broomstick. At the end of six months you shall go to the Buckingham Palace in a carriage, beautifully dressed. If the King finds out youre not a lady, you will be taken by the police to the Tower of London, where your head will be cut off as a warning to the other presumptuous flower

[186] Mrs. Pearce protests that he "cant walk over everyone like this", asking him to be reasonable (41). This view will also be expressed by Mrs. Higgins later on in Act III.

girls. If you are not found out, you shall have a present of seven-and-sixpence to start life with as a lady in a shop. If you refuse this offer you will be a most ungrateful wicked girl; and the angels will weep for you. (45-46)

This statement establishes Higgins as a sort of dictator. Higgins indicates that it is a waste of time explaining things to Eliza, who is unable to express herself except through inarticulate sounds such as "Ah-ah-ow-oo!", because she is incapable of understanding anything. Eliza's linguistic deficiencies put her at a disadvantage and defenseless against Higgins' verbal manipulations which continues throughout much of the play. In this scene taking place in the study, Higgins exercises verbal violence by a variety of means such as insults in the form of jokes, classifying her as a drunk and claiming that she is incapable of understanding anything. In fact, as long as Eliza continues to express herself inefficiently, she will continue to be observed as a 'nobody' in his eyes and be subjected to his verbal attacks. In such situations her linguistic deficiency puts her at a disadvantage and defenseless against Higgins.

Mrs. Pearce leads Eliza to take a bath to change her "from a frowzy slut to a clean respectable girl fit to sit with the gentlemen in the study." (48). In the meantime, Eliza's father Alfred Doolittle pays Higgins a visit[187], leaving with £ 5 in exchange for his daughter. The social "battering" Eliza goes through in Act II, the burning of her clothes and hot bath amount to purifying "rigors quite necessary to cleanse both soul and body" (Berst, 1973: 205). After this step directed at changing

[187] Alfred Doolittle, Eliza's father, arrives to see Higgins. Higgins guesses that Doolittle, a navy who works as a dustman, has come to blackmail him in some way and tells Doolittle to take his daughter back. Doolittle protests that he has been misunderstood. When Higgins and Pickering ask him what he has come for, he answers "'I'm willing to tell you: I'm wanting to tell you: I'm waiting to tell you" (55) which Higgins defines as sentimental rhetoric. He seems to be Higgins' match (55). He asks for £ 5 in exchange for his daughter who he has raised with the "sweat of his brow" (57). Higgins suggests that it is immoral to pay for a person, but Doolittle mockingly replies that middle class morality is only an excuse to never give money to the poor and receives the desired amount (58). We later encounter Mr. Doolittle a second time in Act V. He arrives to Mrs. Higgins' house dressed in a wedding suit. He accuses Higgins of ruining his happiness by making him a member of the middle class: "[you] [d]estroyed my happiness. Tied me up and delivered me into the hands of middle class morality" (115) Doolittle has inherited three thousand pounds a year from an American philanthropist who was told by Higgins that Doolittle was the most original moralist in England. Doolittle laments the new responsibilities he must take on as a member of the middle class, including marrying his girlfriend, but confesses that he cannot resist accepting the money. "I'll have to learn to speak middle class language from you, instead of speaking proper English." (116). Similar to Eliza, he has noticed the connection between language and prestige.

her external appearance, her education in phonetics and etiquette begins the next day and continues for several months before her first presentation in society.

Eliza's first public test takes place in Act III at Mrs. Higgins' drawing room. The guests that Higgins' mother is entertaining happen to be Mrs. Eynsford, Clara and Freddy, the same persons who Eliza came in contact with during the rainstorm in Covent Garden, but nothing in Eliza's present physical appearance, diction or manners reminds them of their previous meeting. Higgins limits the range of her conversation to 'safe' topics such as 'health' and the 'weather'. All goes well so long as she 'parrots' the standard manners and language taught to her by Higgins. However, she fails to pass the test on surpassing her restrictions by speaking in a Cockney jargon about her aunt being "done in" (killed) for a "straw hat" (77). The situation becomes worse when Eliza, on being asked by Freddy about whether she will walk through the park on her departure, replies: "Walk! Not bloody likely". [Sensation] I'm going to take a taxi." (78). The use of the word 'bloody' might not be creating a strange effect in our time, but it caused quite a controversy at the time the play was first staged[188]. In the play, however, Eliza's use of the improper "bloody" is explained by Higgins as the "new small talk" adopted by the upper-middle class. Furthermore, Clara seems eager to master Eliza's "new small talk", which Higgins explains is in vogue (77) and Freddy is charmed by Eliza's beauty and peculiar ways.

Eliza's 'mishaps', however, are not overlooked by Mrs. Higgins, who is acquainted with Eliza's past. When the guests leave, Higgins, Mrs. Higgins and Pickering discuss the experiment. Mrs. Higgins indicates that Eliza is a triumph of their "art" and "of her dressmaker" but gives herself "away in every sentence she utters" (80). She accuses them of being a pair of babies playing with their live doll. Higgins disagrees, describing his experience concerning Eliza and what she represents as follows:

> Playing! The hardest job I ever tackled: make no mistake about that, mother. But you have no idea how frightfully interesting it is to take a human being and change her into a quite different human being by

---

[188] The fact that such an expression was expressed by a woman and acted out by a married actress with children stirred a lot of controversy. The day following its staging, bishops wanted to ban the play, the Women's Purity League protested to the prime minister and *The Daily Express* found a real Covent Garden flower girl called Eliza, took her to the show and reported that she'd been shocked (Sierz, 2000: 12-13).

creating a new speech for her. It's filling up the deepest gulf that separates class from class and soul from soul. (81-82)

This is one of the most significant points in the play, which stresses the importance of not only language and education as a means of transforming people and abolishing class differences (a reflection of Shaw's ideas as a socialist), but also of the 'standardization' of human beings –a Foucauldian concept. Higgins and Pickering, unable to foresee the final effect that this transformation will have on Eliza in the future indicate that they spend their time teaching Eliza, dressing Eliza and "inventing new Elizas" (82) as if she were a doll. They also express their belief that she will be able to "go her own way" after the experiment "with all the advantages" bestowed on her (84). Mrs. Higgins, however, states that she will end up with the manners and habits of a fine lady that will disqualify her from working and thus, lead her to poverty as she will not be provided with a "fine lady's income!" (84) The two gentlemen defend themselves by saying that they will find some light work for her without realizing that Eliza will adopt the values and ideas inherited in the language that she is learning.

Eliza's lessons continue for six-months, and Higgins and Pickering take her to the Embassy ball. Although all the Embassy guests seem to be composed of the upper-social class, they are a mixed social group including both "upstarts" who have mastered refined speech and aristocrats who never learned to speak it; here Shaw openly attacks the view that genteel speech is acquired 'naturally' by the higher social class. As expected by Higgins and Pickering, Eliza's lessons pay off and the Ambassador's wife, along with the other guests is impressed with Eliza's highly refined speech. For Reynolds, she is nevertheless a "linguistic criminal" who uses the language habits of the wealthy without having been born to the privilege while Higgins is also a linguistic criminal for teaching phonetics to pretentious upstarts (1999: 45).

In Act IV, Eliza, Pickering and Higgins are back in Higgins' house late in the night after the party. Pickering congratulates Higgins on his success and Higgins thanks "god" that "its over!" (98). Eliza, on the other hand, has taken up a reserved attitude and remains intact.

At this most crucial turning point in the play, it would serve well to make an overall evaluation of what has happened throughout the story. To begin with language has been presented as 'etiquette' associated with the formal rules of correct and polite behavior in the Victorian society or 'milieu'. Thus, failure to use proper language is considered to be a great class barrier. As a poor female, Eliza stands outside the traditional British elite that depend heavily on the use of fine linguistic skills. At the beginning she is imprisoned in poor living conditions due to her lack of proper verbal skills ("the English" that will keep her in the gutter to the end of her days," [27] as Higgins puts it). Through his education in phonetics, Professor Higgins is able to transform the "lisping, drawling sing-song of the slum" (Cockney dialect) spoken by Eliza into the "dialect of the drawing-room" (Massingham, 1976: 227). For Higgins and Pickering, Eliza's learning to "talk more genteel" has been the only problem at hand.

The rest of the play, however, shows that as her awareness of language increases, she is both empowered and alienated. After Pickering goes to bed, Higgins asks for his slippers. It is then that Eliza throwing Higgins' slippers in a fit of desperation, demands to know what is to become of her. Although he tells her that "theres nothing more to worry about", Eliza wishes she were "dead." (101), asking the vital question put forth earlier by Mrs. Pearce and Mrs. Higgins, women of two different classes: "What am I fit for? What have you left me fit for? Where am I to go? What am I to do? Whats to become of me?" (102). Thus, in a Foucauldian sense, the focal point is not her success at the ball, but the final position in which her education has left her. After Higgins has taught her to speak the prestigious 'standard' dialect, she realizes that she cannot return to her initial position.

As Eliza's awareness of language and society grew, her taste and conception of 'normal' has changed. As a result, she is unable to return to her old habits after the experiment is concluded. Thus, Higgins' education in phonetics surpasses its initial aim and, in opposition to his original claim, transforms her to a 'normal' integrated subject. Eliza, who has initially set out to improve her living conditions, has not only surpassed this simple motive, but has found herself conforming to accepted social codes. Thus, the process of developing her linguistic skill has unexpectedly resulted in her being 'standardized' and 'normalized' in terms of the clichés of the late Victorian society.

Higgins now proposes an arranged marriage for her. This suggestion is immediately rejected by Eliza who complains that she sold flowers as a flower girl, but as a 'lady', she is threatened with the prospect of having nothing to sell but herself (102). Eliza was able to work as a female member of the lower social class, but now she has lost this freedom[189]

From this point on, Eliza treats Higgins as if he were her employer, by speaking in a formal manner which emphasizes their class difference. She informs him about her decision to leave his house, requesting to know which of her clothes belong to her in order not to be accused of stealing. She also returns the jewelry, so as not to run the risk of them being missed, due to her position as a "common ignorant" girl: "in my station I have to be careful. There cant be any feelings between the like of you and the like of me." (104). Her last sentence is a reference to her prior position in Act I. Higgins gets angry and resorting to the position of the 'competent speaker' of English who feels free to abuse those learners who are not thankful for the education he has provided. He states he would "ram" the jewels down her "ungrateful throat" if they were not rented (104). She also returns a ring he bought for her in Brighton. He dashes the ring violently into the fireplace, and turns her so threateningly that Eliza exclaims "Don't hit me" (104). Higgins is hurt by such an accusation and ends up calling her "infamous creature" and damns himself for "having lavished my hard-earned knowledge and the treasure of my regard and intimacy on a heartless guttersnipe" (104-105). Higgins leaves the room furiously, and she gets her things together and leaves the house.

Eliza encounters Freddy on her way out. She protests when he calls her "Miss Doolittle" indicating that "Eliza" is "good enough" for her (106). On Freddy's inquiry about her plans, she first indicates that she is going to the river "to make a hole in it" (commit suicide) (107) but then decides to go to Mrs. Higgins in the morning for advice. Even though Eliza's departure and refusal to be called "Miss Doolittle" might be viewed as her rebellion against Higgins' education and authority, her alternatives (to commit suicide and then to seek advice from Mrs. Higgins) show her failure to gain her autonomy.

The next morning, in Act V, Higgins arrives at his mother's house with Pickering. When Mrs. Higgins informs them that Eliza will come downstairs if Higgins promises to behave, he mocks Eliza through the verbal violence he deliberately employs: "[...] Let us put on our best Sunday manners for this creature

[189] Shaw notes in Act II of his early play, *Mrs. Warren's Profession* that in the late Victorian period the only decent chances of work for a young girl from the lower-class were becoming a singer (is she had a good voice), an actress (if she had the talent for acting), and a journalist (if she had a gift for writing) (1948: 245)

that we picked out of the mud." (119) Eliza eventually joins them in a lady-like fashion of a typical Victorian female. Higgins' furious reaction at Eliza for playing the role he has taught shows that he cannot be classified as a 'standardizer' and 'normalizer' in the Foucauldian sense:

> You will jolly soon see whether she has an idea that I havnt put into her head or a word that I havnt put in her mouth. I tell you I have created this thing out of a squashed cabbage leaves of Convent Garden; and now she pretends to play the fine lady with me. (120-121)

According to Higgins' statement, it is impossible for Eliza to have any personal ideas that have not been imposed upon her by himself through his instruction of language. This is exactly the view put forth by Foucault in his discussion of 'knowledge' or 'education' (1991: 27). However, Shaw makes it clear that the education Eliza received has not brainwashed her into a blind conformity with the codes of the middle-class society. Therefore, it appears that in *Pygmalion* the two protagonists Higgins and Eliza present themselves not only as specimens of 'educator' and 'learner' in the Foucauldian sense, but also stand apart from the 'norms' of such specimens. It follows that, in spite of Higgins' godly claim that Eliza is a complete creation of his genius, he is no advocate of 'standardization' and 'normalization' in the Foucauldian sense. Eliza, on the other hand, falls short of being a typical product of such processes as she still remains the 'rebel' she was at the beginning of the play, this time she is much better equipped –thanks to Higgins' teaching– with the linguistic tools of expression.

The encounter at Mrs. Higgins' drawing room marks the beginning of a verbal duel between Higgins and Eliza. Eliza, as the pupil, strives to free herself from the grasp of her instructor while Higgins, the teacher, fights for his dominance over her. However, compared to their encounter in Act I, Eliza is linguistically much better equipped, and is able to both defend herself and attack Higgins to a certain point.

Eliza attempts to hurt Higgins by commenting that she could not have learned proper manners without the presence of Pickering because "he [Pickering] treats a flower girl like a lady" (126). But Higgins who treats "a lady like a flower girl", indicates that the important point is "having the same manner for all human souls:

behaving as if you were in Heaven, where there are no third-class carriages, and one soul is as good as another" (126)[190].

When Higgins indicates –on being left alone with Eliza in Mrs. Higgins' drawing room– that he shall miss her, Eliza suggests that he can listen to her voice on the gramophone and look at her photographs. He continues to appeal to her emotions by his remark: "I cant turn your soul on. Leave me those feelings; and you can take away the voice and the face. They are not you." (127), but Eliza is now educated enough to recognize his rhetorical technique:

> oh, you are a devil. You can twist the heart in a girl as easy as some could twist her arms to hurt her. Mrs Pearce warned me. Time and again she has wanted to leave you: and you always got round her at the last minute. And you dont care a bit for her. And you do not care a bit for me. (127)

Eliza portrays Higgins simply as a man of science who views individuals as specimens without any regard for their feelings. Higgins, similar to Foucault's idea of the 'state' ignores individuals (Foucault, 1991: 14) by establishing his classification of people according to their intellect and verbal skill. Additionally, by teaching phonetics, Higgins also teaches these 'standards' to his pupils.

Now, Eliza feeling trapped in her present status, accuses Higgins of robbing her of her freedom and making her a slave through his education:

> Oh! If I only could go back to my flower basket! I should be independent of both you and father and all the world! Why did you take my independence from me? Why did I give it up? I'm a slave now, for all my fine clothes. (129)

She also indicates her future plan to marry Freddy as soon as she is able to support him as he cannot offer her economic security. Although Higgins calls Freddy a "fool", she claims that Freddy will make her "happier" than her "betters" that "bully" her and "don't love her" (129). All the same, she cannot help saying that she wants a

---

[190]Although Higgins' claim that one soul is as good as another seems democratic and convincing, he has created another classification system based on people's intellect and linguistic skills. Professor Higgins is defined by Evans as a "bully, a ramping, swearing boor" (1976: 228)

little kindness even though she is only a "common ignorant girl" and he a "book-learned gentleman", pointing out that he has no right to treat her like "dirt" under his "feet." (130). Higgins calls her a fool, suggesting that she can return to the "gutter" if she does not prefer his ways. Her reply to this, illustrates how she has been transformed through her education:

> Oh, you are a cruel tyrant. I cant talk to you: you turn everything against me: I'm always in the wrong. But you know very well all the time that you are nothing but a bully. You know I cant go back to the gutter, as you call it, and that I have no real friends except for you and the Colonel. You know well I couldnt bear to live with a low common man after you two; and it's wicked and cruel of you to insult me by pretending I could. You think I must go back to Wimpole Street because I have nowhere else to go but father's. But dont you be too sure that you have me under your feet to be trampled on and talked down. I'll marry Freddy, as soon as I'm able to support him. (131)

The next point to be considered is how Eliza will earn her living. She points out that she will make a living by teaching others phonetics:

> [...] Aha! Now I know how to deal with you. [...] You cant take away the knowledge you gave me. You said I had a finer ear than you. And I can be civil and kind to people, which is more than you can. Aha! [*Purposely dropping her altches to annoy him*] Thats done you, Enry Iggins, it az. Now I dont care that for your bullying and your big talk. (131-132).

Although Higgins becomes angry and calls her a "damned impudent slut" (132), he is, nevertheless, impressed. Now, he calls her a "tower of strength", but she coldly indicates in a formal manner that she shall not see him again (132).

The Epilog[191], which has been provided for only the readers of the play, indicates that Eliza marries Freddy and they first open a flower shop and then try their hand at being greengrocers with Pickering's financial assistance. Thus, Eliza exchanges her marginal status as an artificial duchess for a legitimate position as a middle class business owner. All the same, Higgins, who has succeeded in elevating Eliza's linguistic performance has not created a genuine middle class woman content with her middle class way of life. For, Shaw makes it clear that at the end of the play Eliza does not seem to be fully oriented to her newly acquired status. She has gone through a process of 'normalization' under the supervision of Higgins, who

[191] The original play did not have an epilogue, but when the actor playing Higgins (Sir Herbert Tree) in the production cast a rose to the departing Eliza, thus suggesting their marriage, Shaw wrote another ending. The original ending was as follows:

> *Mrs. Higgins:* I'm afraid youve spoilt that girl, Henry. But never mind, dear. I'll buy you the tie and gloves.
> *Higgins:* [*sunnily*] Oh, dont bother. She'll buy em all right enough. Goodbye.
> *They kiss, Mrs Higgins runs out. Higgins, left alone, rattles his cash in his pocket; chuckles; and disports himself in a highly self-satisfied manner.* (Gibbs, 1983:173).

In a letter written to Mrs. Patrick Campbell written on December 19, 1915, he expresses his thoughts concerning this subject:

> Besides, I have passed *Pygmalion* for press among the sheets of my new volume of plays; and it now has a sequel, not in dialogue, but in prose, which you will never be able to live up to. It describes in an absolutely convincing manner how Eliza marries Freddy; how she realized her dream of a florist's shop; how neither of them knew how to keep the shop; how she had to beg from the Colonel again and again to avert bankruptcy; how the wretched pair had to go to shorthand and typewriting commercial schools to learn; how they went even to the London School of Economics and to Kew Gardens simultaneously to learn about business and flowers and combine the information; how Eliza wrote such a shameful hand that she had to abase herself to Higgins to be taught his wonderful Italian handwriting; how Clara was converted by H. G. Wells and Galsworthy and went into a shop herself and saved her soul alive; how the flower shop started to pay at last when they tried asparagus and Freddy became Mr. Hill, greengrocer; how Eliza never got out of nagging Higgins that she acquitted in the forth act, and, though deeply interested in him, did not quite like him any more than she liked her father, who was rejected by the middle classes and forced into the highest society, where he was a huge success but poorer than he had ever been in his life before on his four thousand a year. The publication of that sequel will be the end of the romance of Sir Herbert Tree; and you will have to play Eliza properly and seriously for ever after which is impossible. (Alexander, 1988: 22)

Even though they do not come together in the play, both the film version (produced with Shaw's consent) and *My Fair Lady* (1964), the musical film adaptation, conclude open-ended without a narrative about Eliza's marriage to Freddy.

throughout the story remains an advocate and representative of the linguistic standard only rather than an agent of education in the Foucauldian sense. Thus, Bernard Shaw leaves his discussion of language, class and power at the level of fantasy which does not fully pave the way to a Foucauldian act of 'standardization' and normalization', which will find its expression in Harold Pinter's *The Birthday Party* to be studied in the next chapter.

CHAPTER 3

"YOU'LL BE INTEGRATED": LINGUISTIC VIOLENCE AND LOSS OF INDIVIDUALISM IN HAROLD PINTER'S *THE BIRTHDAY PARTY*

Harold Pinter's *The Birthday Party,* a play in three acts covering a time span of 24 hours, was written in 1957 and first produced on May 19, 1958 in London. The play, characterized as a "play of language"[192], incorporates linguistic features from a variety of theatrical movements such as 'social realism', 'angry' and 'absurd' theatre[193]. Also, as a "play of violence"[194], it illustrates the destructive force of daily language in the form of verbal violence.

In the play, Stanley "a man in his late thirties", a non-conformist who presents himself as a pianist, has been living peacefully at a seaside boarding house run by Meg "a woman in her sixties" and Petey "a man in his sixties" until the arrival of two new lodgers, Goldberg and McCann. Although the history of their acquaintance is not clarified, Goldberg and McCann appear to be particularly interested in Stanley and upon learning from Meg that it is his birthday, they convince her to throw a party for him. In the evening of the same day, Stanley and the new lodgers come face to face for the first time in the play. Stanley claims that it is not his birthday and takes a stand against them, indicating that he does not fear them. In response, Goldberg and McCann conduct a cross-examination involving linguistic torture, after which Stanley loses all his ability to speak and goes through a nervous breakdown. The scene of interrogation is followed by the scene of the birthday party in which Stanley, not opening his mouth for once, resorts at times to physical violence. The morning after the party Stanley comes to the kitchen wearing a suit resembling Goldberg and McCann's and uttering meaningless mumblings. He is then taken away by the two

[192] (Misra, 1992: 64)

[193] According to Misra, Pinter employs:

> colloquial speech which did not sacrifice the dramatic elegance and precision, poetic imagery which did not become ostentatious, absurd babblings, contradictions and repetitions which were not over-mannered or too ambiguous and eloquence which did not appear contrived and rhetorical. (1992: 63)

[194] (Misra, 1992: 67)

men in their van.

The Birthday Party is a typical specimen of the theatre of the Absurd in that it lacks a straightforward story and characters that can be clearly identified. It is through working with the clues that Pinter has provided in the dialogues that we can get to the core of the play.

The Birthday Party which stands as a "kind of dramatized theory of power" (Silverstein, 1993: 26) illustrates the process through which individuals are inserted into the dominant order through language. Language as a representative of dominant power and the state, dramatizes "man's loss of autonomy and selfhood through the normative pressures, reductive tendencies, or pre-determination of language" (Malkin, 1992: 8)[195].

The play begins at the breakfast table at the boarding house where Petey and Meg discuss general topics such as cornflakes, the weather and the news. Petey mentions that two men approached him about a room, to which Meg is surprised at first, but later affirms that their "house is on the list" (12) (This 'list' can be a reference to a number of things such as the yellow pages, list of lodgings in a tourist guide book. It may also imply a 'darker' list kept by the mafia or police.). Petey leaves and Stanley, their sole lodger, comes down for breakfast unshaven and in pajamas. He complains about the defects and the unsatisfactory service of the boarding house (the "horrible" cornflakes, tea like "gravy") and about Meg's qualities as a wife (not making tea for her husband and serving him sour milk), calls her a "succulent old washing bag" and tells her "violently" to clean his room (14-19). In spite of all his complaint, however, he does not seem to be planning to leave.

When Meg mentions that she must go shopping to get things for the two new coming lodgers, Stanley seems to be alarmed about them:

Stanley:	What two gentlemen?
	[...]
Stanley:	(*grinding his cigarette*) When was this? When did he see them?
Meg:	Last night.
Stanley:	Who are they?
Meg:	I don't know.

[195] Language is represented in the play as public language-model sentences which induce model behaviour, and thus become, like language itself, well-formed and orderly. It sets out to transform the characters into a single model who speak, act, like language, that is, well-formed and orderly.

Stanley: Didn't he tell you their names?
Meg: No.
[...]
Stanley: But who are they?
Meg: You'll see when they come.
Stanley: (*decisively*). They won't come.
[...]
Stanley: They won't come. Someone's taking the Michael. Forget all about it. It's a false alarm. A false alarm. (*He sits at the table.*) (20-21)

The above passage changes the initial impression Stanley has made earlier at the breakfast table. No longer sounding like a spoiled (son-like) lodger who complains about services all the time, he now seems to be worried about the two new lodgers that have not yet arrived. He implies that they may be people he already knows. He asks about their names. Then he wants to assure himself that they will not come as if he knew who was coming. He implicitly states the fact that he does not want them. The negative attitude he has assumed brings to mind a good number of questions. Does Stanley have an idea who the new lodgers are? Has he met them before? Has he been expecting them? Why does he reject the idea that they are coming? Why does he dismiss the fact of their coming as a "false alarm" ("alarm" implying a state of panic)? By bringing such questions to mind, Pinter seems to convey the clues concerning Stanley's position and identity –perhaps a runaway, possibly responsible for some sort of criminal act and expecting to be caught and punished.

This impression, however, changes when Stanley once more goes back to domestic matters. When Meg tells him that she took his tea away because he didn't want it, Stanley suddenly employs the voice of a superior with an important identity:

Stanley: (*quietly*). Who do you think you're talking to?
Meg: (*uncertainly*). What?
Stanley: Come here.
Meg: What do you mean?
Stanley: Come over here.
Meg: No.
Stanley: I want to ask you something. (*MEG fidgets nervously. She does not go to him.*) Come on. (*Pause.*) All right. I can ask it

> from here just as well. (*Deliberately.*) Tell me, Mrs Boles, when you address yourself to me, do you ever ask yourself who exactly you are talking to? Eh? (21)

He seems to be trying to hold on to the status of an authority.

Meg changes the subject to Stanley's playing the piano. Then Stanley goes on talking about a long and successful career as a pianist giving concerts all over the world. His authoritative attitude continues until Stanley's mentions his piano recital in Lower Edmonton where "they" "carved" him up:

> carved me up. It was all arranged, it was all worked up. My next concert. Somewhere else it was. In winter. I went down there to play. Then, when I got there, the hall was closed, the place was shuttered up, not even a caretaker. They'd locked it up. (Takes off his glasses and wipes them on his pyjama jacket.) A fast one. They pulled a fast one. I'd like to know who was responsible for that. All right, Jack, I can take a tip. They want me to crawl down on my bended knees. (23)

What has happened? Why has Stanley been hindered? Who are "they" who have "carved him up" and why do they want him to "crawl down" on his "bended knees"? Pinter is not interested in satisfying the audience's curiosity. For, all these questions will remain unanswered.

Meg then indicates that the two gentlemen are coming in a van with a wheelbarrow in it, and Stanley claims that "They're looking for someone. A certain person." (24) This echoes Pinter's statement in *Various Voices* that:

> the hierarchy, the Establishment, the arbiters, the socio-religious monsters arrive to effect alteration and censure upon a member of the club who has disregarded responsibility (that word again) towards himself and others. (1998: 11)

Stanley's alarm due to the arrival of the two men becomes more apparent at this point. Yet, the implicit signs concerning whether he is a criminal hiding from the authorities or who the two men soon to arrive at the boarding house are, have not been clarified. On the arrival of the expected lodgers, Goldberg and McCann, Stanley puts on his glasses and slides out the kitchen door (30).

The dialogue between the new lodgers at the front door is proof that they have come with a purpose. McCann worries about whether they have come to the right house and whether this "job" will resemble the other ones. To this, Goldberg answers in a "quiet, fluent, official tone" (30) with a kind of professional jargon that seeks to obscure rather than clarify:

Goldberg:	This main issue is a singular issue and quite distinct from your previous work. Certain elements, however, might well approximate in points of procedure to some of your other activities. All is dependent on the attitude of our subject. At all events, McCann, I can assure you that the assignment will be carried out and the mission accomplished with no excessive aggravation to you or myself. Satisfied?
McCann:	Sure. Thank you, Nat. (30)

Goldberg's discourse brings to mind George Orwell's celebrated article "Politics and the English Language" in which he suggests a list of ways to establish clear and honest communication:

1. Never use a metaphor, simile, or other figure of speech which you are used to seeing in print[196].
2. Never use a long word where a short one will do[197].
3. If it is possible to cut a word out, always cut it out[198].
4. Never use a passive where you can use the active[199].
5. Never use a foreign phrase, a scientific word, or a jargon word if you can think of an everyday English equivalent[200].

---

[196] Thomas and Wareing claim that this is a warning against the use of pre-constructed phrases in which commonly made associations and assumptions are reiterated, not challenged (39)

[197] The first short version should be preferred for clarity: help/assistance, end/conclusion, work with/collaboration with, break/adjournment, last/preceding.

[198] Although it sounds more impressive and intimidating, it is harder to understand, unnecessary words.

[199] Passive constructions often sound more formal, more convoluted, and given slightly less information, harder to understand.

[200] Communicate clearly to a wide audience, everyday terms are often more effective. Jargon is appropriate in special fields, but outside that area makes audience feel bored, intimidated, unimportant or stupid.

6. Break any of these rules sooner than say anything outright barbarous[201]. (1946: 6)

Goldberg's discourse in the above quotation, however, functions in the opposite direction of what has been suggested by Orwell. He speaks by generalizing without any specific references and by using "implicature" (anything that is inferred from an utterance that is not a condition for the truth of the utterance). The "job" is reworded as a "main issue" in which all depends on the cooperation of the "subject" resembling law jargon. According to Malkin, their language is "a sophisticated mixture of corporate jargon, gangster slang, and social pieties. Goldberg, the more verbose of the two, tends toward long, evasive speeches" (1992: 54).

Foucault indicates that power, instead of being instituted by the source, is always instituted by the subject on behalf of the source. Foucault sees power emerge frequently from the bottom-up of a hierarchy; instead of powerless individuals doing the will of those with power, these so-called powerless figures attempt to find the norm, and then self-regulate their behaviour to follow it (1995: 14-15). Two such figures are Goldberg and McCann. They have been sent to the Boyles' house to do a job, but the nature of the job, its purpose, the identity of the "subject", and the relationship between Stanley and the newcomers remain purposely obscure. In a speech made by Pinter at the National Student Drama Festival in Bristol in 1962, he touches upon the subject of language:

> Language [...] is a highly ambiguous business. So often, below the word spoken, is the thing known and unspoken. My characters tell me so much and no more, with reference to their experience, their aspirations, their motives their history. Between my lack of biographical data about them and the ambiguity of what they say lies a territory which is not only worthy of exploration but which it is compulsory to explore. You and I, the characters which grow on a page, most of the time we're inexpressive, giving little away, unreliable, elusive, evasive, obstructive, unwilling. But its out of these attributes that a language arises. A language, I repeat, where under what it said, another thing is being said. (Pinter, 1998: 19)

---

[201] With 'barbarous', he means that statements should be in support of equality and freedom.

Also, concerning Pinter's plays, Brown states that "[i]n effect, Pinter seems to play a game with the audience, giving only a few signposts on the way, a few landmarks or buoys to distinguish the hidden rock and sand. Like his characters, he seems to evade, to obscure intentionally, to blaze false trails." (1987: 35)

The first thing that Goldberg and McCann do on entering the house is to inquire about Petey's occupation and the lodger staying at the boarding house (Stanley Webber). In response, Meg tells them that Petey is a "deck-chair attendant" and that Stanley is a pianist[202], expressing her wish about Stanley playing that night on his birthday. Goldberg then convinces Meg to organize a party for Stanley. Goldberg's purpose in organizing a party is expressed as "will bring him [Stanley] out of himself. Were you going out?" (33), a remark that produces further questions concerning the relationship between Stanley and the two men, who have not yet met each other at the boarding house.

Stanley enters by the back door and inquires about "who" the two gentlemen are, what they want and how long they plan to stay. Meg presents Stanley with a gift of a boy's drum with two drumsticks, even though Stanley indicates that it is not his birthday. He hangs the drum around his neck tapping it gently at first and then becoming "*erratic, uncontrolled*", his "*face and the drumbeat [...] savaged and possessed*"[203] right before the first act is concluded (30). Act I ends without any face to face contact between Stanley and the two new lodgers.

The first contact between Stanley and the two men takes place in Act II, on the evening of the same day. Stanley goes to speak to McCann, who is tearing sheets of newspaper into five equal strips, which is an indication of order and 'sameness'. McCann receives Stanley in a polite manner offering his good wishes on his birthday: "I'm glad to meet you, sir. (*He offers his hand. STANLEY takes it, and MCCANN holds the grip.*) Many happy returns of the day. (*STANLEY withdraws his hand. They face each other.*)" (37). However, McCann becomes more aggressive when Stanley

---

[202] Meg's version of the story is as follows:

> (*falteringly*). In [...] a big hall. His father gave him champagne. But then they locked the place up and he couldn't get out. The caretaker had gone home. So he had to wait until the morning before he could get out. (*With confidence.*) They were very grateful. (*Pause*) And then they all wanted to give him a tip. And so he took the tip. And then he got a fast train and then came down here. (32)

[203] Pinter's emphasis.

indicates that he is not going to be present at the party taking place that night because he prefers to celebrate it quietly (38): "McCann: Where are you going?/Stanley: I want to go out./McCann: Why don't you stay here?" (39). Stanley indicates that he has a feeling that they have met before, asking him if he ever went to Maidenhead where there is a Fuller's teashop, but McCann denies knowing those places (39). Then the conversation is directed to Stanley's birthday:

> *McCann*: You know, sir, you're a bit depressed for a man on his birthday.
> *Stanley*: *(sharply)*. Why do you call me sir?
> *McCann*: You don't like it?
> *Stanley*: *(to the table)* Listen. Don't call me sir.
> *McCann*: I won't, if you don't like it.
> *Stanley*: *(moving away)*. No. Anyway, this isn't my birthday.
> *McCann*: No?
> *Stanley*: No. It's not till next month.
> *McCann*. Not according to the lady. (41)

Stanley, who has denied that it is his birthday earlier (to Meg), and who then told McCann that he prefers to celebrate it alone, now tells McCann that it is not his birthday.

Stanley then asks McCann whether his friend, who is not present in the room, has told him what they have come for, whether he has told him anything, whether he knows what they are there for, but McCann denies knowing anything. At this point, that Stanley is fearful about what the two men may do to him has become an open fact:

> *Stanley:* (*whispering, advancing*). Has he told you anything? Do you know what you're here for? Tell me. You needn't be frightened of me. Or hasn't he told you?
> *McCann:* Told me what?
> *Stanley:* (*hissing*). I've explained to you, damn you, that all those years I lived in Basingstoke I never stepped outside the door. (42)

Their dialogue is broken up with the arrival of Goldberg and Petey. Goldberg tells a story about his relationship with a female Sunday school teacher emphasizing that he did not take liberties with her because of the key word 'respect'. Then Goldberg continues with an anecdote about his mom calling him 'Simey' in the past: "'Simey!' my old mum used to shout, 'quick before it gets cold.' And there on the table what would I see? The nicest piece of gefilte fish you could wish to find on a plate." (43) McCann indicates that he thought his name was Nat, but Golding claims that his mom called him "Simey". Such 'civil' conversation functioning towards emphasizing good morals and family life continues until Petey exits, leaving Stanley, Goldberg and McCann alone. Stanley suddenly confronts them about not being afraid of them:

> Let me–just make this clear. You don't bother me. To me, you're nothing but a dirty joke. But I have a responsibility towards the people in this house. They've been down here too long. They've lost their sense of smell. I haven't. And nobody's going to take advantage of them while I'm here. (*A little less forceful.*) Anyway, this house isn't your cup of tea. There's nothing here for you, from any angle, any angle. So why don't you just go, without any more fuss? (45)

Stanley's outburst puts forth his difference from the Boyles, who have, unlike him, "lost their sense of smell". This statement together with his prior questioning of McCann and Meg is an indication that Stanley is stands apart from the other inhabitants of the house as a free individual who would not allow the newcomers to act the way they want. After Stanley's threat, Goldberg puts aside his manners and begins giving orders:

Goldberg:	Mr Webber, sit down.
Stanley:	It's no good starting any kind of trouble.
Goldberg:	Sit down.
Stanley:	Why should I?
	[...]
Goldberg:	Sit down.
Stanley:	No. (45-46)

Goldberg then assigns to McCann the task of making Stanley sit down, thus asserting his dominance over him as well:

> *Goldberg:* Ask him to sit down.
> *McCann:* Yes, Nat. (*McCann moves to STANLEY*) Do you mind sitting

down?

Stanley: Yes, I do mind.

[...]

McCann: (*to STANLEY*) Sit down.

Stanley: Why?

McCann: You'd be more comfortable.

[...]

McCann: Get down in that seat!

Goldberg: (*crossing to him*). Webber. *(Quietly.)* SIT DOWN. *(Silence. STANLEY begins to whistle "the Mountains of Morne". He strolls casually to the chair at the table. They watch him. He stops whistling. Silence. He sits)* (46-47)

Although Stanley successfully resists Goldberg's invitation to sit down at first, he later obeys him. As observed in the above dialogue, neither Goldberg nor McCann employ any physical force to make Stanley sit down. They use verbal violence in the form of language instead. While it took pleasant manners on the part of Pickering to convince Eliza to sit down on her first visit to Wimpole Street, Stanley is now persuaded by linguistic force. With Stanley's acceptance to sit down an interrogation begins. The interrogation aims at verbally breaking down Stanley's character, or in Foucault's words "the heart, the thoughts, the will, the inclinations" that make up his character. The cross-examination of Stanley first includes questions about his physical appearance, past occupation, family life, marital status, name, religious belief and is followed by absurd questions that have no answers with the aim of verbally destroying Stanley's mental health.

The first part of the interrogation is about Stanley's physical appearance and his possible connection with the 'organization':

Goldberg: What did you wear last week, Webber? Where do you keep your suits?

McCann: Why did you leave the organization?

Goldberg: What would your old mum say, Webber?

McCann: Why did you betray us?

Goldberg: You hurt me, Webber. You're playing a dirty game.

McCann: That's a Black and Tan fact.

Goldberg: Who does he think he is?

McCann: Who do you think you are? (48)

Such questions are meaningless and are put forth to unnerve Stanley. Although Goldberg and McCann's reference to the "organization" and their accusation of Stanley with betrayal raises questions about Stanley's past, they, nevertheless, remain unanswered even at the end of the play. The second topic that they take up is his family life and marital status:

Goldberg:	Where was your wife?
Stanley:	In–
Goldberg:	Answer.
Stanley	*(turning, crouched).* What wife?
Goldberg:	What have you done with your wife?
McCann:	He's killed his wife!
Goldberg:	Why did you kill your wife?
Stanley.	*(sitting, his back to the audience).* What wife?
McCann:	How did he kill her?
Goldberg:	How did you kill her?
McCann:	You throttled her.
Goldberg:	With arsenic.
McCann:	There's your man!
Goldberg:	Where's your old mum?
Stanley:	In the sanatorium.
McCann:	Yes!
Goldberg:	Why did you never get married?
McCann:	She was waiting at the porch.
Goldberg:	You skeddadled from the wedding.
McCann:	He left her in the lurch.
Goldberg:	You left her in the pudding club.
McCann:	She was waiting at the church. (49-50)

They accuse Stanley of poisoning his wife and of putting his mom in the sanatorium. Then they question him about why he has remained a "bachelor" and afterwards accuse him of leaving his fiancé at the altar by 'skeddadling' (running away) to avoid getting married. Such paradoxical claims pointing towards an irrational way of thinking and questioning on the part of Goldberg and McCann, contribute to the verbal violence on stage. According to Brown, falsehoods are important in the play:

> Contrary statements, falsehood, half-truths and absence of verification raises suspicions about statements that could be possibly true, might be significant. So the audience doubts and questions the characters' progress through the play, the clues they seem to drop, the assurance they seem to possess. Their words are determined, their credit is short (1987: 39)

Also Bloom puts forth the ambiguity in the play as follows:

> The menace of what they are doing is tangible but unexplained; it is the irruption of a bizarre and arbitrary violence into an ordinary life. The structure of feeling is familiar: the precarious hold on reality, the failures of communication, the inevitability of violence and exploitation. (Bloom, 1987: 19)

The questions that follow are aimed at Stanley's identity, namely his name, which is considered to be the fundamental signifier of existence:

Goldberg:	Webber! Why did you change your name?
Stanley:	I forgot the other one.
Goldberg:	What's your name now?
Stanley:	Joe Soap
Goldberg:	You stink of sin.
McCann:	I can smell it. (50)

At this point, it is not apparent whether his real name is "Stanley Webber", "Joe Soap" or some other name. Stanley's inability to affirm his name is an indication that they are successful in their verbal torture. The next aspect questioned by the two men is Stanley's spiritual or religious beliefs and practice:

Goldberg:	Do you recognize an external force?
Stanley:	What?
Goldberg:	Do you recognize an external force?

McCann:	That's the question!
Goldberg:	Do you recognise an external force, responsible for you, suffering for you?
Stanley:	It's late.
Goldberg:	Late! Late enough! When did you last pray?
McCann:	He's sweating!
Goldberg:	When did you last pray?
McCann:	He's sweating!
	[...]
Goldberg:	Right? Of course right! We're right and you're wrong, Webber, all along the line.
McCann:	All along the line! (50-51)

In the above lines, Stanley starts to break down. He is sweating. The agents of violence have been using language to destroy Stanley's sense of security.

The cross-examination eventually turns into a grotesque display of cliché verbal patterns. The topic discussed becomes in turn extremely absurd:

Goldberg:	Speak up, Webber. Why did the chicken cross the road?
Stanley:	He wanted to–he wanted to–he want to...
McCann:	He doesn't know!
Goldberg:	Why did the chicken cross the road?
Stanley:	He wanted to–he wanted to...
Goldberg:	Why did the chicken cross the road?
Stanley:	He wanted...
McCann:	He doesn't know. He doesn't know which came first!
Goldberg:	Which came first?
McCann:	Chicken? Egg? Which came first?
Goldberg and McCann:	Which came first? Which came first? Which came first?
	STANLEY Screams. (51-52)

"Why did the chicken cross the road" jokes is linked to the fact that it resembles the 'fill in the blank' structure with endless joke possibilities. Also, the question that follows about whether the chicken or the egg comes first, an endless cycle, is a riddle impossible to answer. Both these are pre-constructed verbal patterns, which make up Goldberg and McCann's discourse and the discourse of authority. In this private meeting, Goldberg and McCann, parroting the 'superior' language of authority, are able to dominate, manipulate and 'break' Stanley. Stanley, unable to stand the verbal torture any longer, screams.

In the dialogue full of verbal assault, language is used as a medium of violence. According to Misra, Goldberg and McCann's style composed of "quick-fire succession" of questions "effect in the victim a sense of mysterious dread and incertitude" instead of being genuine points of inquiry (1992: 68). Malkin defines their style as a "quick, gapless rhythm, a totalitarian style which allows no space for response and no option for self-defense" (1992: 57). The vagueness of simple questions, statements and commands that make up Goldberg and McCann's discourse create a sense of incertitude for Stanley leading to his total loss of control and the break-down of his psychology. Stanley does not speak after he screams, but Goldberg and McCann continue with their linguistic torture, this time, their questions aiming at Stanley's physical identity and his citizenship:

> *Goldberg:* He doesn't know. Do you know your own face?
> *McCann:* Wake him up. Stick a needle in his eye.
> *Goldberg:* You're a plague, Webber. You're an overthrow.
> [...]
> *McCann:* You betrayed your land.
> *Goldberg:* You betrayed your breed. (52)

They call him a "plague" and a traitor who has betrayed his "land" and "breed". They then question his whole existence concluding that he is dead:

> *McCann:* What are you, Webber?
> *Goldberg:* What makes you think you exist?
> *McCann:* You're dead.
> *Goldberg:* You're dead. You can't live, you can't think, you can't love. You're dead. You're a plague gone bad. There's no juice in you. You're nothing but an odour! (52)

McCann and Goldberg have entered into warfare with Stanley, using language as their sole weapon. As Misra indicates "The invaders are always more facile in speech.[...] They empower their victim more by violent impact of their language than by any physical action as in the case of Goldberg and McCann" (1992: 67). Stanley, on the other hand, is unable to defend himself verbally and thus, resorts to physical violence. He kicks Goldberg in the stomach and covers his head with a chair as if to protect himself from being brainwashed. His petty condition is illustrated by McCann who indicates that "the bastard [...] is sweating like a pig" (53).

As for Goldberg and McCann, physical violence seems unnecessary as it has been greatly replaced by linguistic violence. Their position can be associated with Foucault's discussion in *Discipline and Punishment.* Foucault indicates that the concept of physical torture has disappeared as a public spectacle (such as executions) and the "expiation that once rained down on the body" was "replaced by a punishment that acts in depth on the heart, the thoughts, the will, the inclinations" (1995: 16). In other words, "the heart, the thoughts, the will, the inclinations" were now to be disciplined and/or punished through linguistic devices of suppression. A civilized kind of inflicting violence is made possible through linguistic means based on a special kind of 'knowledge' or 'discourse' that common people cannot easily gain access to[204]. The practice of such linguistic violence may turn out to be most effective in controlling, punishing and changing the identity of individuals.

Following the scene of linguistic torture, the guests for Stanley's birthday party arrive. This social event gives us a further insight into Goldberg's linguistic skills. At the party, Lulu (with whom Goldberg flirts throughout the party, makes her sit on his lap and possibly sleeps with) comments that Goldberg is a marvelous speaker inquiring about where he learned to speak in that manner, and he indicates that he first gave a lecture at Ethical Hall about "The Necessary and the Possible". It is

---

[204] In *Discipline and Punish* Foucault indicates that 'discourse' includes those who are familiar with its particular jargon and excludes or eliminates the rest. For example, the language of the law falls short of being clearly comprehended, because its formal style cannot be understood by the general public with poor linguistic skills:

> How are we, with our prudish, contemptuous languages, overloaded with formality, to make ourselves understood by those who have never heard anything but the crude, poor, irregular, but lively, frank picturesque dialect of the market, the tavern and the fair [...](1995: 276)

And the inability to understand and grasp meaning leads to getting empowered.

interesting that he has spoken at "Ethical" Hall and on the "Necessary" and the "Possible", which are all direct reference of 'order'.

Lulu asks Goldberg if he has a wife, and his response is exactly the same story as he told McCann on page 43 about his mother, a preconceived story. The only difference is that he has replaced "mom" with "wife":

Goldberg:	I had a wife [...] "Simey", my wife used to shout, "quick before it gets cold!" And there on the table what would I see? The nicest piece of rollmop and pickled cucumber you could wish to find on a plate,
Lulu:	I thought your name was Nat.
Goldberg:	She called me Simey. (59)

Such a reply illustrates that Goldberg is used to employing cliché phrases, sentences and thoughts instead of using more original or personal structures. While Goldberg mingles with the guests, Stanley remains silent.

Close to the end of the party Meg expresses her wish to play a game. To this, McCann suggests to play "hide and seek" while Lulu prefers "blind man's buff". It is noteworthy that both these games refer to 'sight' or 'blindness' ("Seek" and "Hide") which is a direct reference to Stanley, who has been hiding until he was found by Goldberg and McCann. They decide to play "blind man's buff". Meg goes first and is followed by McCann and Stanley. When it is Stanley's turn, McCann takes his glasses off in order to blindfold him, which acts as a metaphor for the destruction Stanley's of the world. McCann places the drum (Meg's present) sideways in Stanley's path, to which Stanley walks into and falls over with his foot caught in it (63). McCann breaks Stanley's glasses by snapping the frames, and leads Stanley to fall into the drum. Yet, he does not use violence directly on Stanley. Then Stanley moves towards Meg, dragging the drum on his foot, and attempts to strangle her until McCann and Goldberg rush forward and throw him off (63-64). Suddenly, there is a blackout and the two men get a "torch" and shine it on Stanley, to discover that Lulu is lying "spread-eagled" on the table with Stanley bent over her. It is apparent that Stanley, who has been left 'without a voice' at the scene of the cross-examination has been continuously resorting to physical violence. Thus, Pinter chooses to pinpoint Stanley's act of physical violence as one directly proportional to his linguistic deficiency. As soon as the torchlight hits him, Stanley begins to giggle and "flattens against the wall." As for McCann and Goldberg, the stage direction says "[t]heir figures converge upon him [...]" (66), thus concluding act II. Stanley's silence at the party increases and his unbalanced behavior, his tendency towards violence together with his giggling points to the destruction of his sanity. The rest of the scene takes place offstage and what has happened remains obscure.

Stanley's loss of identity is signified by his silence and broken glasses. The verbal torture conducted by Goldberg and McCann has reached its aim. The birthday party, which is also the name of the play, is of central importance. Although a party generally denotes a celebration and connotes a new beginning, this party, ironically, represents Stanley's symbolic death as a non-conformist and re-birth as a conformist that has surrendered to authority. Raymond Williams indicates that "The birthday party, with its drum, its switching-off of lights, its game of blind-man's bluff, releases the violence [...]" (1987: 20). The extent of Stanley's conformity to the rules and values represented by Goldberg and McCann, however, is further illustrated in Act III.

In the last act, Meg and Petey are sitting at the breakfast table the next morning and talking about the party. Meg points out that although Stanley generally sleeps in late, he was speaking to the two gentlemen that morning. Meg goes out for groceries. Goldberg comes down to join Petey. Petey asks him how Stanley is and Goldberg replies in a fashion that is full of eloquent but meaningless jargon:

> (*a little uncertainly*). Oh... a little better, I think, a little better. Of course, I'm only really qualified to say, Mr Boles. I mean, I haven't got the... the qualifications. The best thing would be if someone with the proper...mnn...qualifications...was to have a look at him. Someone with a few letters after his name. It makes all the difference. (71)

Goldberg states that Stanley feels a little better, but that he needs someone with qualifications, defined as a person with a few letters after his name referring to degrees. Goldberg goes on to point out that Stanley had a nervous breakdown because the birthday celebration was more than he could handle. Petey inquires about what could have brought on such a sudden breakdown and Goldberg, again, answers vaguely, making fragmented statements and imitating the tone of an authority in the subject:

> *(rising, and moving upstage).* Well, Mr Boles, it can happen in all sorts

> of ways. A friend of mine was telling me about it only the other day. We'd both been concerned with another case–not entirely similar, of course, but... quite alike. *(He pauses.)* Anyway, he was telling me, you see, this friend of mine, that sometimes it happens gradual–day by day it grows and grows and grows...day by day. And then other times it happens all at once. Poof! Like that! The nerves break. There's no guarantee how it's going to happen, but with certain people...it's a foregone conclusion. (71-72)

His claim that this "breakdown" might happen day by day or at an instance, shows the arbitrariness of the violence exerted on Stanley and its potential to be directed to everyone. Petey wonders if people recover from such a condition, and Goldberg indicates that they sometimes might "one way or another". He does not clarify what these 'ways' are (73). This "recovery" might be a direct reference to the 'standardization' of the members of society. Petey becomes even more concerned and offers to get a doctor to come in the afternoon, but Goldberg tells him that it is taken care of. So, due to Goldberg's interference, Petey is prevented from receiving any clear or concrete information about Stanley.

McCann comes down, on being asked when Stanley will be ready, he informs Goldberg that he gave Stanley his glasses:

Goldberg:	Wasn't he glad to get them back?
McCann:	The frames are bust.
Goldberg:	How did that happen?
McCann:	He tried to fit the eyeholes into his eyes. I left him doing it. (74)

Stanley's attempt to fit the eyeholes of the glasses into his eyes portrays an unstable psychology. Petey offers to stick it with sellotape, but Goldberg rejects the idea saying that it will keep Stanley "quiet for the time being, keep his mind off other things" (74) as if he were a child. Petey, again, insists that Stanley needs a doctor, but McCann states that he will take him to "Monty" (74). The name can be "Monty" associated with the head of the organization, or Goldberg and McCann's boss.

McCann and Goldberg decide to finish "the bloody thing" (76) (previously called the "job on their arrival [58]) and go. But before McCann goes up, Goldberg orders him to look at his teeth, in order to express his thoughts about the advantages of a life without change:

> You know what? I've never lost a tooth. Not since the day I was born. Nothing's changed. (*He gets up.*) That's why I've reached my position, McCann. Because I've always been as fir as a fiddle. All my life I've said the same. Play up, play up, and play the game. Honour thy father and thy mother. All along the line. Follow the line, the line, McCann, and you can't go wrong. What do you think, I'm a self-made man? No! I sat where I sold to sit. I kept my eye on the ball. School? Don't talk to me about school. Top in all subjects. And for why? Because I'm telling you, I'm telling you, follow the line? Follow my mental? Learn by heart? Never write down a thing. And don't go too near the water. And you'll find–that what I say is true.
> Because I believe that the world ... (*Vacant*)....
> Because I believe that the world...(*Desperate.*)....
> BECAUSE I BELIEVE THAT THE WORLD...(*Lost.*).... (77-78).

Goldberg's language is full of clichés and worn out phrases that reveal that he is parroting the dominant values in the society. This does not only illustrate that Goldberg lacks genuine values of his own, but also the extent to which Goldberg has been brainwashing McCann with such ideas. According to Prentice:

> Goldberg's blind adherence to authority, like Stanley's rebellion against it, mirrors the same unconscious response to received values; both reflexively attack whatever does not conform to that self. The struggle for dominance that defines identity inevitably and irrevocably intensifies into a life-and-death battle over what each character regards as his own deepest values, ultimately indistinguishable from the self. (2000: 35)

Additionally, Goldberg tells about McCann about his father's advice to him at his deathbed:

> [...] Go home to your wife. I will, Dad. Keep an eye open for low-lives, for schnorrers and for layabouts. [...] Do your duty and keep your

> observations. Always bid good morning to the neighbors. […] I swore on the good book. And I knew the word that I had to remember– Respect! (78)

Although Goldberg puts forth high morals represented by 'being faithful', 'dutiful', 'a good neighbor' and emphasizes the word "respect", his behavior is far from reflecting such virtues. When Lulu comes to accuse Goldberg of using her, he deflects the attack by putting the blame on her. McCann is no better than his senior partner asks as he also instructs Lulu to get down on her knees and confess, and finally tells her to get out of his sight.

Eventually Stanley is brought down by McCann. Stanley has cleaned up his appearance and is dressed in a dark well cut suit holding his broken glasses. His physical appearance conforms to the business-like appearance of Goldberg and McCann. Goldberg, continuing his 'polite appearance' asks Stanley if he is feeling better and about his broken glasses, but Stanley just stares blankly. Goldberg continues to indicate that Stanley needs new glasses: "Stan, it's about time you had a new pair of glasses" (82). Since the glasses symbolize sight and vision, Goldberg's last remark illustrates that they have succeeded in imposing upon Stanley, the rules, views and values they cherish:

McCann:	You can't see straight.
Goldberg:	It's true. You've been cockeyed for years.
McCann:	Now you're even more cockeyed.
Goldberg:	He's right. You've gone from bad to worse.
McCann:	Worse than worse.
Goldberg:	You need a long convalescence.
McCann:	A change of air.
Goldberg:	Somewhere over the rainbow.
	[…]
Goldberg:	You're on the verge.
McCann:	You're a dead duck. (82)

Goldberg and McCann define Stanley's world view (glasses) to have been "cockeyed or years" making him see worse and worse, and for this reason point out to the fact that he needs "a change of air". According to them, Stanley is "on the verge", a "dead duck" which they can be saved through 're-orientation':

Goldberg:	But we can save you.
McCann:	From a worse fate.
	[...]
Goldberg:	we'll watch over you.
McCann:	Advise you.
	[...]
Goldberg:	We'll make a man of you.
McCann:	And a woman.
Goldberg:	You'll be re-orientated.
McCann:	You'll be rich.
Goldberg:	You'll be adjusted.
McCann:	You'll be our pride and joy.
Goldberg:	You'll be a mensch.
McCann:	You'll be a success.
Goldberg:	You'll be integrated.
McCann:	You'll give orders.
Goldberg:	You'll make decisions.
McCann:	You'll be a magnate.
Goldberg:	A statesman.
McCann:	You'll own yachts.
Goldberg:	Animals.
McCann:	Animals. (82-84)

Their future plans include saving Stanley, looking after him, giving him advice, supervising him and making a "man" and a "woman" out of him. By making him a "man" and a "woman", they seem to be referring to a person who shares their ideology and 'speaks' their discourse. Pinter defines Goldberg and McCann as: "Dying, rotting, scabrous, the decayed spiders, the flower of our society. They know their way around. Our mentors. Our ancestry. Them. Fuck'em" (1998:10). Although McCann seems to be Goldberg's partner, instead of two persons working together, they should be viewed as one body with one brain, one view, one soul in which Goldberg dominates, abuses and manipulates. As Raymond Williams also states "The menace of what they are doing is tangible but unexplained; it is the irruption of a bizarre and arbitrary violence into ordinary life" (1987: 19).

Their world view is illustrated by their future prospects for Stanley. They indicate that after his re-orientation, Stanley will be "rich", "integrated", "make decisions" and "give orders", become a "statesman" and own "yachts" and "animals". They ask his opinion, but Stanley is unable to offer a personal view because he has lost his power of speech:

> *Stanley*: Uh–gug…uh-gug…eeehhh–gag…(*On the breath*) Caahh…caahh….
> […]
> *Stanley*: Ug–gughh…uh–gughhh. …
> *McCann*: What's your opinion, sir?
> *Stanley*: Caaahhh…caaahhh. …(84-85)

Stanley is only able to make mumblings at this point. Pinter's thoughts about what such unclear sounds signify are as follows:

> In the third act Stanley can do nothing but make a noise […] But does this sound signify anything? It might very well. I think it does. He is trying to go further. He is on the edge of utterance. But it's long, impossible edge and utterance, were he to succeed in falling into it, might very well prove to be only one cataclysmic, profound fart. You think I'm joking? Test me. In the rattle in his throat Stanley approximates nearer to the true nature of himself than ever before and certainly ever after. But it is late. Late in the day. He can go no further. (1998: 10)

Petey, who was absent from the party, finally voices his discomfort: "Leave him alone!" (85), but is helpless when they threaten to take him as well (86). They take away Stanley. After they exit, Petey picks up the paper, Meg returns from her shopping and they continue their usual breakfast conversations. When Meg inquires about Stanley, Petey tells her that "He's…still asleep," adding "Let him…sleep" (87), which refers to Stanley's final condition.

In a letter to Peter Wood, director of the play, Pinter summarized the play as follows: "Goldberg and McCann turned up. They had come with a purpose, a job in hand –to take Stanley away. This they did, Meg unknowingly, Petey helpless, Stanley sucked in. Play over." (Pinter, 1998: 8)

The Birthday Party dramatizes the tragic conflict between the individual and society, the process of integrating people into society, and the destruction of 'individualism'. Goldberg and McCann emerge from nowhere and use verbal violence to control, manipulate and rob Stanley of his individuality. They never employ physical violence. Even when Stanley tries to escape before the party, McCann threateningly requests, but does not force him to stay. Their style is full of 'bookish' metaphors, similes and figures of speech, more and longer words than necessary, cliché phrases and a combination of legal, medical, religious, political and popular jargon expressed in passive structures. Thus, the language of authority, represented by Goldberg and McCann, is characterized by 'implicature', aggressive questioning and giving orders. Since they are only agents of authority, power works through them. In *Discipline and Punishment* states that:

> power is exercised rather than prossessed; it is not the 'privilege', acquired or preserved, of the dominant class, but the overall effect of its strategic position– an effect that is manifested and sometimes extended by the position of those who are dominated. Furthermore, this power is not exercised simply as an obligation or a prohibition on those who 'do not have it'; it invests them, is transmitted by them and through them; it exerts pressure upon them, just as they themselves, in the struggle against it, resists the grip it has on them (1995: 26-27)

As such, Goldberg and McCann do not produce power and ideology, but instead, power works through them. So, their present status as model-citizens instead of unique individuals, make them victims as well. Authority in the form of language has taken over their souls and as its product and victims their sole weapon is language. They do not use direct physical violence. As Brown points out: "speech is warfare, fought on behalf of thoughts, feeling and instincts." (Brown, 1987: 26) By such a process, they contribute to the construction of 'discourse', 'ideology' and 'authority', and the creation of one kind of language and one type of human being.

Goldberg and McCann inflict verbal violence through ordinary vocabulary, where they create a sense of uncertainty and chaos. The language constructs authority and secures power by setting certain value systems or ideologies[205] as 'natural' or 'common sense', and forcing subjects to such rules, structure and limitations. One of

---

[205] 'Ideology' can be defined is as any set of beliefs which appear to be logical and natural to the people who hold them (Thomas and Wareing, 1999: 34)

the ways in which language (discourse/ideology) gains momentum and power is through the use of 'implicature', the method of obscuring information by the unclear use of language. Since information is expressed unclearly[206], it makes it hard to reject an idea that cannot be identified[207]. At the end, Stanley has been reduced to a broken, possibly blind, mumbling subject, who has conformed to the rules and regulations of the dominant order (represented by the two men). The violence in Pinter's play is related to the "existential fear of self-hood slipping away from one's grip" (Misra, 1992: 67). The verbal violence in Pinter's play is established through the incertitude in the use of language brought about by the techniques opposing the ones put forward by Orwell for clarity of expression. This incertitude creates a sense of fear and violence[208].

In the study of *Pygmalion* and *The Birthday Party* the aim was to show how authority is constructed through language and how violence is exerted through the same means. In *The Censor*, which will be the subject of the next chapter, however,

[206] In all societies where power is not maintained exclusively by physical force, political language will attempt to produce a "common-sense consensus" view shared by at least a significant section of the population (Andersen, 1988: 259). In his essay "Politics and the English Language" George Orwell reflects how 'euphemism', substitution of a mild and pleasant expression for a harsh and blunt one, is used in politics in order to defend the indefensible:

> In our time, political speech and writing are largely the defence of the indefensible. Things like the continuance of British rule in India, the Russian purges and deportations, the dropping of the atom bombs on Japan, can indeed be defended, but only by arguments which are too brutal for most people to face, and which do not square with the professed aims of the political parties. Thus political language has to consist largely of euphemism, question-begging and sheer cloudy vagueness. Defenceless villages are bombarded from the air, the inhabitants driven out into the countryside, the cattle machine-gunned, the huts set on fire with incendiary bullets: this is called pacification. Millions of peasants are robbed of their farms and sent trudging along the roads with no more than they can carry: this is called transfer of population or rectification of frontiers. People are imprisoned for years without trial, or shot in the back of the neck or sent to die of scurvy in Arctic lumber camps: this is called elimination of unreliable elements. Such phraseology is needed if one wants to name things without calling up mental images of them. (1961: 358)

With these lines Orwell expresses the use of pleasant expressions and general definitions of situations used by governments to conceal the truth of the situation.

[207] For example, the British Labor Party indicated that when they say that they "will save the NHS [British National Health Service], funded by public money, they imply that it needs saving, or that the present government is damaging the NHS (Thomas and Wareing, 1999: 35)

[208] As Bloom indicates, the "menace is of the agents of an unnamed organization, and the fact that it is unnamed allows every effect at once: criminal, political, religious, metaphysical" (1987: 21).

the focus will be on a different use of verbal violence, namely on how verbal violence is employed to question and to deconstruct authority and defy order.

CHAPTER 4

"OVERSTEPPING THE MARK": VERBAL VIOLENCE AS A MEANS OF DEFYING AUTHORITY IN ANTHONY NEILSON'S *THE CENSOR*

Anthony Neilson's *The Censor* was first published in 1997 and originally produced by the Red Room on April 1, 1997 at Finborough Theatre in London. The play then transferred to the Duke of York's Theatre. The Director Stephen Daldry converted the 600-seat theatre into a sixty-seat one (placing both the audience and actors on stage), and put on a short season of theatre called 'Behind the Safety Curtain' in the scope of which the play was performed.

In the play, the Censor works in an office dealing with hardcore pornographic material with almost no chance of getting a license. Miss Fontaine, a filmmaker, comes to see the Censor about the licensing of her movie classified as 'hard-core pornography' by the Board of Classification. She claims her work is a love story, not 'pornography' and asks the Censor to prepare a recommendation in order to make the Board see her perspective. Alongside the Censor's dealings with Miss Fontaine, the play also shows brief instances of the Censor's 'cold' and distant married life. The conversations between the Censor and his wife reveal that they lack a physical relationship due to the Censor's impotence and that his wife has affairs with other men (with his knowledge). Miss Fontaine helps the Censor overcome his impotence by discovering that his secret fantasy is watching women defecate and the two make love. Miss Fontaine later leaves to work on an exhibition in New York, and soon after, the Censor finds out that she has been beaten to death at a hotel room.

The Censor, as the title clearly reveals, dwells on the subject of censorship (intellectual and artistic censorship and the one that exists in our daily lives –daily language, social and private relations, sexuality–). It illustrates how people are verbally and physically 'censored' by authority (through its social institutions and norms).

'Censorship' may be defined as the supervision and control of artistic, intellectual, political and religious[209] ideas, which may exist in the form of books,

[209] Leon L., 1987: vol. v, 411

periodicals, plays[210], films, news reports etc., for the purpose of altering or suppressing parts considered to be objectionable, immoral, obscene, offensive, harmful or vulgar. Some of the categories of censorship include military censorship (keeping military intelligence and tactics confidential), political censorship (governments holding back secret information from their citizens), religious censorship (removing any material objectionable to a certain faith as in the example of Salman Rushdie's *Satanic Verses*) and moral censorship (censoring the body or pornography), which is the topic of the play.

In *The History of Sexuality: The Will to Knowledge (Vol. I)*, Foucault states that after the seventeenth century, it was more difficult and costly to call 'sex' by its name than ever before:

> As if in order to gain mastery over it [sex] in reality, it had first been necessary to subjugate it at the level of language, control its free circulation in speech[211], expunge it from things that were said, and extinguish the words that rendered it too visibly present. And even these

---

[210] Sammells indicates that the concept of 'censorship' had an important impact on the history of English theatre. Following the Stage Licensing Act of 1737, the text of any play to be performed in the UK before a public audience had to be submitted to the Lord Chamberlain, one of the senior members of the royal household, in advance of the performance. This Act gave him a right to ban anything "as often as he shall think fit" (1992:2) The 'censoring committee' was made up of the Lord Chamberlain, appointed by the monarch from the ranks of senior courtiers, and comptrollers chosen by the Chamberlain to work in this department (Hyland & Sammells, 1992: 3). These comptrollers were mostly composed of upper-middle-class and retired senior officers from the armed services. Thus, both the Lord Chamberlain and the comptrollers generally held views of a conservative aristocracy, showing little appreciation of the modern movement in literature, drama, art and music (Hyland & Sammells, 1992: 3).

The process that was followed by the Chamberlain's Examiner of plays, that is the reason for censoring the play or deleting scenes, words or incidents were not publicly revealed or discussed with the playwright. The Lord Chamberlain's judgment was final and no court of appeal or questions about his decision could be discussed in the House of Commons or the Lords (Jongh, 2000: x). The Lord Chamberlain's files were withheld from the public until 1991. For example, Edward Garnett, the playwright, insisted on knowing why his play *The Breaking Point* (1907) was banned and the Lord Chamberlain's Examiner, George Redford wrote to the playwright saying that in England, one was allowed to read what could not be said or depicted on stage. The ban of the play was not lifted until 1957 (Jongh, 2000: x).

There were four parliamentary inquiries into stage censorship between 1853 and 1909, and it was lifted in 1967. (Sammells, 1992:1).

[211] As Fairclough has pointed out questions of language and power are fundamental to understanding the new order and to the politics of the new order, because language is becoming increasingly important in social life. Struggles to impose or resist the new order are partly struggles over language, both over new ways of using language, and over linguistic representations of change (Fairclough, 1989; 2001: 204). The 'turn to language' means that the struggle to impose or resist the new order is in large part a struggle for or against a new language. (Fairclough, 1989; 2001: 208).

prohibitions, it seems, were afraid to name it. Without even having to pronounce the word, modern prudishness was able to ensure that one did not speak of sex, merely through the interplay of prohibitions that referred back to one another: instances of muteness which, by dint of saying nothing, imposed silence. Censorship. (1998: 17)

Foucault adds that at the beginning of the 18th century sex became a political topic that was studied throughout:

At the heart of the economic and political power of population was sex: it was necessary to analyze the birth rate, the age of marriage, the legitimate and illegitimate births, the precocity and frequency of sexual relations, the ways of making them fertile and sterile, the effects of unmarried life or of the prohibitions, the impact of contraceptive practices [...] (1998: 25-26)

And thus, "between the state and the individual, sex became an issue, and a public issue no less; a whole web of discourses, special knowledges, analyses, and injunctions settled upon it." (Foucault, 1998: 26). Subsequently, the discourse on 'sex'[212] was produced in the 18th and 19th centuries, and has been highly regulated by the state since that time, whether it be written, visually displayed or performed.

---

[212] According to Foucault, the following discourses on sex were produced in the eighteenth and nineteenth centuries:

First there was medicine, via the "nervous disorders"; next psychiatry, when it was set to discovered the etiology of the mental illnesses, focusing its gaze first on "excess," then onanism, then frustration, then "frauds against procreation," but especially when it annexed the whole of the sexual perversions as its own province; criminal justice , too, which had long been concerned with sexuality, particularly in the form of "heinous" crimes and crimes against nature, but which, toward the middle of the nineteenth century, broadened its jurisdiction to include petty offences, minor indecencies, insignificant perversions; and lastly, all those social controls, cropping up at the end of the last century, which screened the sexuality of couples, parents and children, dangerous and endangered adolescents –undertaking to protect, separate, and forewarn, signaling perils everywhere, wakening people's attention, calling for diagnoses, piling up reports, organizing therapies. These sites radiated discourses aimed at sex, intensifying people's awareness of it as a constant danger, and this in turn created a further incentive to talk about it. (1998: 31)

On the relationship between 'sex', 'power' and repression (censorship), Foucault points out that 'prohibition', and 'censorship' are the forms in which power is exercised in society (1998: 10). He states that power over sex is exercised in the same way at all levels, in whichever device or institution it relies on and operates "according to the simple and endlessly reproduced mechanism of law, taboo, and censorship" (1998: 84).

According to Aleks Sierz, "British culture was the most highly censored in Europe" in the 1990's[213] (2000: 80). Even though certain 'censorship' laws are loosened or lifted at times, Jongh claims that censorship "never really goes away: it just changes its form." For example, he indicates that 21 years after the abolition of stage-censorship (lifted in 1967), the Broadcasting Standards Council appeared in its place: "We get rid of the Lord Chamberlain, and get Lord Rees-Mogg instead" Sammells, 1: 1992).

Anthony Neilson, in an interview with Sierz, states that he has been interested in censorship since his childhood. He used to write to the British Board of Censors when he was 10 years old to inquire about why a film had been given a certain certificate. The Board did not only reply to his questions but also sent him a folder about how they operate (Sierz, 2000: 83). In order to question the topic of 'censorship', Neilson dwells on. He indicates that "the main purpose [in his plays] has been to move away from the notion that sex and violence have to be seen as extremes" (Sierz, 2000: 88).

The Censor illustrates that verbal violence, generally used to dominate and manipulate others into accepting 'standardization', can also work to deconstruct, reveal and resist authority. In contrast to the other two contemporary plays studied in this book, *Pygmalion* and *The Birthday Party*, in which representatives or agents of the system use verbal violence to 'standardize' individuals (into accepting 'standard' ideas and values), in *The Censor* Miss Fontaine, a filmmaker, employs linguistic violence to rebel against the dominant value system exercised by the Board of Classification, or other social 'standards' that may function to robotize humans. She

[213] Jongh claims that "Relatively speaking, the twentieth-century English stage was subject to more censorship than in the reigns of Elizabeth I, James I and Charles I. Furthermore, he claims that Britain's "repressed" theatre became a "reactionary, unintellectual outpost of Europe, scarcely involved with the modern theatre movement". (2000: xv)

uses language to transform the Censor, from a standardized subject into an individual who is able to 'see' through the workings of the dominant order.

The play begins with a kind of prologue in which the Censor narrates his views about Miss Fontaine's movie:

> It started with a pornographic film. And I swear to God, it was a porn film like any of the hundreds I'd seen.
>
> No: There were differences –strange edits and inflections– but at the time I put it down to poor technique.
>
> No: I'll be honest with you –I put it down to the fact it was made by a woman.
>
> The film was hard-core and unpassable as it stood but she requested a meeting with me to challenge the ruling. (245)

The Censor clearly indicates that her movie is a "hard-core" pornographic movie like many that he has viewed before and cannot possibly receive a license. The Censor's employment of the word "challenge" instead of 'inquiry', or 'change', connotes defiance on the part of the female director (Miss Fontaine). In fact, the play will show that apart from her wish to "challenge the ruling", Miss Fontaine will also "challenge" the existing order.

Scene 1, the first of fourteen, begins with the Censor and Miss Fontaine's initial meeting about her movie. Her half-naked greeting of the Censor in his office, shows that she is anything but 'normal'. He tells her to put back her skirt on, but she asks him if he is "married" or "gay" (245). He tries to persuade her further by telling her that she is embarrassing him and making a fool of herself suggesting that she leaves. She puts her skirt back on and asks him whether he thought about the things she said about her movie, as if nothing has happened. The Censor is "*at a loss for words*" at her indifference while Miss Fontaine, referring to the Censor's earlier statement about being embarrassed, says: "I'm not going to be ashamed. Waste of time being ashamed" (247). Miss Fontaine's 'free' ways and outspoken style stands in contrast with the Censor's embarrassment and discomfort.

Scene 2 shows that the Censor is actually, as Miss Fontaine correctly guessed, married. The Censor and his wife have a quite distant and 'censured' dialogue from which we infer that she is possibly having an affair with a man called "David" (247) Such conversations between them also take place in scene 4[214], 6[215], 8[216] and 11[217]. The Censor's conversation with his wife is followed by the time-coding of the action in Miss Fontaine's film by the Censor:

> Fifteen forty-seven: outer labia.
> Sixteen o two: inner labia. Penetration by inorganic device.
> Sixteen twenty-three: anal penetration by same. Digital insertion to vagina.
> Additional oral stimulation of vagina –sixteen forty–two.
> Seventeen ten: masturbation of erect penis.
> Seventeen twenty-six: oral stimulation of erect penis.
> Seventeen fifty-one: repetition of anal insertion sequence.
> Eighteen o three: repetition of oral sequence. (247-248)

With medical jargon such as "outer labia", "inorganic device" and "repetition of the oral sequence", the censor's notes resemble a surgical procedure, a dissection or a highly technical matter instead of intercourse. The dialogue between the Censor and his wife, and the time-coding, both composed of 8 lines, lack intimacy.

On the next meeting between the Censor and Miss Fontaine (scene 3), she accuses him of lying about not being married (scene 1). He reminds her about their agreement about not talking about the "other night" (their meeting in scene 1). His reference to their embarrassing prior meeting as the "other night" without naming it clearly illustrates his self-censorship. The Censor suggests that they return to her film, explaining that it might be recommended for viewing with a "Restricted 18" rating if they cut somewhere "in the region of ....thirty-five minutes" (248). The

---

[214] In Scene 4, we get another glimpse at the Censor's married life. In this scene, composed of five lines, his wife indicates that "he" (the person she is having an affair with) wants to speak to him about the "situation". His wife's preference not to name her lover and reference to her affair as the "situation" show how people employ censorship in their daily lives.

[215] In Scene 6, another instance between husband and wife is shown. The Censor's wife states that "he" (her lover) does not want to be his (the Censor's) enemy but wishes to show that there are "feelings involved". The Censor asks what she "wants" and she replies "Yes, I want that too" (262).

[216] In Scene 8, the Censors wife asks him whether he will meet "him" (her lover) and when he doesn't reply, she says "Say something!" (271)

[217] In Scene 11, his wife tells him that he can have it his own way, and that they can just continue pretending that nothing has happened.

Censor's abstaining from naming the sexual action that takes place around "thirty-five minutes" seems to support Foucault's view that the system "subjugate[s] it [sex] at the level of language, control its free circulation in speech, expunge it from things that were said, and extinguish the words that rendered it too visibly present" in order to gain "mastery" over it (1998: 17). The Censor says that her movie can be sold in "licensed video stores" with certain cuts, but she protests that he means "sex shops". He is surprised at her reaction to it being sold in sex shops when in fact her film is composed of nothing but "one sex scene after another" without character or plot. He accuses her of wanting to cause a "fuss" and indicates that the question of whether her film is "art" and "pornography" is "academic", but what is allowed to be shown is a matter of "*law*":

> [...] Look –with all due respect– what did you think was going to happen? Your film is just one sex scene after another. There's no plot, there's no character, there's no nothing. So what did you expect? A tie-in with Burger King?
>
> No: You knew exactly what would happen –that it would cause a fuss, get you some attention. Well it's achieved all that. But whether your film is art, Miss Fontaine, or whether it's pornography, is academic: there are things you just *cannot legally* show here, and that isn't a matter of opinion, it's a matter of *law*." (249)

The Censor's view emphasizing the regulation of what can be shown according to the "law" brings to mind Foucault's claim that power over sex is realized through law:

> Power is essentially what dictates its law to sex. Which means first of all that sex is placed by power in a binary system: licit and illicit, permitted and forbidden. Secondly, power prescribes an "order" for sex that operates at the same time as a form of intelligibility: sex is to be deciphered on the basis of its relation to the law. And finally, power act by laying down power's hold on sex is maintained through language, or rather through the act of discourse that creates, from the very fact that it is articulated, a rule of law. It speaks, and that is the rule. The pure form of power resides in the function of the legislator;

> and its mode of action with regard to sex is of a juridico-discursive character (Foucault, 1998: 83-4)

Miss Fontaine asks the Censor whether her movie could be shown in movie clubs with "less cuts" and the Censor indicates that he would have to present a strong case (in the form of a recommendation) to the Director, but that it would be a waste of time and energy because "whole films have known to just disappear in this system." (249-250) Yet, she insists on trying her luck. The Censor gathering that she does not comprehend the impossibility of the situation feels the need to further clarify it:

> Has nobody explained this to you? (*Pause.*) D'you know what they call this place, Miss Fontaine? (*Pause.*) 'The *shit hole*.' All we get sent is the sickest, most extreme material. Ninety per cent of what we see is never legally released. Seven per cent of it results in criminal prosecution. About three per cent makes it back into the stream. (250)

The kind of material ("sickest", the "most extreme material") exemplified by the Censor show how marginal her movie is according to the classification system of the board and the destiny of her film sent to the "*shit hole*".

Since the Censor has been working at "bottom level" for six years without getting his due transfer, she suggests that a successful "recommendation" would be good for his advancement. He agrees, but states that in order to write a recommendation for her movie, he must first be convinced that it serves another purpose except "titillation" (251). Although he admits that some points in the film are unusual, it is still pornography:

> It's unusual. I'll admit. Using the same two actors throughout –not always ending in ejaculation, the order of the episodes…You might be subverting conventions –but at the end of the day, it's still hard-core pornography. […] Let's not pretend its groundbreaking art, as if I'm so green I won't know the difference. *That* is just a wee bit too *insulting.* (251)

He then confesses that he called her in again because he guessed that she thought he was a "prude", "a stuffed shirt" and "some sort of repressed, anally retentive apparantchik" (251). The topic of their conversation moves back to the topic of their last meeting and the Censor expresses his discomfort of her "outrageous behavior":

Censor: [...] I know you walked out of here the other night thinking you'd oh–so–cleverly shown me up for what I am–
Fontaine: I wondered when we'd get back to that.
Censor: Well yes because it's outrageous behaviour –I mean, what am I supposed to do, this woman I've never met before just starts taking her *clothes* off –I mean *anyone* would be a bit...*taken aback* by that, but to you it just confirms this smug, simplistic notion that anyone who does this job must be some...sort of...
Fontaine: Repressed anally retentive apparatchik? (251-252)

As the Censor has indicated in the above dialogue, Miss Fontaine's unconventional and marginal character makes him uncomfortable. He even tells her that he doesn't like being made a "fool" of. In return, she speaks to him in a manner that intimidates the Censor:

Fontaine: So that's why you called me back? To tell me I couldn't make a fool of you?
Censor: Yes –well, no –to tell you the –the reasons for –my decision–
Fontaine: I don't believe you.
Censor: Miss Fontaine–
Fontaine: You thought of me, didn't you?
Censor: No I didn't –well yes obviously I did –but not in the way–
Fontaine: The little seeds turned into a beanstalk like I knew they would. (252)

Although he claims that he didn't think of her "in that way" (romantically or sexually), she nevertheless exclaims: "The little seeds turned into a beanstalk like I knew they would" and puts her hand on his "crotch" (252). He feels uncomfortable and asks her not to do so, but she says "stop me.", continues to unzip his "fly", and smells her hand scented with talcum powder (253). While he states that getting sexually intimate with him won't help change her case, she claims that she knows him "a lot better than if I'd kept my shirt on." (253). Her last remark puts forth her philosophy about sex as a universal language. The Censor tells her how peculiar he finds her: "Miss Fontaine –I can honestly say– that you are one of the most bizarre people I've ever met–" (255). She speaks further to emphasize the importance of her movie to both herself and the world, but the Censor is not able to see what she sees: "That I don't see. I'm sorry, but I don't" (255). To this, Miss Fontaine, full of confidence, says: "You will" (6).

Her view of sex as a language and the importance she attaches to her movie make her seem "bizarre" to the Censor. In fact, people who hold views that do not comply to the set orders often do seem 'different', 'abnormal' and 'bizarre'. According to Thomas and Wareing, "People who question the dominant ideology often appear not to make any sense; what they say won't sound logical" and might even appear mad to anyone who does not hold that ideology (1999: 35). So while it is possible to question the dominant ideology, "there is often a price to be paid for doing so." (Thomas and Wareing, 1999: 35). As in this case, Miss Fontaine's ideas that defy the dominant order appear abnormal to the Censor because he does not share her views. In the course of the play, it will be seen that Miss Fontaine's work is not a piece of pornography but a representation of the beginning and development of an affair between a woman an a man, illustrating the stages of their relationship.

The two start editing the movie in scene 5. The Censor suggests beginning with the 'editing' of the last section, but she cannot understand why he wants to start with the end of the "story". The Censor, perceiving her movie only as pornography, sarcastically asks her what the plot is about. She tells him that it is a love story and then they start with the editing of scene 1 of the movie:

The Censor:	[...] That is scene one, isn't it? It's not a prologue? Man is masturbated by woman.
Fontaine:	Is that all you saw?
Censor:	There wasn't much else to see.
Fontaine:	Because your eye stops at the image.
Censor:	Most people's would.
Fontaine:	Because they've lost the ability to see. (257)

The Censor gets fed up and asks her what there is to "see" in a 'penis': "A penis is a penis, is it not?", but Miss Fontaine employs verbal violence by making reference to his wife's affair: "What about when it's your wife's lover's penis?" (257). After a short pause, the Censor warns her not to overpass the boundaries: "You're overstepping the mark, Miss Fontaine" (257).

The two continue watching the movie. The Censor asks her about the plot. Miss Fontaine prefers to guide him through the scene in order to make his own inferences, instead of telling him directly. She indicates that the male's penis hardens and softens repeatedly and asks him why that is. He suggests that there might be several possibilities such as the man being "camera-shy" or a lack of skill on the part of the woman. Instead of confirming his theory, she makes him put his finger "inside" her:

> *Fontaine:* Just hold it there. That's nice.
> *Pause.*
> All right: her strokes were erratic, random. She didn't know his rhythm. So that means...?
> *Pause.*
> So that *means*–?
> *Censor*: Uh –that means– they haven't...done it...before?
> *Fontaine*: (*nods*) This is the early part of the relationship. They're still learning about each other.
> Deeper.
> *He pushes his fingers deeper. She winces, laughing at his mistake.*
> Deeper into the *story*... (258-9)

Miss Fontaine inquires whether he noticed that "the man's penis only stiffens when he could see her stroking?" explaining his action by the fact that the man is "visual rather than tactile" (259). The Censor attentively asks her why he didn't "keep...looking at her?" She answers that he didn't want her to see that he watches a lot of pornography in his eyes and feel like a "whore" because he thinks that they might have a future together. The Censor is very interested and is eager to get more information:

> *Censor*: What else?
> *Fontaine*: You want me to tell you?
> *He nods.*
> Are you sure?
> *He nods.*

He's wary of people, solitary.
Parents were cerebral rather than physical and he's the same.
When he lived at home, his bedroom was next door to theirs.
One parent was very ill–
He *withdraws his fingers. Pause.*

Censor: Are you playing some sort of trick on me, Miss Fontaine?
Pause.
Has someone put you up to this?
Pause.
You were describing the character in your film?

Fontaine: Why? Does he sound familiar?
Pause. (260)

He wonders how people can understand all these details just by watching the film. Her reply makes reference to the Censor's earlier question "A penis is a penis" (257): "A penis is not just a penis". The Censor comments: "Well you might as well say a hatstand's not a bloody...hatstand!", giving a chance for Miss Fontaine to come to the crucial point of her argument about censorship: "The difference is we're allowed to see hatstands."(260). He tells her that she doesn't need genitalia to get her point across, explaining the necessity of 'censorship':

Censor: I'm just saying that...censorship isn't necessarily such...a bad thing. Without censorship, there'd be no allegory, no metaphor, no restraint– I mean– *Brief Encounter*[218] is a story about two lovers, but you don't have to see Trevor Howard's penis thrusting in and out of Celia Johnson, do you? (261)

According to the Censor, all sexual relations do not have to be shown on stage. Scene 7, however, illustrates that Miss Fontaine has been getting through to the Censor, who obviously holds conventional views about sex and censorship,

---

[218] The film was directed by David Lean and released in 1945. In the film, Laura Jesson, a housewife, meets doctor Alec Harvey at café at a railway station. Although they are both married to others, they gradually fall in love with each other. Although they know that realizing their love is impossible, they continue to meet every Thursday at the small café.

In this scene, the Censor places a bottle of wine and two glasses on the desk while awaiting her arrival, but then changes his mind. Miss Fontaine arrives an hour late, bringing him flowers. He tries to find something to put them in, and not succeeding in finding anything "*he lays them down on the desk*" (262). Then he brings out the wine with two glasses, but feels the need to explain his action by the fact that "it's after hours..." (262). She doesn't drink, he pours a glass for himself and tells her that it is hard for him to imagine her leading a normal ordinary life:

Censor: [...] You know it's a funny thing, Miss Fontaine, but I can't imagine you travelling here. I can't imagine you sitting on a bus or going shopping. Doing anything normal.
I suppose you've got friends you go out with, that sort of thing?
Fontaine shrugs.
Fontaine: You're not the only person that finds me bizarre.
Censor: Well, I wouldn't say *bizarre* exactly: you just take a bit to get used to.
Fontaine: And are you? Used to me?
Censor: I'm...getting there.
Pause. (263)

In return, Miss Fontaine questions how long he will continue 'censoring' in an aggressive manner:

Fontaine: So when are you going to hang up your scissors, Mr Censor? When people just give up having sex altogether? Will that be the job done?
Censor: No, no, not at all. We'll move on to humour next. Eventually we'll have eradicated all pleasure from the world. It's called Scottish expansionism.

She shows no sign of amusement.

No, nobody's trying to eradicate sex, Miss Fontaine.

> There's just a few of us who still believe it should be about love. I know that's terribly old-fashioned... (263)

Miss Fontaine claims that it is "not old-fashioned" but "stupid": "It's just completely stupid. Love is an emotion, sex is a means of expression. You can't restrict a language to one emotion. (264) He asks what the thing they have (Miss Fontaine touching his penis etc.) done expresses. She says it expresses "trust", "curiosity" and "many things" to which he answers "good, good". (264)

They continue with 'editing' "scene two" of the film. The Censor proceeds by consulting his clipboard; "intercourse", "Eight o six: erect penis–/Eight eighteen: inner labia-/Eight thirty-one: vaginal penetration" (264) and the position being "missionary", the most traditional position. When Miss Fontaine questions him about why they have chosen such a traditional position, the Censor guesses that it is because "they know each other better?". She is not satisfied with that answer, and the Censor frustrated about losing time, asks her to just tell him. Miss Fontaine explains that she wants him to "see" it for himself instead of simply "time" coding "every genital interplay" in the movie:

> *Fontaine*: Because I want you to *see*! You time code every single detail of genital interplay, but you don't see the *looks* that pass between them, the *breathing*, the *rhythms*–!
>
> *Censor*: Because those are not my *concerns*, Miss Fontaine! The looks, the breathing, the rhythms aren't the reason your film can't be passed! You have to be *practical* about it! It doesn't matter *how* sincere you are, we can't change the *law!* (265)

Although the Censor is still strict about obeying the law, different from his earlier remark in scene 3 ("it's a matter of *law*."), he now states that "we" "cant' change the *law*!" implying a change in his attitude and a certain sympathy towards her cause.

She proposes to have sex with him to prove her point, but he refuses. He first claims that it is not "right" to which Miss Fontaine employs a violent reaction:

> It's not right, it's not right. Your *job* isn't *right*, Mr Censor! Your *marriage* isn't *right*! And if we're talking about ethics, then buying that

> bottle of wine probably wasn't *right*, was it? For someone who's always talking about what's *right*, you seem to have an awful lot *wrong*! (265)

The Censor indicates that it is not about "ethics", but that he has been suffering from an infestation. But she is not the kind of woman to take 'no' for an answer without penetrating through to the core of the problem. She questions whether he got the infestation from his wife, tells him that she did not see him scratch himself even once, and asks him what is the reason which is "strong enough to use 'infestation' as a cover" (267). He then suggests that perhaps he is not attracted to her and she rejects such as possibility: "no". He resorts to other reasons such as the atmosphere being too "clinical", that he is not the kind of man that can do it "at the drop of a hat", but, she openly tells him that he is "impotent". He tries to justify himself by saying that he is not easily "*stimulated*" but she continues to make him uncomfortable by asking whether the size of his penis worries him or whether his wife's infidelities affected his "libido". He says that he was never a "physical" sort of person while his wife is rather "physical", indicating that he has chosen to stay with her knowing that she has had relations with other men. Miss Fontaine, not convinced by his arguments, bluntly says "You're impotent, aren't you." (269). He tells her that she is "about the most arrogant person" he ever met. Miss Fontaine gets saddened and tells him that he is not able to "see", but the Censor is apparently more enthusiastic about the project:

> *Censor:* But I *do* see! I know I'm making out that I don't – but I just want to give you the –you know– the other angle. I mean it's an interesting idea but you know –it's not exactly beyond my grasp. And you have a point. You do.
> I think we should try to get it through.
>
> *She looks at him, dubious.*
>
> Really. I think I can even draft something up for the next session. I just need to watch it again. Just let me do that. (270)

And the Censor presents his 'recommendation' to Miss Fontaine in Scene 9:

[…](*Reads*) 'Miss Fontaine's intention is to depict the course of a relationship, from courtship, from courtship to separation, by focusing exclusively on the couple's sexual activity.

'Thus, the masturbation and oral sex denote courtship, and intercourse in the missionary position symbolises a *traditional* vow of commencement. During this stage of infatuation, with the future uncertain, the sexual activities are essentially conservative.
'But as trust deepens, and a sense of ownership develops, the activities become more various and individualised, the bodies more objectified.' – Yes?

She remains impassive.

All right, I don't know about this, listen to this: 'An aggressive note is introduced as the couple pass through their first betrayal. –'

'This disillusionment opens a phase of experimentation now more animalistic, more overtly passionate and more stereotypically divided along crude gender lines.

'*But*– whilst this new element of distrust invigorates the sexuality, the spiritual basis of the relationship erodes until copulation becomes their only cement.

'As a result, we enter the realms of depersonalisation: the sexuality intensifies, becoming more abusive, more fetishistic, a rehearsal for separation. And even after this separation, they still participate in sporadic erotic encounters until new partners are found.

'*Finally*' –and this bit took me ages to get– 'we see each partner participate in solitary acts of masturbation, their memories of each other now just the fuel of their fantasies.'

–Now *that* sounds like art, doesn't it? (271-272)

At this point in the play, the Censor has moved considerably beyond the official discourse related to pornography and has almost reached the point where his language violates the limits of that discourse.

The Censor is pleased with himself, but she still says 'Is that all you saw?' (272). She indicates that he only wrote down what was already obvious asking him where the "characters", "the subtext", "the details" are. The Censor becomes furious: "The character, the –?!! Are you being serious?! It's two people, on a bed– wanking and shagging and sucking each other off!! That's all it is! There isn't even any dialogue!!" (273). But, she states that he does not "see it". He tells her that he can't help her anymore, but she claims that he must because the movie is important to the world:

> You think the world will stay this way?
> You think this is the highest level we'll reach?
> Read the newspapers, Mr Censor: artificial insemination, cloning, male contraception–
> Very soon, sex will be completely divorced from reproduction.
> You think it'll just disappear?
> No, It'll be free to evolve into the most sophisticated level of interaction attainable: a completely universal non-verbal language. [...] No more repression! No more witch-hunts- A world absolutely without guilt or shame! And one by one all the institutions that've got fat on that shame- the church, the courts, the social services, even this rotten building we're in now– they'll fall, Mr Censor! They'll come crashing down!
>
> And the people we dare to call perverts and deviants –the victims of this war– the good humane people we've criminalized and traumatised, they'll be recognized for what they truly are: Visionaries! *(Pause)* Visionaries.(273-274)

Her explanation shows her defiance against authority and stands in line with Foucault's criticism of sexual repression exercised by social institutions. She indicates that with "artificial insemination, cloning, male conception", the function of sex will lose its function in reproduction and the discourse exerted by institutions such as the Church, the courts and social services for the repression and control of sex will be eliminated. She points out that her movie is as "rich", "moving" and as "detailed" as *Brief Encounter*, which contains no scenes of intercourse. She also claims that her movie is a symbol of future freedom:

> *Fontaine*: This film is the first artifact of a truly liberated future. And the day it can be shown in every multiplex in the land to every man, woman and child is the day we'll know the human race has come to age. (273)

The point she is making here can be associated with Foucault's assertion that speaking on sex in forbidden terms is "a deliberate transgression":

> If sex is repressed, that is, condemned to prohibition, nonexistence, and silence, then the mere fact the one is speaking about it has the appearance of a deliberate transgression. A person who holds forth in such language places himself to a certain point extent outside the reach of power; he upsets established law; he somehow anticipates the coming freedom. When they allude to it, the first, the first demographers and psychiatrists of the nineteenth century thought it advisable to excuse themselves for asking their readers to dwell on matters so trivial and base. But for decades now, we have found it difficult to speak on the subject without striking a different pose: our tone of voice shows that we know we are being subversive, and we ardently conjure away the present and appeal to the future, whose day will be hastened by the contribution we believe we are making. Something that smacks of revolt, of promised freedom, of the coming age of a different law, slips easily into this discourse of sexual oppression. (Foucault, 1998: 6-7)

Miss Fontaine then explains why she is not wholly satisfied with the Censor's interpretation of her film:

> Now, it's good that you see the relationship, but that's only the first level. Could you tell, for instance, that the man's previous girlfriend was Asian? That the woman had been brought up in care? Could you see any of that?

Long pause

Censor: No (*Pause*) I couldn't.
Fontaine: It's there, right in front of your eyes. If you can see beyond the image. (274)

To prove her point, she is determined to resolve his 'sexual' case and 'break' all his defenses and justifications. He asks her why it is so important for him to see, indicating that he does not have any power at the board. She "*kneels down in front of him, puts her hand on his crotch.*" and attacks him verbally in order to apply her philosophy and convince him of his importance. She tells him that she was right about his being impotent and about his parents. He says that she's only making a "guess" about his impotence and that some-one has told her about his parents' illness (275). However, she is determined to resolve his case:

Fontaine: [...] You have a fantasy you're ashamed of.

You think of your wife as this deeply sexual being but you know even she wouldn't approve of it. Maybe you even asked her to do it once.

Yes and she was disgusted, wasn't she? And if this highly sexual woman could be so disgusted, who else would ever be different?
[...]
If it was sado-masochistic you could easily indulge it with prostitutes, and anyway you're visual not tactile. This is about watching. Watching something taboo. Somewhere in your childhood, you saw this thing and had your first strong sexual feeling. You haven't buried it. (275-6)

Like a therapist, she makes a detailed psychological analysis of the Censor. Her verbal control of the situation breaks him down. While Stanley screams at the final point of the inquisition in *The Birthday Party*, the Censor gets sexually aroused. Subsequently, in Scene 10, the two make love (267-7). Miss Fontaine's therapy has produced positive results.

On their next meeting which takes place in scene 12, she says that she is going to an instillation at an art gallery in New York. The Censor, who has just recently become revolutionized through her verbal attack and his sexual experience, tries to touch her, but she seems lost in thought. He tells her that he will sort it out with his wife, she expresses her consent and leaves. This scene shows that the Censor has changed from a subject with 'censored' thoughts and fantasies to one that has started to discover and accept his desires.

The Censor's confident attitude is also reflected on his relationship with his wife. In Scene 13, the Censor talks to his wife is in a more assertive manner and they actually have a long conversation. The scene starts with all the short conversations they had in scene 1, scene 4, scene 6, scene 8 and scene 11 placed one after another up till the line where his wife asks him to say something. He keeps silent and she tells him that they will pretend that nothing has happened and hope for it to go away like "always" (283). But this time the Censor breaks the silence: "No, I'll say something." He starts speaking by stating that "There's no point in meeting him [her lover]". He is in the verge uttering his true feeling which he 'censored' :"There's no point in meeting him because–" (283) when his wife, reading the newspaper, points out that "Shirley" Fontaine, "working on an exhibition– whose 'controversial film which was recently banned by the Board of Classification'" was murdered. She indicates that Miss Fontaine was beaten to death at a hotel room in New York. (284). The wife then asks him if he met her and he says "Um....no...not really...I...um..." (284). He tries to control himself but the tears come. She thinks that he is sad about her infidelity and comforts him: 'We'll work it out. We always do'.

On one hand, scenes 12 and 13 illustrate the lifting of censorship from the Censor's life. On the other hand, Miss Fontaine, a misfit, has been eliminated by a murder, the cause of which remains a mystery. Authorities that disagree with her ways or people she had sexual dealings with may be reasonable for her death, but what matters is that she has been eliminated. According to Sierz, she is "a sexual Joan of Arc", a "fanatic" on a mission to show her film to the world because she believes that sex will soon be completely divorced from reproduction and therefore, will be free to evolve into a completely universal non-verbal language. The person resisting, questioning and working against the dominant order has been eliminated. Nevertheless, although she is no longer alive, her ideas have left an important impact on the Censor who in scene 14 "*sits in his office, watching the film. And, after a while, he smiles*" (285). Thus, although she dies, she is able to make him see beyond the obvious images.

To sum up, the Censor is an archetype representing the values of the Board of Classification and the 'system' based on 'censorship' and 'prohibitions'. The Censor, who is not even given an individual name, is an example of how the 'system' changes individuals into stereotypes representing concepts, ideologies and regimes. Neilson himself defines the Censor as a metaphor for all the things that individuals "hold down" and "cut out" of their minds (Sierz, 2000:83). Miss Fontaine, in contrast, is an 'individual' and free soul who rejects being dominated by the system and puts forth a theory based on sexuality that stands in contrast to it. Miss Fontaine exerts verbal violence on the Censor through the use of the forbidden language concerning sex by producing verbal shock, digging deep into 'indecent' topics which he has for long repressed or censored. Miss Fontaine's aim in exerting verbal violence on the Censor is to enable him to 'see' beyond the existing categories, definitions, rules and value systems imposed upon individuals as part of power strategies in the society he lives in. Her employment of linguistic violence that violates the accepted restrictions concerning the discussion of sex, contributes to her determination to do away with such values in the process of changing the Censor from a 'standardized' human being into a unique individual who is able to come to terms with his 'non-standard' state of being.

The result is that, the ethical point of view on which the Censor's act depends has been de-constructed by an opposing/alternative discourse that eliminates the validity of the 'norm' set by censorship.

CONCLUSION

In accordance with its aim to study verbal violence (both as a sophisticated means of persuasion and manipulation, and as a means of verbal assault and verbal shock) as a construction of authority in Renaissance and contemporary English drama, this book has focused on the reading of dramatic texts representing different approaches towards the manifestation of power through language. With this purpose, the texts have been handled in two parts.

Part I has been devoted to the study of verbal violence in the form of rhetoric in Renaissance dramatic dialogue, treated according to various Classical theories on language and rhetoric. In ancient times, philosophers such as Plato, Aristotle, Cicero and Quintilian produced works on the effective use of language by the mastering of the techniques of 'rhetoric'. They also dwelled on the relationship of language with 'truth' and the potential danger of the use of rhetoric by persons lacking 'good' character. The Renaissance philosopher Niccolo Machiavelli stressed the importance of good verbal skills in the gaining and maintaining of power by rulers. In contrast to that of the Classical writers, his emphasis was, however, on the use of language to trick, manipulate and dominate others in every way possible. Accordingly, a historical survey of rhetoric, with special reference to Classical texts on rhetoric has been made in the first chapter of Part I.

Part I, chapter 2 has focused on Christopher Marlowe's *Tamburlaine the Great, Part I,* the first English play to have been written in blank-verse and chapter 3 on William Shakespeare's *Richard III,* a masterpiece in the use of rhetoric in blank-verse. These two plays have been especially selected because, although they both deal with fighting and war, violence in both is exerted through verbal means instead of any physical action represented on the stage. In these plays, verbal violence is employed by characters in the form of rhetoric in order to attain power, to trick, manipulate and abuse others.

In *Tamburlaine, Part I,* Christopher Marlowe glorifies rhetoric and draws a parallel between rhetorical skills and military power, and between 'word' and 'sword'. In fact, all of Tamburlaine's battles are fought verbally, rather than physically on the stage. The rulers who are more competent as rhetoricians, get the upper hand, and destroy opponents with low verbal competence. Although almost all of the characters in the play use a rhetorical style to a certain extent, they do not have the same degree of skill. Tamburlaine is singled out as having an extensive ability for rhetoric (and warfare) to the point of persuading both the Persian lords and Cosroe (brother to the Persian king Mycetes) to join him against kingly brother, then manipulating the Persian lords into joining him against Cosroe, winning in term the heart of Zenocrate (daughter of the Soldan of Egypt) and, finally proves his ultimate power by beating an opponent like Bajazeth, who matches him in verbal skills and military power.

In William Shakespeare's *Richard III*, the second Renaissance play studied in Part I, Richard as the protagonist and the dominant speaker, exploits the frontiers of deception, and acts out multiple characters, such as the 'reliable brother', 'passionate lover', 'offended friend' and 'honest courtier' through an elaborate use of rhetoric in the Machiavellian sense. In this way, he is able to trick others, so as to remove the obstacles on his path to the English throne. As in *Tamburlaine, Part I,* Shakespeare's drama lacks any scenes of physical fighting (with the exception of a few final scenes on the battlefield) although it depicts an episode in the War of Roses, a tragic civil war which has caused an awful amount of bloodshed for many years.

In the play, the rhetorical skill presented is directly proportional to the intellectual capacity of the main character. Thus, although Richard is able to manipulate others through his linguistic virtuosity in the first half of the play, both his intellectual power and rhetorical skills begin to decline after he becomes king. When, in fear of losing his crown, he becomes preoccupied with eliminating potential threats against his kingship, he also loses his control ever his speech. On the other hand, as his rhetorical skill diminishes, so does his power. It follows that young Richmond, who has a claim to the English throne, uses rhetoric in a positive moral attitude and is thus able to prove his superiority to Richard, both verbally and physically. In *Richard III*, therefore, political power is also identified and matched with a powerful verbal style.

While the Classical theories on the concept and practice of rhetorical language have served as the basic guideline for the study of the two verse plays in Part I, those studied in Part II have been associated with the social theories of the French philosopher Michel Foucault on power as a social force as included in his works *History of Sexuality, Civilization and Madness* and *Discipline and Punish* illustrating the function of knowledge, discourse and social institutions in creating standards, controlling and shaping subjects. In addition, Andersen's book *Power and the Word* and Fairclough's *Language and Power* have also been used because they emphasize the connection between social power and language, which is at times implied by

Foucault. The same chapter also includes an introduction to contemporary English plays exemplifying Foucault's theories such as Stoppard's *Every Boy Deserves a Favor* (1997), Churchill's *Vinegar Tom* (1976) and Whiting's *The Devils* (1961), and continuing with a general overview of the physical and verbal violence in contemporary English drama with reference to plays such as Osborne's *Look Back in Anger* (1956), Bond's *Lear* (1971) and *Saved* (1965), Orton's *Entertaining Mrs Sloane* (1964) McDonagh's *The Cripple of Inishmaan* (1997) and Sarah Kane's *Blasted* (1995).

Part II includes a study of verbal violence in three contemporary English plays in prose: Bernard Shaw's *Pygmalion*, Harold Pinter's *The Birthday Party* and Anthony Neilson's *The Censor.* Similar to Part I, contemporary English plays containing little or no physical violence have been chosen so as to avoid any convergence of physical and linguistic violence. The plays selected for this purpose demonstrate forms of man's domination and subjugation through language. In these plays, institutions and related discourses function to set up norms or standards against which people are judged and punished.

In contemporary English plays, the violence of language not only contributes to the creation of a realistic spectacle, but also –and more importantly– to the process of replacing free critical thinking by automatic preconceived patterns of thought and speech. In turn, such pre-constructed thought and speech function to re-shape, redefine and transform individuals' character and do away with their autonomy. In these plays, linguistic violence is employed to promote conformity to social order. Language, which is a part of the legal and social structures, forces the individual to comply with socially accepted norms set by those in power. This acceptance, on the part of the individual, manifests itself as voluntary obedience to standardization. In both *Pygmalion* and *The Birthday Party,* language functions to violate and destroy man's autonomy and individuality. The characters Eliza and Stanley are victimized through imposed or inherited verbal structures of standardization reflected through language. They go through a form of verbal re-construction which re-shapes and reduces them to products of the dominant linguistic order. In contrast, the linguistic violence employed by Miss Fontaine in *The Censor* functions to deconstruct the dominant order of the state, and change the 'standardized' and 'censored' Censor to an 'individual' coming to terms with his own non-standard characteristics.

Pygmalion illustrates the transformation of Eliza as a result of the instruction on phonetics that she receives from Professor Higgins. At the beginning, her non-standard Cockney accent makes her an outcast of the system and subjected to verbal abuse by Higgins. As Eliza's education in phonetics advances and command of languages increases, she is both empowered and alienated. Despite her success at the Embassy reception, Eliza remains a declassed flower girl who will never be completely accepted in upper-middle class British society. Furthermore, she continues to be verbally bullied by Higgins. Although she is finally able to stand up against Higgins, the ideas and values making up her arguments are only a kind of 'parroting' of those taught by her instructor. Thus, although Higgins' intentions in educating Eliza did not aim at forcing her to conformity with the upper-middle class milieu, she is nevertheless 'standardized' through her instruction in the proper use of the English language.

The process of 'standardization' is taken to an extreme level in *The Birthday Party,* where language functions to torture and destroy Stanley, a so-called nonconformist, so as to orient him towards full conformity to accepted norms. Goldberg and McCann, the linguistic torturers, employ the language of authority, characterized by a style full of 'bookish' metaphors, figures of speech, long words and sentences, cliché phrases and a combination of legal, medical, political and popular jargon that work to obscure, and create a sense of chaos rather than clarifying or producing 'meaning'. Thus, verbal violence in Pinter's play is realized through the incertitude of language realized by the techniques that stand in full opposition to the ones mentioned by Orwell for clarity of expression in his essay "Politics and the English Language".

In Pinter's play, the power of authority is exercised and transmitted through daily language. Goldberg and McCann, who turn out to be the agents of authority (of some kind), use verbal violence to control, manipulate and rob Stanley of his individuality. In fact, they never employ physical violence, even when Stanley tries to get out of their sight. McCann threateningly requests him to stay, but does not force him to do so. Although no physical violence has been exerted upon him, Stanley is reduced to a mumbling subject all the same. It is apparent that Stanley's final position is that of a person who is ready to take in and conform to the rules and regulations of the dominant order represented by the language of authority practiced by Goldberg and McCann.

The Censor, on the other hand, stands in contrast to *Pygmalion* and *The Birthday Party* in that verbal violence in this play is used to question and deconstruct authority and to defy order. The Censor, who is an archetype representing the values of the Board of Classification and the 'system' based on 'censorship' and 'prohibitions' at the beginning of the play, experiences an 'awakening' due to the verbal harassment exerted on him by Miss Fontaine, a film-maker.

Miss Fontaine's linguistic manipulation includes verbal violence in the form of daring questions, foul language and slang in order to deconstruct the existing 'system'. As a result, she enables the Censor to 'see' beyond the existing categories, definitions, rules and value systems, transforming him from a 'standardized' human being to a unique 'individual' who is able to come to terms with his 'non-standard' ways.

The plays discussed in this study have helped to signify the fact that language, in representing the process of power struggle on the stage, can serve as powerful a weapon as that produced by physical force. Through its institutions, authority works to create 'discourse' that is spread by and through language. In everyday life, this fact is hardly noticed since the destructive effects of language are less recognized than those caused by physical violence. It is the particular characteristic of dramatic language and action on the stage that brings this fact to the foreground. Thus, verbal violence in Renaissance English plays is matched with military and political power, while in contemporary English plays it functions to construct authority or to resist it.

SOURCES

A-PRIMARY SOURCES

ARDEN, John. "Sergeant Musgrave's Dance". *Arden Plays: One*. London: Eyre Methuen: 1960. 9-111.

ARISTOTLE. *Aristotle on Rhetorics: A Theory of Civil Discourse.* Trans. George A. Kennedy. New York: Oxford University Press, 1991.

- - -. *Treatise on Rhetoric.* Trans.Theodore Buckley. New York: Prometheus Books, 1995.

AYCKBOURN, Alan. *The Norman Conquests.* Harmondsworth: Penguin Books, 1975.

BECKETT, Samuel. *The Unnamable.* Trans. Samuel Beckett. New York: Grove Press, 1958.

- - -. *Waiting for Godot.* New York: Chelsea House Publishers, 1987.

BOND, Edward. *Plays: One; Saved, Early Morning, The Pope's Wedding.* London: Methuen, 1977.

- - -. *Lear.* London: Eyre Methuen Ltd., 1979.

CHURCHILL, Caryl. "Vinegar Tom". *Plays: One.* London: Methuen Drama, 1985. 127-181.

CICERO. *De Inventione, De Optimo Genere Oratorum, Topica.* Trans. H. M. Hubbell. London: Harvard University Press, 1993.

- - -. *De Oratore Books I-II.* Trans. E. W. Sutton. London: Harvard University Press, 1996.

FOUCAULT, Michel. *Discipline and Punish: The Birth of Prison.* Trans. Alan Sheridan. London: Penguin Books, 1995.

- - -. *The Foucault Reader.* Ed. Paul Rabinow. London: Penguin Books, 1991.

- - -. *Madness and Civilization.* New York: Trans. Richard Howard. Vintage Books, 1973.

- - -. *The History of Sexuality: The Use of Pleasure.* Trans. Robert Hurley. New York: Vintage Books, 1990.

- - -. *The History of Sexuality: The Will to Knowledge.* Trans. Robert Hurley. London: Penguin Books, 1998.

- - -.*Aesthetic, Method, and Epistemology*. Trans. Robert Huxley. New York: The New York Press, 1998.

KANE, Sarah. "Blasted". *Complete Plays.* London: Methuen Drama, 2001. 1-63.

MACHIAVELLI, Niccolo. *The Prince and the Discourses.* Toronto: Random House, Inc., 1950.

- - -.*The Art of War.* Trans. Ellis Farneworth. New York: A Da Capo Paperback, 1965.

- - -. *The Prince.* Trans. George Bull. Harmondsworth: Penguin Books, 1995.

MARLOWE, Christopher. *Christopher Marlowe: The Complete Plays.* Harmondsworth: Penguin Books, 1980.

- - -. *Tamburlaine the Great.* Manchester: Manchester University Press, 1981.

MCDONAGH, Martin. *The Beauty Queen of Leenane.* New York: Dramatists Play Service Inc., 1996.

- - -. *The Cripple of Inishmaan.* New York: Vintage Books, 1997.

MENANDER. *Plays and Fragments.* Trans. and Ed. Norma Miller. Harmondsworth: Penguin Classics, 1987.

NEILSON, Anthony. "The Censor". *Plays: 1.* London: Methuen Drama, 1998. 243-285.

ORTON, Joe. "Entertaining Mr Sloane". *Penguin Plays: New English Dramatists 8.* Harmondsworth: Penguin Books, 1965. 159-236.

ORWELL, George. "Politics and the English Language". *The Orwell Reader: Fiction, Essays and Reportage.* U.S.A: Mariner Books: 1961. 355-367.

OSBORNE, John. *Look Back in Anger.* London: Faber, 1956.

PINTER, Harold. *The Birthday Party.* London: Samuel French, 1959.

- - -. *Mountain Language.* London: Faber and Faber, 1988.

- - -. *Homecoming.* London: Faber and Faber, 1991.

- - -. *Various Voices Harold Pinter: Prose, Poetry, Politics.* New York: Grove Press, 1998.

- - -. "The Caretaker". *The Essential Pinter.* New York, Grove Press: 2006. 103-181.

- - -. "One for the Road". *The Essential Pinter.* New York, Grove Press: 2006. 319-337.

PLATO, *Gorgias.* Trans. W. Hamilton. Harmondsworth: Penguin Books, 1960.

- - -. *Philebus.* Trans. Robin A.H. Waterfield. London: Penguin Books, 1982.

- - -. *Symposium and Phaedrus.* Trans. Benjamin Jowell. New York: Dover Publications, Inc., 1993.

PUTTENHAM, George. *The Arte of Poesie Book I.* London: Richard Field, 1589.

QUINTILIAN. *Institutio Oratoria I-III.* Trans. H. E. Butler. London: Harvard

University Press, 1996.
- - -. *Institutio Oratoria IV-VI.* Trans. H. E. Butler. London: Harvard University Press, 1996.
- - -. *Institutio Oratoria VII-IX.* Trans. H. E. Butler. London: Harvard University Press, 1996.
- - -. *Institutio Oratoria X-XII.* Trans. H. E. Butler. London: Harvard University Press, 1998.
SENECA, Lucius Annaeus. "Medea". *Roman Drama.* Trans. Samuel Lieberman and Frank Justus Miller. New York: Bantam Books, 1964. 349-375.
- - -.*Four Tragedies and Octavia.* Trans. E. F. Watling. London: Penguin Books, 1966.
- - -. *Seneca, the Tragedies Volume I.* Ed. and Trans. David R. Slavitt. Baltimore: Johns Hopkins University Press, 1992.
SHAKESPEARE, William. "*Henry VI, Part* 3". *The Complete Works of William Shakespeare.* Ed. W. J. Craig. London: Pordes, 1914. 609-644.
- - -. *King Lear.* Ed. Eric A. McCann. Toronto: Academic Press, 1964.
- - -. *King Richard III.* Ed. E. A. J. Honigmann. Harmondsworth: Penguin Books, 1985.
- - -. "Julius Caesar". *Three Roman Plays.* Ed. Norman Sanders. Harmondsworth: Penguin Books, 1994.
- - -. *Hamlet.* Ed. T.J.B. Spencer. Harmondsworth: Penguin Books, 1996.
- - -. *King Richard III.* Ed. Anthony Hammond. London: Methuen & Co. Ltd., 2006.
SHAW, Bernard. *The Intelligent Woman's Guide to Socialism and Capitalism.* New York: Brentanos, *1928*
- - -. "Mrs. Warren's Profession". *Plays Unpleasant.* Middlesex, Penguin Books: 1948. 179-283.
- - -. *Pygmalion.* Harmondsworth: Penguin Books, 1957.
SOPHOCLES. *The Three Theban Plays. Antigone, Oedipus the King, Oedipus at Colonus.* Trans. Robert Fagles. Harmondsworth: Penguin Books, 1984.
STOPPARD, Tom. *Every Good Boy Deserves Favor and Professional Foul.* New York: Grove Press: 1978.
WESKER, Arnold. "Roots". *The Wesker Trilogy Volume 1.* Harmondsworth: Penguin Books, 1979. 79-151.
WHITING, John. *The Devils.* London: Heinemann Educational Books,1978.

B-SECONDARY SOURCES

ABRAMS, M. H. *A Glossary of Literary Terms*. London: Brace College Publishers, 1999.

AIJMER, Goran and Jon ABBINK. *Meanings of Violence: A Cross Cultural Perspective*. New York: Oxford, 2000.

ANDERSEN, Roger. *The Power and the Word*. London: Paladin, 1988.

ARTUN, Unsal. "Genişletilmiş Bir Siddet Tipolojisi". *Cogito*. 6-7. Istanbul: Yapi Kredi Yayinlari, 1996. 29-36.

BANKS, R. A. *Drama and Theatre Arts*. London: Hodder and Stoughton. 1986.

BENDER, David and Bruno Leone. *Censorship: Opposing Viewpoints*. San Diego: Greenhaven Press, Inc., 1990.

BERGER, Arthur Asa. *Narratives in Popular Culture, Media and Everyday Life*. London: SAGE Publications Inc., 1997.

BERGER, Fred R. *Freedom, Rights and Pornography: A Collection of Papers by Fred R. Berger*. Ed. Bruce Russell. London: Kluwer Academic Publishers, 1990.

BERST, Charles A. *Bernard Shaw and the Art of Drama*. Urbana: University of Illinois Press, 1973.

BIRRINGER, Johannes H. "Marlowe's Violent Stage: "Mirrors" of Horror in Tamburlaine". *ELH* 51.2 (1984). 219-239.

BIZELL, Patricia and Bruce HERZBERG. *The Rhetorical Tradition*. Boston: Bedford Books of St. Martins Press, 1900.

BOYLE, A.J. *Tragic Seneca: An essay in the theatrical tradition*. London: Routledge, 1997.

BROOKE, Nicholas. "Linguistic Contrasts in Richard III". *Critical Essays on Shakespeare's Richard III*. Ed. Hugh Macrae Richmond. New York: G. K. Hall, 1999. 161-169.

BROWN, J.A.C. *Techniques of Persuasion: From Propaganda to Brainwashing*. Harmondsworth: Penguin Books, 1963.

BROWN, John Russell. "Words and Silence". *Harold Pinter: The Birthday Party, The Caretaker, The Homecoming*. London: Macmillan, 1986. 87-99.

BURKE, Kenneth. *The Rhetoric of Motives*. New York: George Braziller, 1955.

CAMURDAN, Esen. *Şiddet ile Oynamak*. Istanbul: Mitos Boyut Yayınları, 2004.

CLARE, Janet. "Marlowe's 'theatre of cruelty' ". *Constructing Christopher*

Marlowe. Ed. J. A. Downie and J. T. Parnell. Cambridge: Cambridge University Press, 2000. 74-87.

CLEMEN, Wolfgang H. *Shakespeare's Soliloquies*. Trans. Charity Scott Stokes. London: Methuen & Co. Ltd., 1987.

- - -. "Richard III: Act I, Scene One". *Critical Essays on Shakespeare's Richard III*. Ed. Hugh Macrea Richmond. New York: G. K. Hall & Co., 1999, 64-72.

CORRIGER, Robert Willough. *Classical Tragedy. Greek and Roman*. New York: Applause Theatre Books, 1990.

CRANE, W. G. *Wit and Rhetoric in the Renaissance*. New York: Columbia University Press, 1937.

CRAWFORD, Fred D. "Shaw's British Inheritors". *Shaw and Other Playwrights*. Ed. John A. Bertolini. Pennsylvania: The Pennsylvania State University Press, 1993. 101-111.

CROMPTON, Louis. *Shaw the Dramatist*. Lincoln: University of Nebraska Press, 1970.

CUDDON, J.A (ed.) *The Penguin Dictionary of Literary Terms and Literary Theory*, Oxford: Blackwell Publishers Ltd., 1998.

CUNNINGHAM, J. S. and Roger WARREN. "Tamburlaine the Great Rediscovered". *Marlowe: Tamburlaine the Great, Edward the Second and The Jew of Malta*. London: Macmillan, 1991. 127-140.

DILLON AND GERGEL. *The Greek Sophists*. London: Penguin Books 2003.

DERRIDA, Jacques. *Positions*. Trans. Alan Buss. London: Athlore Press, 1981.

DUKORE, Bernard F. *Bernard Shaw, Playwright Aspects of Shavian Drama*. Colombia: University of Missouri Press, 1973.

EINSTEIN, Albert. *Ideas and Opinions*. New York: Crown Publications, 1986.

ENRIGHT, D. J. and Ernst De Chickera. *English Critical Texts: 16th Century to 20th Century*. London: Oxford University Press, 1962.

ESSLIN, Martin. *The Theatre of the Absurd*. London: Methuen, 2001.

EVANS, Ifor. *The Language of Shakespeare's Plays*. Westport: Greenwood Press Publishers, 1964.

FAIRCLOUGH, Norman. *Language and Power*. Essex: Pearson Education Limited., 2001.

FOWLES, Roger (ed.). *A Dictionary of Modern Critical Terms*. New York: Routledge, 1987.

GALBRAITH, John Kenneth. *The Anatomy of Power*. Boston: Houghton Mittlen Company, 1985.

GIBBS, A. M. *The Art and Mind of Shaw*. Macmillan: Gill and Macmillan, 1983.

GILBERT, Anthony J. *Shakespeare's Dramatic Language*. Lewiston: The Edwin Mellen Press, 1997.

GRANDE, Troni Y. *Marlovian Tragedy: The Play of Dilation*. London: Associated University Presses, 1999.

GREGOR, McLennan, David HELD and Stuart HALL. *The Idea of the Modern State*. Philadelphia: Open University Press, 1987.

HALLIDAY, F. E. *A Shakespeare Companion 1564-1964*. Harmondsworth: Penguin Books, 1964.

HASSEL, R. Chris (Jr.). *Songs of Death: Performance, Interpretation, and the Text of Richard III*. London: University of Nebraska Press, 1987.

HAY, Malcolm and Philip ROBERTS. *Bond: a study of His Plays*. Eyre Methuen: London, 1980.

HEIDEGGER, Martin. *On the Way to Language*. Trans. Peter D. Hertz. New York: HarperSanFransisco, 1971.

HONEY, John. *Does Accent Matter? The Pygmalion Factor*. London: Faber and Faber, 1989.

HUGHES, Nancy Scheper. "Sacred Wounds": Making Sense of Violence. *Drama and Violence*. Theatre Symposium, Vol 7. Tuscaloosa: The University of Alabama Press: 1999. 7-31.

HUSSEY, S. S. *The literary language of Shakespeare*. London: Longman, 1982.

JARDINE, Lisa. *Francis Bacon: Discovery and the Art of Discourse*. Cambridge: Cambridge University Press, 1975.

JONGH, Nicholay de. *Politics, Prudery and Perversions: The censoring of the English Stage 1901-1968*. London: Methuen, 2000.

KAHN, Victoria. *Machiavellian Rhetoric: from the Counter Reformation to Milton*. Princeton: Princeton University Press, 1994

KELLY, Michael (ed.). *Critique and Power: Recasting the Foucault/Habermas Debate*. London: The MIT Press, 1994.

KENNEDY, Andrew. "In Search of Language". *Harold Pinter: The Birthday Party, The Caretaker, The Homecoming*. London: Macmillan, 1986. 61-71.

KENNEDY, George. *The Art of Rhetoric in the Roman World*. New Jersey: Princeton University Press, 1972.

KNIGHTS, L. C. *Shakespeare: The Histories*. London: Longmans, Green & Co. Ltd, 1965.

LANHAM, Richard A. *A Handbook of Rhetorical Terms*. London: University of California Press, 1991.

LECERCLE, Jean-Jacques. *The Violence of Language*. New York: Routledge, 1990.

LEVENSON, Jill L. " 'Working Words': The Verbal Dynamic of Tamburlaine". *"A Poet and a filthy Play-maker" New Essays on Christopher Marlowe*. New York: AMS Press, Inc., 1988. 99-115.

MALKIN, Jeannette R. *Verbal Violence in Contemporary Drama: From Handke to Shepard*. Cambridge: Cambridge University Press, 1992.

MASSINGHAM, H. M. "H. W. Massingham, in an initial notice, *Nation* [18 April 1914, vol. XV, 3, 93]". *Shaw: The Critical Heritage*. Ed. T. F. Evans. London: Routledge, 1976. 226-9.

MCADAM, Ian. *The Irony of Identity: Self and Imagination in the Drama of Christopher Marlowe*. London: Associated University Presses, 1999.

MC CORMICK, Samuel. "Earning One's Inheritance: Rhetorical Criticism, Everyday Talk, and the Analysis of Public Discourse". *Quarterly Journal of Speech* Vol. 89.2 (2003). 109-131.

MCDONALD, Russ. *The Bedford Companion to Shakespeare: An Introduction with Documents*. Boston: Bedford Books, 1996.

MISRA, Chittaranjan. *Harold Pinter, the Dramatist*. New Delhi: Creative, 1992.

MORGAN, Margery M. *Bernard Shaw II: 1907-1950*. Berkshire: Profile Books, 1992.

NAISMITH, Bill. *Harold Pinter: The Caretaker, The Birthday Party, The Homecoming*. London: Faber and Faber, 2000.

NIGEL, Alexander. "The Play of Ideas". *Modern Critical Interpretations. George Bernard Shaw's Pygmalion*. Ed. Harold Bloom. New York: Chelsea House Publishers, 1988. 19-44.

OHLANDER, Stephen. *Dramatic Suspense in Euripides' and Seneca's Medea*. New York: P.Lang, 1989.

OUSBY, Ian. *The Wordsworth Companion to Literature in English*. Cambridge: Cambridge University Press, 1988.

PARR, Johnstone. "Tamburlaine's Malady". *Marlowe: Tamburlaine the Great, Edward the Second and The Jew of Malta*. London: Macmillan, 1991, 113-127.

PARROTT, Thomas MARC and Robert Hamilton BALL. *A Short View of Elizabethan Drama*. New York: Charles Scribner's Sons: 1958.

PLATT, Peter G. "Shakespeare and Rhetorical Culture". *A Companion to Shakespeare*. Ed. David Scott Kastan. Malden: Blackwell Publishers, 1999. 277-296.

PRENTICE, Penelope. *The Pinter Ethic: The Erotic Aesthetic*. New York: Garland Publishing, Inc. 2000.

PRESTON, John (ed.). *Thought and Language*. Cambridge: Cambridge University Press, 1997.

PRIOR, Moody E. *The Language of Tragedy*. London: Indiana University Press, 1966.

RAPPORT, Nigel. " 'Criminals by Instinct': On the 'Tragedy' of Social Structure and the 'Violence' of Individual creativity". M*eanings of Violence: A Cross Cultural Perspective*. Ed. Göran Aijmer and Jon Abbink New York: Oxford, 2000. 39-54.

REYNOLDS, Jean. *Pygmalion's Wordplay: The Postmodern Shaw*. Gainesville: University Press of Florida, 1999.

RUSINKO, Susan. *British Drama 1950 to the Present*. Boston: Twayne Publishers, 1989.

SALES, Roger. *Christopher Marlowe*. London: Macmillan, 1991.

SALMI, J. *Violence and Democratic Society: New Approaches to Human Rights*. London: Zed Books, 1993.

SAMMELLS, Neil. "Chapter 1: Writing and Censorship: an introduction". *Writing and Censorship in Britain*. Ed. Paul Hyland and Neil Sammells. London: Routledge, 1992.1-20.

SEDER, John W. *Shakespeare's Book of Insults, Insights and Infinite Jests*. Springfield, Octavo Pres: 1984.

SILVERSTEIN, Marc. *Harold Pinter and the Language of Cultural Power*. Lewisburg: Bucknell University Press, 1993.

STYAN, J. L. *Shakespeare's Stagecraft*. London: Cambridge University Press, 1979.

THOMAS, Linda and Shan WAREING. *Language, Society and Power: An Introduction*. London: Routledge, 1999.

THOMAS, Vivien and William TYDEMAN. *Christopher Marlowe: The Plays and Their Sources*. London: Routledge, 1994.

TILLYARD, E. M. W. "Richard and the First Tetralogy". *Critical Essays on*

Shakespeare's Richard III. Ed. Hugh Macrae Richmond. New York: G. K. Hall & Co: 1999. 117-127.

TRUSSEL, Simon. *Edward Bond*. Essex: Longman Group Ltd., 1976.

UZMEN, Engin. *Shakespeare'in Tarihi Oyunları: Kaynaklar Işığında Başlıca Kişiler*. Ankara: Hacettepe Universitesi Yayınları, 1973.

VANDERVEKEN, Daniel. *Meaning and Speech Acts Volume I Principle of Language Use*. Cambridge: Cambridge University Pres, 1990.

VAN HOOK, J. W. "The Rhetoric of Marlowe's Orations". *"A Poet and a filthy Play-maker" New Essays on Christopher Marlowe*. New York: AMS Press, Inc., 1988. 49-61.

VANNIER, JEAN. "Langages de L'avant-garde". *Théâtre Populaire*. 18 (1956). Paris: 30-39.

VICKERS, Brian. "Shakespeare's Use of Rhetoric". *A Reader in the Language of Shakespearean Drama*. Comp.Vivian Salmon and Edwina Burness. Amsterdam: John Benjamins Publishing Company, 1987. 391-406.

- - -. *In Defence of Rhetoric*. Oxford: Clamdan Press: 1988.

WAITH, Eugene M. "Marlowe's Herculean Hero". *Marlowe: Tamburlaine the Great, Edward the Second and The Jew of Malta*. London: Macmillan, 1991. 87-113.

WEINTRAUB, Stanley (Ed.). *British Dramatists Since World War II 1900-1945 Part 1 and 2. Detroit: Gale Research Co., 1982.*

WESTWOOD, Sallie. *Power and the Social*. London: Routledge, 2002.

WILLIAMS, Raymond. "The Birthday Party: Harold Pinter". *Modern Critical Views: Harold Pinter*. New York, Chelsea House Publishing, 1987. 19-22.

WITTGENSTEIN, Ludwig. *Philosophical Investigations*. Trans. G. E. M. Anscombe. Oxford: Blackwell Publishers Ltd., 1999.

WORTHEN, W.B. *The Harcourt Brace Anthology of Drama*. London. Harcourt Brace College Publishers, 2000.

WOUDHUYSEN, H. R. (ed.). *Samuel Johnson on Shakespeare*. Harmondsworth: Penguin Books, 1989.

***ibidem*-Verlag**

Melchiorstr. 15

D-70439 Stuttgart

info@ibidem-verlag.de

www.ibidem-verlag.de
www.ibidem.eu
www.edition-noema.de
www.autorenbetreuung.de